MASTERING RISK

FINANCIAL TIMES

MASTERING RISK

Volume 2: Applications

editor

Professor Carol Alexander
Chair of Risk Management,
ISMA Centre, University of Reading, UK
www.ismacentre.rdg.ac.uk

FINANCIAL TIMES
Prentice Hall

London New York San Francisco Toronto Sydney Tokyo Singapore
Hong Kong Cape Town Madrid Paris Milan Munich Amsterdam

PEARSON EDUCATION LIMITED

Head Office:
Edinburgh Gate
Harlow CM20 2JE
Tel: +44 (0)1279 623623
Fax: +44 (0)1279 431059

London Office:
128 Long Acre
London WC2E 9AN
Tel: +44 (0)20 7447 2000
Fax: +44 (0)20 7240 5771

Website: www.financialminds.com

First published in Great Britain in 2001

© Pearson Education Limited 2001 except where otherwise indicated

ISBN 0 273 65436 5

British Library Cataloguing in Publication Data
A CIP catalogue record for this book can be obtained from the British Library.

10 9 8 7 6 5 4 3 2 1

Typeset by Land and Unwin (Data Sciences) Limited, Bugbrooke
Printed and bound in Great Britain by Ashford Colour Press Ltd

The Publishers' policy is to use paper manufactured from sustainable forests.

Contents

Introduction

Mastering Risk Volume 1: Concepts provides a comprehensive overview of the important concepts in risk management, including: risk measurement and management; risk strategy; operational risk; regulation; political risk; insurance and systemic risk. These concepts touch on a wide range of disciplines, such as psychology, law, marketing and statistics. There are many short articles that are written at a non-technical level by leading academics and specialist practitioners working in the field of risk management.

Mastering Risk Volume 2: Models also contains contributions from leading academics and top industry practitioners working in the field of risk management. However each of the 14 chapters are written at an advanced level that assumes readers are somewhat familiar with the area. Several chapters have a high mathematical content; these aim to provide an in-depth understanding of the latest issues and the most important practical problems in risk measurement and management. The book has been divided into three parts, covering market, credit and operational risks. Detailed summaries of each chapter are given in the part introductions.

Market risks have been the subject of extensive research for many years, with option pricing and risk measurement being the main focus of theoretical and quantitative analysis. As market become more liquid and open, much data are available for this analysis. The net result is that huge progress has been made towards our understanding of market risks during the last two decades. We now view the Black-Scholes formula as only a crude approximation to reality in many cases and the same could be said of the standard "historical" statistical measures of risk. This has been a driving force behind a vast international research effort into better pricing models and better risk models.

The chapters in the first part of the book represent some of the most important recent contributions towards an advanced understanding of market risks.

Each has been written by acknowledged experts in their field. Two chapters examine the pricing of options under more realistic assumptions for price processes, showing how they may be mispriced if traditional methods are used. Three of the chapters introduce new and more effective methods for measuring market risks. The last chapter focuses on model risk, which concerns both option pricing and risk measurement.

The second part of the book contains four chapters on credit risks. During the last few years there has been an enormous resurgence of interest in this area, driven in part by the imminent changes by regulators for credit risk requirements in the Basel 2 Accord. Many different theoretical models for pricing the risks of default have been proposed during the last few years, but data that are relevant for modeling credit default and credit migration are relatively difficult to obtain; consequently it is not yet clear which models perform best.

The first chapter in Part 2 provides a general framework for credit risk measurement by portfolio models. Portfolio models of credit risks are still at an early stage of development and more work is essential before credit VaR type models will be acceptable for the measurement of credit risk capital. The other three chapters focus on the estimation of default and migration probabilities and the pricing of credit risky products: new models for pricing collateralized bond obligations; an extensive and critical survey of the many different models for pricing default risk; and a clear explanation of the difference between real-world and risk-neutral default probabilities and the circumstances in which each should be applied.

The last part of the book is about "operational risk", a term that has become a catch-all for financial risks that are not market or credit risks. Last year it became clear that the Basel committee will introduce minimum capital requirements to cover operational risks in the Basel 2 amendment that is due for implemention in 2004. Naturally this has been a catalyst for an intense research effort into this area. However there are many different types of operational risks and they have quite diverse characteristics; consequently a rather wide variety of financial and mathematical models are currently under consideration. Several aspects of measuring and managing operational risks are surveyed in this book: the response to the proposed changes in regulations; the insurance and securitization of operational risks; the design of an operational risk system; and an introduction to Bayesian methods and how they may be applied to the measurement and management of operational risks.

This book brings together recent cutting-edge research in financial risk measurement and management by some of the leading experts in their fields. I would like to thank all the authors for their excellent contributions, and the editorial staff at Pearson Education for bringing the book to publication. I would also like to thank Rosalind Oxley and Julian T. Kirby of ICBI, a leading producer of finance conference forums in Europe. Every year ICBI host several large summits on risk management and financial derivatives and this book began as a collection of papers that were presented at ICBI forums in 1999 and 2000. For many years ICBI have provided a forum for leading experts to show case their latest research and this book is testimony to the extremely high calibre of speakers and presentations at their events.

Carol Alexander
Professor of Risk Management,
ISMA Centre, University of Reading, UK

MARKET RISKS

Contributors

Paul Glasserman is the Jack R. Anderson Professor of Risk Management at Columbia Business School. His research focuses on methods for valuing derivative securities and measuring their risks. He has published numerous research articles and two books, and has served on the editorial boards of several academic journals. He has been a consultant to financial and management consulting firms.

Philip Heidelberger has been a research staff member at the IBM Thomas J. Watson Research Center in Yorktown Heights, New York since 1978. He is the General Chairman of the ACM SIGMETRICS/Performance 2001 conference and has served as the Program Chairman of the 1989 Winter Simulation Conference, and the Program Co-Chairman of the ACM SIGMETRICS/Performance '92 Conference. He is also a Fellow of the ACM and the IEEE.

Perwez Shahabuddin is an Associate Professor of Industrial Engineering and Operations Research at Columbia University, New York. His research interests include stochastic modeling methodologies, and Monte Carlo and discrete event simulation methodologies for financial engineering, telecommunications and reliability applications. His research has been funded by National Science Foundation (NSF), AT&T, IBM and AUM Systems. He serves on the editorial board of several academic journals.

Carol Alexander is Professor of Risk Management at the ISMA Centre at the University of Reading. She was also formerly a Director and Head of Market Risk Modeling for Nikko Global Holdings and Academic Director of Algorithmics Inc. Her research interests include volatility and correlation analysis, high frequency price prediction, alternative investment strategies and quantification of operational risks. She is the author of *Market Models: a guide to financial data analysis* (Wiley, 2001).

Emanuel Derman is a Managing Director in Firmwide Risk at Goldman Sachs, and was named the IAFE/SunGard Financial Engineer of the Year 2000. He obtained a PhD in theoretical physics from Columbia University. Prior to joining Goldman Sachs in 1985, he held a number of academic positions where he did research in theoretical particle physics, as well as working at Bell Laboratories. The co-author of this chapter, Joe Zou, is a Vice President at the Equity Volatility Trading Department of Goldman Sachs & Co. He holds a PhD in theoretical physics from Princeton University.

Ernst Eberlein is Professor for Stochastics and Mathematical Finance at the University of Freiburg. He studied Mathematics and Physics in Erlangen and Paris, and held positions at the Department of Economics, University of Bonn, and at the Swiss Federal Institute of Technology, Zurich. In 1994 he was co-founder of the Center for Data Analysis and Model Building, University of Freiburg. His current research interests are realistic models in finance, risk management, and pricing and hedging of derivative products.

Jin-Chuan Duan holds the Manulife Chair in Financial Services at Joseph L. Rotman School of Management, University of Toronto. He is also a Professor of Finance with Hong Kong University of Science and Technology (on leave). He has a PhD in Finance from the University of Wisconsin-Madison. His research covers pricing of derivative securities, time-series econometrics and banking.

Dr Riccardo Rebonato is Group Head of Market Risk, and Head of the Quantitative Research Center for the Royal Bank of Scotland Group. He is a Visiting Lecturer at Oxford University (Mathematical Finance) and Visiting Fellow at the Applied Mathematical Department. He is the author of *Interest-Rate Option Models, Volatility and Correlation in Option Pricing* and of *Modern Pricing of Interest-Rate Derivatives*.

Contents

Introduction

Market risks have been the subject of extensive research for many years and the industry has gained much expertise in this area. Most large banks employ highly sophisticated mathematical and statistical techniques to understand how to price financial products, measure their market risks and hedge them in an uncertain environment. The chapters in this part of the book represent some important and recent contributions towards an advanced understanding of market risks.

It begins with a chapter on Monte Carlo methods for computing the market Value-at-Risk (VaR) of a portfolio. Paul Glasserman, Philip Heidelberger and Perwez Shahabuddin are acknowledged experts in this field. Recently they have developed new techniques for speeding up Monte Carlo VaR calculations that are based on importance sampling and stratified sampling to generate changes in risk factors. The approach that is described in this chapter uses the delta-gamma approximation to guide the sampling of market scenarios; it does not need to be used as an approximation to portfolio value changes. However, when the delta-gamma approximation holds exactly the new method that is introduced in this chapter will be close to optimal (see pp. 7–20).

The second chapter, written by myself, describes a new method for generating large covariance matrices that is based on principal component analysis. The title of the chapter is "Orthogonal GARCH", but the method may be also applied with exponentially weighted moving averages to great effect. In this case the orthogonal EWMA covariance matrix will not need to use the same smoothing constant for each volatility and correlation; in fact the smoothing constant will be determined by the correlation in the system. The orthogonal GARCH model represents an important development in multivariate GARCH, since it allows large GARCH covariance matrices to be generated using only univariate GARCH models. All the advantages of GARCH convergent term structure forecasts are maintained, the modeler may also tailor the amount of "noise" by choosing more or

less principal components and there are many other advantages. The model is supported with empirical validation on systems of the main asset types (see pp. 21–38).

The third chapter is written by Joseph Zou and Emanuel Derman of Goldman Sachs, NY. The chapter explains how an option investor can measure the cheapness or expensiveness of an option, relative to the other options in the market. The method involves using historical data on an equity to compute a "fair" volatility smile for any option on that equity; then the relative value of the option is determined by comparing the current market implied volatility and its "fair" volatility. Fair volatility smiles are obtained by estimating a risk-neutral distribution for valuing options that takes into account the historical behaviour of the equity price including any price jumps. The method is particularly useful to gauge the relative value of illiquid or thinly traded options (see pp. 39–55).

The next chapter, written by Ernst Eberlein of the University of Freiberg, explains why the hyperbolic density is so useful for modeling financial returns. Many returns, and high frequency data in particular, exhibit fat-tailed density functions that are not well approximated by normal assumptions. The hyperbolic density is a four parameter family of density functions; in addition to the location and scale parameters the two shape parameters allow these densities to fit financial return data extremely well. Eberlein shows that the asset price process corresponding to the hyperbolic density is the generalized hyperbolic Levy motion; this is a purely discontinuous process which is shown to capture the microstructure of certain price fluctuations extremely well. Having defined the price process, the chapter continues with a discussion of the risk-neutral evaluation of derivatives based on the hyperbolic model and compares the Black-Scholes option prices with generalized hyperbolic option prices (see pp. 56–72).

In the next chapter Jin-Chuan Duan of the University of Toronto explains how cointegration between asset prices occurs naturally in financial markets: yields of different maturities, spot and futures prices, option prices on the same underlying asset; all these assets are tied together in the long run. Individually each price may be a random walk, and therefore difficult to predict over the longer term; but if prices are cointegrated then one thing is certain: that the prices will be close to each other however far away the forecasting horizon. Jin-Chuan's chapter explains how cointegration can be incorporated into diffusion models; he applies it to the valuation of derivative contracts on multiple assets, showing that the theoretical value will depend on a cointegration premium as well as the usual risk premium when volatilities are not constant (see pp. 73–83).

The final chapter in part 1 is about managing model risk, perhaps one of the least understood concepts in risk management. Riccardo Rebonato of the Royal Bank of Scotland argues that risk mangers should be concerned about the possibility of mispricing not only today, but also with future distributions of profit and losses over a suitably chosen holding period that may be far longer than the usual one-day or ten-day holding periods that are normally used for market risk assessment. He recommends that the approach used by middle office risk management should not be the same as that used by front office traders; the model validation unit will not necessarily benefit from using the same sophisticated models as those that might be used by the front desk. This extensive chapter begins by quantifying model risk with a distribution of differences between model and market values; it then draws the link between model risk and asset pricing in incomplete markets, where model risk reflects the view that today's chosen pricing measure could change in the future. Using some well chosen examples, Riccardo describes how the market price of a complex instrument can reflect the different perspectives of the trader and the risk manager. This chapter is beautifully written and will be a classic reference for those wishing to understand the most important conceptual aspects of model risk management. (see pp. 84–115)

Carol Alexander
Professor of Risk Management,
ISMA Centre, University of Reading, UK

Efficient Monte Carlo methods for Value-at-Risk

by Paul Glasserman, Philip Heidelberger and Perwez Shahabuddin

The calculation of Value-at-Risk (VaR) for large portfolios of complex derivative securities presents a tradeoff between speed and accuracy. The fastest methods rely on simplifying assumptions about changes in underlying risk factors and about how a portfolio's value responds to these changes in the risk factors. Greater realism in measuring changes in portfolio value generally comes at the price of much longer computing times.

The simplest methods – the "variance-covariance" solution popularized by RiskMetrics, and the delta-gamma approximations described by Britten-Jones and Schaefer (1999), Rouvinez (1997) and Wilson (1998) – rely on the assumption that a portfolio's value changes linearly or quadratically with changes in market risk factors. These assumptions limit their accuracy. In contrast, Monte Carlo simulation is applicable with virtually any model of changes in risk factors and any mechanism for determining a portfolio's value in each market scenario. But revaluing a portfolio in each scenario can present a substantial computational burden, and this motivates research into ways of improving the efficiency of Monte Carlo methods for VaR.

Because the computational bottleneck in Monte Carlo estimation of VaR lies in revaluing a portfolio in each market scenario sampled, accelerating Monte Carlo requires either speeding up each revaluation or sampling fewer scenarios. In this article, we discuss methods for reducing the number of revaluations required through strategic sampling of scenarios. In particular, we review methods developed in Glasserman, Heidelberger, and Shahabuddin (2000ab) – henceforth referred to as GHS2000a and GHS2000b – that combine *importance sampling* and *stratified sampling* to generate changes in risk factors.

This approach uses the delta-gamma approximation to guide the sampling of market scenarios. Deltas and gammas are routinely calculated for other purposes so we assume their availability, without additional computational overhead, as inputs to the calculation of VaR. We develop sampling methods that are, in a precise sense, close to optimal when the delta-gamma approximation holds exactly. These methods remain attractive so long as the delta-gamma approximation contains useful information about changes in portfolio value, even if the approximation is not accurate enough to replace simulation entirely. Numerical examples indicate that the methods can often reduce by a factor of 20–100 or more the number of scenarios required to achieve a specified precision in estimating a loss probability. Because this means that the number of portfolio revaluations is also reduced by a factor of 20–100 or more, it results in a very large reduction in the computing time required for Monte Carlo estimation of VaR.

The rest of this article is organized as follows. The next section provides some background on Monte Carlo for VaR and on the delta-gamma approximation. After that, we discuss importance sampling and stratified sampling based on the delta-gamma approximation. We then discuss the application of these methods when

7

volatility is included among the risk factors and portfolio "vegas" are available along with deltas and gammas. Numerical examples are included to illustrate the methods. Throughout this article we assume that changes in risk factors are normally distributed. In Glasserman, Heidelberger, and Shahabuddin (2000c), we develop related methods that apply when changes in risk factors are modeled by heavy-tailed distributions.

Background on Monte Carlo and delta-gamma

Before discussing the new methods developed in GHS2000a and GHS2000b, we briefly review basic Monte Carlo estimation of VaR and the delta-gamma approximation. To give a precise formulation of the problem, we let

$$
\begin{aligned}
S &= \text{vector of risk factors} \\
\Delta t &= \text{VaR horizon (e.g., one day or two weeks)} \\
\Delta S &= \text{change in risk factors over } \Delta t \\
L &= \text{loss in portfolio value resulting from change } \Delta S \text{ over } \Delta t.
\end{aligned}
$$

The loss L is the difference between the current value of the portfolio and the portfolio value at the end of the VaR horizon Δt if the risk factors move from S to $S + \Delta S$.

There are two closely related problems associated with the tail of the distribution of L. The first is the problem of estimating a loss probability $P(L > x)$ given a loss threshold x. The second is the inverse problem of finding a quantile x_p for which $P(L > x_p) = p$, given a probability p. The estimation of VaR is an instance of the second problem, typically with $p = 1\%$ or 5%. However, calculating loss probabilities is a prerequisite to calculating quantiles so we focus primarily on the first problem. Given values of $P(L > x)$ for several values of x in the vicinity of x_p it is then straightforward to estimate the quantile itself.

Basic Monte Carlo for VaR

The main steps in a basic Monte Carlo approach to estimating loss probabilities are as follows:

1. Generate N scenarios by sampling changes in risk factors $\Delta S^{(1)},...,\Delta S^{(N)}$ over horizon Δt.

2. Revalue portfolio at end of horizon Δt in scenarios $S + \Delta S^{(1)},...,S + \Delta S^{(N)}$; determine losses $L^{(1)},...,L^{(N)}$ by subtracting revaluation in each scenario from current portfolio value.

3. Calculate fraction of scenarios in which losses exceed x: $N^{-1} \sum_{i=1}^{N} I(L^{(i)} > x)$, where $I(L^{(i)} > x) = 1$ if $L^{(i)} > x$ and 0 otherwise.

To estimate VaR, the last step can be repeated for multiple values of x; the required quantiles can then be estimated by, for example, interpolating between the estimated loss probabilities.

The first step requires some assumptions about market data. In *historical simulation*, the $\Delta S^{(i)}$ are the changes observed (or are obtained from the *percentage* changes observed) in market data over N past periods of length Δt. This implicitly assumes that future changes in risk factors will look like samples from past changes. Alternatively, a statistical model uses historical data to select a distribution with estimated parameters to describe future changes. A simple and widely used assumption is that, conditional on past data, the change ΔS over a short horizon Δt is described by a multivariate normal distribution $N(0, \Sigma_S)$. The conditional covariance matrix Σ_S is commonly estimated from past changes (or returns) using a sample covariance matrix, using an exponentially weighted moving average, or using a GARCH forecast – see Alexander (2001) or Jorion (1997) for a discussion of this issue. We will focus primarily on the case of normally distributed changes in risk factors, but touch on alternative models in our concluding remarks.

Given a covariance matrix Σ_S and the assumption of normally distributed changes in risk factors, it is a simple matter to generate the samples of ΔS required in the simulation above. We factor the covariance matrix to find a matrix C for which $CC' = \Sigma_S$ (the prime denoting transpose) and then set

$$\Delta S = CZ, \tag{1}$$

where Z is a vector of independent, standard (i.e., mean 0, variance 1) normal random variables. For example, assuming Σ_S is positive definite, Cholesky factorization produces a lower triangular matrix C for which $CC' = \Sigma_S$.

The only difficult step in the Monte Carlo algorithm above is the second one – revaluing the portfolio in each scenario. For a large portfolio of complex derivative securities, each revaluation may be very time-consuming, with individual instruments requiring execution of numerical pricing routines or even separate Monte Carlo pricing estimates. The time required to revalue a portfolio is the limiting factor in determining the number of scenarios that can be generated.

The delta-gamma approximation

An alternative to full portfolio revaluation is to use an approximation to how changes in risk factors determine changes in portfolio value. Assuming a linear relation between risk factors and portfolio value leads to the "variance-covariance" method associated with RiskMetrics; assuming a quadratic relation leads to the delta-gamma approximation. In both cases, the approximation makes it possible to find the loss distribution numerically, without Monte Carlo simulation.

The delta-gamma approximation assumes the availability of (i) the vector δ of first partial derivatives of portfolio value with respect to the components of the vector S of risk factors, (ii) the matrix Γ of the corresponding second partial derivatives, and (iii) a scalar Θ giving the partial derivative of portfolio value with respect to time. From these we obtain the Taylor approximation

$$L \approx a_0 - \delta' \Delta S - \tfrac{1}{2} \Delta S' \Gamma \Delta S,$$

where $a_0 = -\Theta \Delta t$. The derivatives appear with minus signs in this approximation because the loss L is the negative of the increase in portfolio value.

Through a change of variables and some matrix algebra, we can rewrite this approximation in the form

$$
\begin{aligned}
L &\approx a_0 + b'Z + Z'\Lambda Z \\
&\equiv a_0 + Q,
\end{aligned}
\tag{2}
$$

where Z is a vector of independent standard normal random variables and Λ is a diagonal matrix,

$$
\Lambda = \begin{pmatrix}
\lambda_1 & 0 & \cdots & 0 \\
0 & \lambda_2 & & 0 \\
\vdots & & \ddots & \vdots \\
0 & 0 & \cdots & \lambda_m
\end{pmatrix},
$$

with $\lambda_1 \geq \lambda_2 \geq \cdots \geq \lambda_m$ the eigenvalues of $-\frac{1}{2}\Gamma\Sigma_S$. This is accomplished by choosing C in (1) to satisfy

$$
CC' = \Sigma_S \text{ and } -\tfrac{1}{2}C'\Gamma C = \Lambda.
\tag{3}
$$

(Calculation of C will be discussed later.) The vector b in the linear term of (2) is then given by $b' = -\delta'C$.

This transformation accomplishes two important simplifications: it replaces the correlated changes in risk factors ΔS with the uncorrelated elements of Z, and it diagonalizes the quadratic term in the approximation. The vector ΔS is recovered from Z through (1), so one may think of the elements of Z as (hypothetical) primitive underlying risk factors driving the market changes ΔS. Notice that the diagonal matrix Λ captures information about both the portfolio (through Γ) and the distribution of risk factors (through Σ_S).

With these simplifications it becomes relatively straightforward to find the characteristic function (Fourier transform) of the delta-gamma approximation – more precisely, of the quadratic Q in (2). Define

$$
\psi(\theta) = \sum_{i=1}^{m} \tfrac{1}{2}\left(\frac{(\theta b_i)^2}{1 - 2\theta\lambda_i} - ln(1 - 2\theta\lambda_i) \right);
\tag{4}
$$

then $E[\exp(\sqrt{-1}\omega Q)] = \exp(\psi(\sqrt{-1}\omega))$. Transform inversion can now be used to calculate values of the distribution $P(Q < x)$. In light of (2), the loss distribution can be approximated using $P(L < x) \approx P(Q < x - a_0)$.

Importance sampling based on the delta-gamma approximation

The main virtue of the delta-gamma approximation is that it can be computed quickly. However, the accuracy of the approximation may not always be satisfactory. Monte Carlo simulation is more accurate but much more time-consuming. Our objective is to use the information contained in the delta-gamma approximation to accelerate Monte Carlo simulation and thus exploit the best features of two methods.

The simplest way to use the delta-gamma approximation in a simulation is to implement it as a *control variate*. In estimating a loss probability $P(L > x)$, this produces an estimator of the form

$$
\frac{1}{N} \sum_{i=1}^{N} I(L^{(i)} > x) - \beta\left[\frac{1}{N} \sum_{i=1}^{N} I(Q^{(i)} > x - a_0) - P(Q > x - a_0) \right].
$$

Here, the $L^{(i)}$ are actual losses calculated in the N simulated scenarios and the $Q^{(i)}$ are the quadratic approximations (see (2)) computed *in the same scenarios*. The true probability $P(Q > x - a_0)$ is computed through transform inversion. The term in square brackets is thus the observed simulation error in the delta-gamma approximation; this observed error is used to adjust the simulation estimate of the true portfolio loss. The coefficient β can be chosen to try to minimize the variance of the combined estimator. Fixing β at 1 should yield most of the benefit of the control variate and avoids issues that arise in estimating an optimal β.

This method was proposed independently in Cardenas et al. (1999) and GHS2000a. It can provide reasonable variance reduction in some examples; but as observed in GHS2000a, its effectiveness diminishes at larger loss thresholds x. Notice that the control variate method uses the delta-gamma approximation to adjust the standard estimator "after the fact" – in particular, the scenarios used are generated in the usual way (i.e., as in our discussion above of basic Monte Carlo). In contrast, the method we describe next uses the delta-gamma approximation *before* any scenarios are generated; it uses the approximation to guide the sampling of scenarios.

Importance sampling: preliminaries

Through (1), the problem of sampling changes ΔS in market risk factors is transformed into a problem of sampling the vector Z of underlying normal random variables. In importance sampling (IS), we change the distribution from which underlying variables are generated in order to generate more samples from "important" regions. We will focus on IS methods that change the distribution of Z from $N(0, I)$ (the standard multivariate normal) to $N(\mu, \Sigma)$ (the multivariate normal with mean vector μ and covariance matrix Σ).

The key identity we need for importance sampling is

$$P(L > x) = \mathrm{E}_{\mu,\Sigma}[l(Z)I(L > x)]. \tag{5}$$

In subscripting the expression on the right by μ and Σ, we are indicating that the expectation is taken with Z sampled from $N(\mu, \Sigma)$ rather than its original distribution $N(0, I)$. To correct for this change of distribution, we must weight the loss indicator $I(L > x)$ by the *likelihood ratio*

$$l(Z) = |\Sigma|^{1/2} e^{-\frac{1}{2}\mu'\Sigma^{-1}\mu} e^{-\frac{1}{2}[Z'(I-\Sigma^{-1})Z - 2\mu'\Sigma^{-1}Z]} \tag{6}$$

which is simply the ratio of the $N(0, I)$ and $N(\mu, \Sigma)$ densities evaluated at Z. On both sides of (5), the loss L is computed from the market changes ΔS which are in turn calculated from Z through (1). Through (5) we are free to sample Z from any $N(\mu, \Sigma)$ and still obtain an unbiased estimate

$$l(Z)I(L > x) \tag{7}$$

of the loss probability.

How should μ and Σ be chosen to produce an estimator with lower variance (and thus greater precision)? Since changing μ and Σ does not change the resulting expectation, comparing variances is equivalent to comparing second moments. The second moment of (7) is

$$E_{\mu,\Sigma}\left[(l(Z)I(L > x))^2\right] = E[l(Z)I(L > x)], \tag{8}$$

the expectation on the right taken with respect to the original $N(0, I)$ distribution. From this we see that the key to reducing variance is *making the likelihood ratio small when $L > x$*. Equivalently, we would like to choose μ and Σ to make scenarios with $L > x$ more likely under $N(\mu, \Sigma)$ than under $N(0, I)$.

Using the approximation

Unfortunately, the expression in (6) provides little insight into what choice of μ and Σ might accomplish this objective. However, we can use the delta-gamma approximation to get a sense for which scenarios tend to produce large losses and use this information in the selection of μ and Σ.

We can write (2) more explicitly as

$$L \approx a_0 + \sum_i b_i Z_i + \sum_i \lambda_i Z_i^2$$

and now ask, what values of Z will tend to make the (approximate) loss expression large? Inspection of this formula suggests that large losses result from

- large positive values of Z_i for those i with $b_i > 0$;
- large negative values of Z_i for those i with $b_i < 0$;
- large values of Z_i^2 for those i with $\lambda_i > 0$.

This describes the regions that should be given greater probability under the IS distribution than under the original distribution. It suggests that we should

- increase the mean of Z_i for those i with $b_i > 0$;
- decrease the mean of Z_i for those i with $b_i < 0$;
- increase the variance of Z_i for those i with $\lambda_i > 0$;

and perhaps

- decrease the variance of Z_i for those i with $\lambda_i < 0$.

We accomplish this in two steps. We first reduce the choice of μ and Σ to the choice of a scalar parameter θ, and then specify the value of this parameter. For any $\theta > 0$ (and $\theta < 1/(2\lambda_1)$ if $\lambda_1 > 0$)

$$\Sigma(\theta) = (I - 2\theta\Lambda)^{-1}, \qquad \mu(\theta) = \theta\Sigma(\theta)b. \tag{9}$$

With these parameters, Z_i becomes normal with mean and variance

$$\mu_i(\theta) = \frac{\theta b_i}{1 - 2\theta\lambda_i}, \qquad \sigma_i^2(\theta) = \frac{1}{1 - 2\theta\lambda_i}, \tag{10}$$

and the Z_i remain independent of each other. Note that with this type of IS, the sampling distribution of Z_i is as suggested; for example, if $\lambda_i > 0$, then the variance of

Z_i is increased, resulting in more samples with large values of Z_i^2. The key observation is that with this change of distribution the likelihood ratio (6) collapses to

$$l(Z) = e^{-\theta Q + \psi(\theta)}. \tag{11}$$

Here, ψ is precisely the function introduced in (4) and may be interpreted as a normalization constant. The remarkable feature of this expression is that the likelihood ratio – which in general could depend on the entire vector Z, as in (6) – now has the scalar Q as its only stochastic element. The estimator associated with this IS distribution is

$$e^{-\theta Q + \psi(\theta)} I(L > x),$$

where the Z used to compute L and Q is now generated using (10). It must be stressed that this estimator is unbiased (in light of (5)) for the exact loss probability $P(L > x)$, even though it involves the delta-gamma approximation.

Recall from the discussion surrounding (8) that an effective importance sampling distribution makes the likelihood ratio small in those scenarios for which $L > x$. Based on (2), we can expect that when $L > x$ we will often have $Q > x - a_0$; in particular, Q will typically be large when L is and in this case the likelihood ratio (11) will indeed tend to be small when $L > x$.

It remains to specify the parameter θ. A consequence of the specification in (9) is that

$$\frac{d}{d\theta}\,\psi(\theta) = E_{\mu(\theta),\,\Sigma(\theta)}[Q]. \tag{12}$$

(In statistical terminology, (9) defines an *exponential family* of distributions with *cumulant generating function* ψ; (12) is a special case of a standard property of exponential families.) We may paraphrase (12) as stating that the derivative of ψ at θ gives the expected delta-gamma approximate loss when Z is drawn from $N(\mu(\theta), \Sigma(\theta))$. Since our objective is to estimate $P(L > x) \approx P(Q > x - a_0)$, we choose θ to be θ_x, the solution to

$$\frac{d}{d\theta}\,\psi(\theta_x) = E_{\mu(\theta_x),\,\Sigma(\theta_x)}[Q] = x - a_0.$$

If we sample Z from $N(\mu(\theta_x), \Sigma(\theta_x))$, scenarios in which $L > x$, which were previously rare, should now be "typical," since the expected value of the approximate loss $a_0 + Q$ is now x.

This choice of parameter θ is shown in GHS2000b to minimize an upper bound on the second moment of the estimator, providing further support for the approach. In addition, both experimental and theoretical results in GHS2000b indicate that the effectiveness of the IS procedure is not very sensitive to the choice of θ. Consequently, we may use a single IS distribution $N(\mu(\theta), \Sigma(\theta))$ to estimate the loss probability $P(L > x)$ for multiple levels of x.

The procedure

We now summarize the importance sampling procedure. We assume the availability of the portfolio delta vector (δ) and gamma matrix (Γ), which would also be required for the delta-gamma approximation.

1. Compute C satisfying (3):
   (a) Find any matrix A satisfying $AA' = \Sigma_S$ (e.g., the Cholesky factor).
   (b) Find V, an orthogonal matrix ($VV' = I$) whose columns are eigenvectors of $-\frac{1}{2}A'\Gamma A$ and Λ, a diagonal matrix of associated eigenvalues (so $-\frac{1}{2}A'\Gamma A = V\Lambda V'$).
   (c) Set $C = AV$ and $b = -\delta'C$.
2. Set $\theta = \theta_x$, the solution to (13).
3. Set $\Sigma(\theta) = (I - 2\theta\Lambda)^{-1}$ and $\mu(\theta) = \theta\Sigma(\theta)b$.
4. Simulate:
   (a) Generate $Z^{(1)}, ..., Z^{(N)}$ independently from $N(\mu(\theta), \Sigma(\theta))$.
   (b) Set $\Delta S^{(i)} = CZ^{(i)}$, $i = 1, ..., N$.
   (c) Calculate portfolio losses $L^{(i)}$ resulting from scenarios $\Delta S^{(i)}$, $i = 1, ..., N$.
   (d) Calculate $Q^{(i)}$ for each $Z^{(i)}$, $i = 1, ..., N$, as in (2).
   (e) Return estimate

$$\frac{1}{N}\sum_{i=1}^{N} e^{-\theta Q(i) + \psi(\theta)} I(L^{(i)} > x). \tag{14}$$

An important feature of this method is that it can be wrapped around an existing implementation of Monte Carlo. The core of the algorithm – the calculation of portfolio losses in each scenario – is exactly the same here as in the basic Monte Carlo method presented earlier in this article. After some preprocessing steps 1–3, the importance sampling algorithm differs only in how it generates scenarios and in how it weights scenarios in (14). As with the basic Monte Carlo method, (14) could easily be calculated for multiple values of the loss threshold x, all based on a single value of θ. If we plan to estimate loss probabilities at large thresholds $x_1 < x_2 < ... < x_k$, we would probably fix θ at θ_{x_1}.

A theoretical analysis of this IS method is reported in GHS2000b. We show there that the method is provably effective, in the sense of substantially reducing variance, as either the loss threshold or the number of risk factors increase. These results are established under the hypothesis that the relation $L = a_0 + Q$ holds exactly rather than merely as an approximation. We interpret these results as evidence that the method should remain effective whenever $a_0 + Q$ provides a reasonable approximation to L, even if it is not sufficiently accurate to replace simulation altogether. The importance of reducing variance in the simulation estimate is that it reduces the number of scenarios required to achieve a desired precision. This can result in substantial reductions in computing times, because revaluing a portfolio in each scenario is the most time-consuming step in estimating loss probabilities through Monte Carlo.

Stratified sampling

Inspection of (14) suggests that to further reduce variance we should reduce variability in the sampling of the quadratic approximation Q. Indeed, if we had $L = a_0 + Q$, then eliminating the variance due to Q would eliminate all the variance in (14). If $a_0 + Q$ only approximates L, reducing the variability from Q should nevertheless result in further overall variance reduction.

Figure 1 : Illustration of equiprobable strata

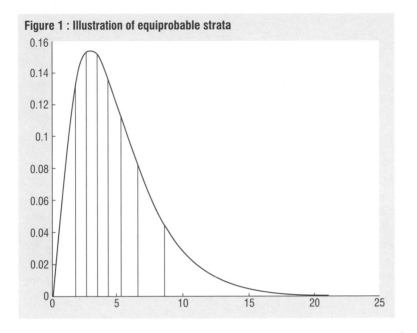

We implement this idea through *stratified* sampling of Q. This mechanism is best explained through reference to Figure 1. The figure shows a hypothetical density for Q. (It is in fact the chi-square density with five degrees of freedom and thus a special case of the density of Q in (2).) More precisely, this should be interpreted as the density of Q under the importance sampling distribution, which is to say with Z drawn from $N(\mu(\theta), \Sigma(\theta))$. The $Q^{(i)}$ used in the algorithm above are independent samples from the density of Q under the IS distribution.

In stratified sampling, rather than drawing the $Q^{(i)}$ randomly and independently we ensure that fixed fractions of the samples fall within specified ranges. For example, the vertical lines in Figure 1 define eight equiprobable bins or strata: the area under the curve between each consecutive pair of lines is $\frac{1}{8}$. If we generate samples $Q^{(i)}$ independently, we cannot expect that exactly $\frac{1}{8}$th of the samples will fall in each of the strata; because the sampling mechanism is random, some strata will end up with too many samples, some with too few. In contrast, using stratified sampling we ensure that exactly $\frac{1}{8}$th of the generated samples do indeed fall in each of the strata. In practice, we typically use 40 equiprobable strata and ensure that $\frac{1}{40}$th of the samples fall within each stratum. With 40 strata, much of the variance in the estimated loss probability due to sampling variability in Q is eliminated.

The first step in implementing this method is to define the strata. In order to define k equiprobable strata, we need to find points $y_1,..., y_{k-1}$ such that

$$P_\theta(Q \le y_i) = i/k, \quad i = 1, ..., k-1.$$

We have subscripted the probability by θ to emphasize that this should hold under the IS distribution. Under the IS distribution, Q remains a quadratic function in normal random variables, so the transform analysis outlined in our discussion of the delta-gamma approximation (after (4)) is still applicable. Using this method we can solve for the required y_i. The intervals (y_i, y_{i+1}), $i = 0,..., k-1$, $(y_0 \equiv -\infty, y_k \equiv \infty)$ then form k equiprobable bins. As discussed in GHS2000b, one could just as easily define strata with any other fixed set of probabilities, but here we focus on the case of equal probabilities for simplicity.

Having defined the strata, it remains to define a sampling mechanism under which an equal fraction of the $Q^{(i)}$ generated fall in each stratum. For this we use a simple if somewhat crude approach. Suppose we want to generate n samples from each stratum for a total sample size of nk. We generate a large number of independent samples Z from $N(\mu(\theta), \Sigma(\theta))$; for each Z generated we evaluate Q and check which stratum it falls in; if we have not already generated n samples for that stratum, we keep the Z generated, otherwise we discard it. We repeat this procedure until we have the required number of samples for each stratum.

Let $Q^{(ij)}$ denote the jth sample from stratum i and let $Z^{(ij)}$ denote the draw from $N(\mu(\theta), \Sigma(\theta))$ that produced this sample. From $Z^{(ij)}$ we get $\Delta S^{(ij)} = CZ^{(ij)}$ as before and compute the corresponding portfolio loss $L^{(ij)}$. The resulting estimator is

$$\sum_{i=1}^{k} \frac{1}{nk} \sum_{j=1}^{n} e^{-\theta Q^{(ij)} + \psi(\theta)} I(L^{(ij)} > x).$$

A bit more generally, if we define strata with probabilities $p_1,..., p_k$ and allocate n_i samples to stratum i, $i = 1,..., k$, the estimator is

$$\sum_{i=1}^{k} \frac{p_i}{n_i} \sum_{j=1}^{n_i} e^{-\theta Q^{(ij)} + \psi(\theta)} I(L^{(ij)} > x).$$

This does not require that the allocations n_i be proportional to the stratum probabilities p_i. Various strategies for choosing the allocations $\{n_i\}$ are investigated in Glasserman et al. (1999). A very simple form of stratified sampling based on the delta-gamma approximation – using just two strata, proportional allocation, and no importance sampling – was proposed independently in Cardenas et al. (1999).

Numerical illustration

Extensive numerical experiments using control variates and a variety of importance sampling and stratified sampling methods have been reported in Glasserman et al. (1999, 2000ab). Here we reproduce one table of results from GHS2000b for illustration.

The results in Table 1 apply to test portfolios defined in GHS2000b, which should be consulted for detailed descriptions. Briefly, each of portfolios (a.1) – (a.14) consists of 150 – 1,000 standard calls and puts distributed over 10 underlying assets; (a.15) has 20 options on each of 100 underlying assets. The options in (a.1) – (a.3) have expirations of 0.5 years; those in (a.4) – (a.6) have expirations of 0.1 years and thus comparatively larger gammas. Portfolios (a.7) – (a.10) are delta hedged. The underlying assets in (a.11) – (a.15) are correlated whereas those in (a.1) – (a.10) are not. All results are based on a VaR horizon Δt of 10 days.

The second column of Table 1 specifies the loss threshold x as x_{std} standard deviations of Q above the mean of $a_0 + Q$. The associated portfolio loss probabilities (all close to 1 percent) are indicated in the third column.

The last two columns of the table are estimates of the ratio of variances in the estimated loss probabilities using standard Monte Carlo and using importance sampling (IS) or importance sampling with stratification (ISS-Q). (The ISS-Q results use 40 equiprobable strata.) These variance ratios indicate how many times more scenarios would have to be generated using standard Monte Carlo to achieve the same precision obtained with the indicated variance reduction technique. Since the bulk of the computational effort in using Monte Carlo with complex portfolios lies in revaluing the portfolio in each scenario, these variance ratios are estimates of the computational speed-up obtained through variance reduction. The results clearly indicate the potential for enormous speed-ups using the methods reviewed here.

Further results and details of the experiments can be found in GHS2000b. The only test portfolios for which we have found results substantially inferior to those in Table 1 are portfolios of digital and barrier options combined to achieve a net delta of 0. Given the nature of these portfolios, it is perhaps unsurprising that a Taylor approximation turns out to be not very informative.

Table 1: Variance reduction estimates for test portfolios

| Portfolio | x_{std} | $P(L > x)$ | Variance ratios | |
			IS	ISS-Q
(a.1)	2.5	1.0%	30	270
(a.2)	1.95	1.0%	43	260
(a.3)	2.3	1.0%	37	327
(a.4)	2.6	1.1%	22	70
(a.5)	1.69	1.0%	43	65
(a.6)	2.3	0.9%	34	132
(a.7)	2.8	1.1%	17	31
(a.8)	1.8	1.1%	52	124
(a.9)	2.8	1.1%	16	28
(a.10)	2.0	1.1%	19	34
(a.11)	3.2	1.1%	18	124
(a.12)	1.02	1.0%	28	48
(a.13)	2.5	1.1%	15	65
(a.14)	1.65	1.1%	14	45
(a.15)	2.65	1.0%	18	28

Including volatility as a risk factor

Thus far, we have interpreted S as a vector of market prices and rates. However, S could also include risk factors associated with levels of volatility rather than prices or rates. The methodology above continues to apply.

We develop this idea through a simple formulation of the problem. Our intent is to illustrate how volatility can be incorporated rather than to propose a specific model. We interpret some of the components of S as asset prices and some as implied volatilities for those assets. For simplicity, we do not incorporate a volatility skew or smile: we assume all options in a portfolio on the same underlying asset have the same implied volatility. In contrast to the previous setting, we now allow the level of implied volatility to change over the VaR horizon. We assume that correlations among prices, among implied volatilities, and between prices and implied volatilities are unchanged over the VaR horizon. We impose this assumption solely for notational simplicity.

Partition the vector S as $(\widetilde{S}, \widetilde{\sigma})$ with $\widetilde{\sigma}_i$ the implied volatility of $\widetilde{S}_i$. We assume that the changes $(\Delta\widetilde{S}, \Delta\widetilde{\sigma})$ over the VaR horizon are conditionally normally distributed, given the current history of prices and implied volatilities, with a conditional mean of 0 and a known conditional covariance matrix. We assume the availability of a vector of "vegas" υ, with υ_i the partial derivative of a portfolio's value with respect to $\widetilde{\sigma}_i$. We continue to assume the availability of the usual δ and Γ with respect to the prices $\widetilde{S}$. It seems less likely that second derivatives involving $\widetilde{\sigma}_i$ would be available as these are not routinely computed for other purposes. We therefore assume these are unavailable and arbitrarily set their values at 0. The quadratic approximation thus takes the form

$$L \approx a_0 - (\delta' \;\; \upsilon') \begin{pmatrix} \Delta\widetilde{S} \\ \Delta\widetilde{\sigma} \end{pmatrix} - \tfrac{1}{2}(\Delta\widetilde{S}' \;\; \Delta\widetilde{\sigma}') \begin{pmatrix} \Gamma & 0 \\ 0 & 0 \end{pmatrix} \begin{pmatrix} \Delta\widetilde{S} \\ \Delta\widetilde{\sigma} \end{pmatrix}.$$

From here on, the analysis proceeds exactly as before.

We tested this method on portfolio (a.1) (0.5 year at-the-money options), (a.4) (0.1 year at-the-money options), and (a.7) (a delta-hedged version of (a.4)). All underlying assets have an initial volatility of 0.30. We also tested the method on a new portfolio that is both delta and gamma hedged. On each of 10 underlying assets with a spot price of 100, the portfolio is short 4.5 calls struck at 110, long 4 calls struck at 105, long 2 puts struck at 95, and short 2.1 puts struck at 90, with all options expiring in 0.5 years. This combination results in deltas and gammas very close to 0.

With each portfolio we consider two levels of the volatility of volatility: 20 percent ("High") and 10 percent ("Low"). We also consider two possible cases for the correlation structure: uncorrelated, and correlated with

$$\text{Corr}[\Delta\widetilde{S}_i, \Delta\widetilde{S}_j] = 0.20, \;\; \text{Corr}[\Delta\widetilde{S}_i, \Delta\widetilde{\sigma}_i] = -0.25, \;\; \text{Corr}[\Delta\widetilde{S}_i, \Delta\widetilde{\sigma}_j] = 0, \;\; \text{Corr}[\Delta\widetilde{\sigma}_i, \Delta\widetilde{\sigma}_j] = 0.6.$$

The interpretation of this case is as follows. All assets are affected by a common "market level" factor inducing a positive correlation in price changes; each asset has a negative correlation with its own implied volatility (so volatility goes up when prices drop); and all implied volatilities are affected by a common "volatility level" factor inducing a positive correlation in volatility changes.

The results are summarized in Table 2. The variance ratios for portfolios (a.1), (a.4), and (a.7) are similar to what we found in the case of constant volatility. We see less variance reduction for the portfolio that is both delta and gamma hedged. For this portfolio the IS and ISS-Q methods rely entirely on vega information as we do not assume the availability of second derivatives involving volatilities. The delta-gamma-vega approximation is therefore less informative in this case than in the others.

Table 2: Variance reduction estimates with volatility as a risk factor

	Portfolio	x_{std}	$P(L > x)$	Variance ratios	
				IS	ISS-Q
(a.1)	Uncorrelated, High	2.5	1.0%	30	244
	Uncorrelated, Low		1.0%	30	291
	Correlated, High	2.6	1.1%	28	281
	Correlated, Low		1.2%	26	285
(a.4)	Uncorrelated, High	2.6	1.1%	23	65
	Uncorrelated, Low		1.1%	23	74
	Correlated, High	3.0	1.1%	19	84
	Correlated, Low		1.1%	19	96
(a.7)	Uncorrelated, High	2.8	1.1%	17	28
	Uncorrelated, Low		1.1%	17	29
	Correlated, High	3.2	1.0%	12	20
	Correlated, Low		1.1%	11	18
$\delta{-}\Gamma$ hedged	Uncorrelated, High	3.3	1.0%	9	8
	Uncorrelated, Low		0.9%	10	13
	Correlated, High	2.7	1.1%	14	21
	Correlated, Low		1.2%	11	19

Conclusion

The methods reviewed in this article attempt to combine the best features of two approaches to calculating VaR: the speed of the delta-gamma approximation and the accuracy of Monte Carlo simulation. We use the delta-gamma approximation not as a substitute for simulation but rather as an aid. By using the delta-gamma approximation to guide the sampling of scenarios – through a combination of importance sampling and stratified sampling – we can greatly reduce the number of scenarios needed in a simulation to achieve a specified precision.

For simplicity, in this article we have restricted attention to methods based on modeling changes in market risk factors over the VaR horizon using a normal distribution. But empirical studies consistently find that market returns exhibit greater kurtosis and heavier tails than can be captured with a normal distribution. In Glasserman, Heidelberger, and Shahabuddin (2000c), we extend the methods discussed here to certain heavy-tailed distributions, including multivariate *t* distributions. This setting poses interesting new theoretical questions as well as having practical relevance. Numerical results indicate that our methods are generally at least as effective in the heavy-tailed setting as in the normal case.

Summary

The calculation of Value-at-Risk for large portfolios presents a tradeoff between speed and accuracy, with the fastest methods relying on rough approximations and the most realistic approach – Monte Carlo simulation – often too slow to be practical. This article describes methods that use the best features of both approaches. The methods build on the delta-gamma approximation, but they use the approximation not as a substitute for simulation but rather as an aid to it. **Paul Glasserman**, **Philip Heidelberger** and **Perwez Shahabuddin** use the delta-gamma approximation to guide the sampling of market scenarios through a combination of importance sampling and stratified sampling. This can greatly reduce the number of scenarios required in a simulation to achieve a desired precision. The authors also describe an extension of the method in which "vega" terms are included in the approximation to capture changes in the level of volatility.

Suggested further reading

Alexander, C. (2001) *Market Models: A guide to financial data analysis*, Wiley, Chichester, UK.

Britten-Jones, M. and Schaefer, S.M. (1999) "Non-linear Value-at-Risk," *European Finance Review*, 2, pp. 161–187.

Cardenas, J., Fruchard, E., Picron, J.-F., Reyes, C., Walters, K. and Yang, W. (1999) "Monte Carlo within a day," *Risk*, 12:2, pp. 55–59.

Glasserman, P., Heidelberger, P. and Shahabuddin, P. (1999) "Stratification issues in estimating Value-at-Risk" in *Proceedings of the 1999 Winter Simulation Conference*, pp. 351–358, IEEE Computer Society Press, Piscataway, New Jersey.

Glasserman, P., Heidelberger, P. and Shahabuddin, P. (2000a) "Importance sampling and stratification for Value-at-Risk" in *Computational Finance 1999 (Proceedings of the Sixth International Conference on Computational Finance)*, Y.S. Abu-Mostafa, B. LeBaron, A.W. Lo and A.S. Weigend, eds, pp. 7–24, MIT Press, Cambridge, Mass.

Glasserman, P., Heidelberger, P. and Shahabuddin, P. (2000b) "Variance reduction techniques for estimating Value-at-Risk," *Management Science*, Vol. 46, pp. 1349–1364.

Glasserman, P., Heidelberger, P. and Shahabuddin, P. (2000c) "Portfolio Value-at-Risk with heavy-tailed risk factors," PaineWebber Finance Working Paper Series PW-00-06, Columbia Business School, New York. Available at www.columbia.edu/cu.business/wp/00/

Jorion, P. (1997) *Value-at-Risk*, McGraw-Hill, New York.

Rouvinez, C. (1997) "Going Greek with VaR," *Risk*, 10:2, pp. 57–65.

Wilson, T. (1998) "Value-at-Risk" in *Risk Management and Analysis*, Vol. 1 pp. 61–124, C. Alexander, ed., Wiley, Chichester, UK.

Orthogonal GARCH

by Carol Alexander

During the past few years there have been many changes in the way that financial institutions model risk. New risk capital regulations have motivated a need for vertically integrated risk systems based on a unified framework throughout the whole office. If the risk exposures in all locations of a large institution are to be aggregated, the risk system must also be horizontally integrated. Internationally, regulators are pushing toward an environment where traders, quants and risk managers from all offices are referring to risk measures generated by the same models. This is a huge task and remains a challenge for many financial institutions, but the result should be useful to manage risks for allocation of capital between different areas of the company, and to set traders' limits as well as levels of capital reserves.

Following the Basel Accord Amendment in 1996 for the calculation of market risk capital using internal models, the Basel Committee on Banking Supervision (1995) recommended two methods for generating a unified set of risk measures on a daily basis. These methods have become industry standards for measuring risk not only for external regulatory purposes but also for internal risk management. The first approach is to calculate a Value-at-Risk (VaR) measure, which is a lower percentile of an unrealized profit and loss distribution. This distribution is based on movements of the market risk factors over a fixed risk horizon. The second approach is to quantify the maximum loss over a large set of scenarios for movements in the risk factors.

Given the huge number of market risk factors affecting the positions of a large financial institution, VaR models and scenario-based loss models may become very complex indeed. In fact, their implementation becomes extraordinarily cumbersome, if not impossible, without making assumptions that restrict the possibilities for movements in the risk factors. For example, at the heart of many risk models there is a covariance matrix that captures the volatilities and correlations between the risk factors. Typically hundreds of risk factors, such as all yield curves, interest rates, equity indices, foreign exchange rates and commodity prices, need to be encompassed by a very large dimensional covariance matrix. It is not easy to generate this matrix and so simplifying assumptions may be necessary. For example, the RiskMetrics methodologies designed by J.P. Morgan use either simple, equally weighted moving averages, or exponentially weighted moving averages with the same smoothing constant for all volatilities and correlations of returns. There are limitations with both of these methods, described in Alexander (2001).

Another example of how the standard methods necessitate simplifying assumptions is in maximum loss calculations. The applicability of maximum loss measures depends on portfolio revaluation over all possible scenarios, including movements in both prices and implied volatilities of all risk factors. In complex portfolios the computational burden of full revaluation over thousands of scenarios would be absolutely enormous, and certainly not possible to achieve within an acceptable time frame unless analytic price approximations and advanced sampling techniques are employed in conjunction with a restriction of the possibility set for scenarios.

The problems outlined in both of the above examples have a common root: the computations, be they volatility and correlation calculations for a covariance matrix or portfolio revaluation for the calculation of maximum loss, are being applied to the full set of risk factors. So the dimensions of the problem become too large to manage and the problem is intractable.

But there is an alternative: to apply computations to only a few key market risk factors that capture the most important uncorrelated sources of information in the data. Such an approach is computationally efficient because it allows an enormous reduction in the dimension of the problem while retaining a very high degree of accuracy. Because the risk factors are uncorrelated it does not significantly increase the computational complexity even if a large number of key risk factors are employed. Normally a sufficient number of key risk factors will be generated so that any movements that are not captured by these factors are deemed to be insignificant "noise" in the system, and by cutting out this noise the risk measures will become more stable and robust over time. Also, being able to quantify how much risk is associated with each key factor is an enormous advantage for risk managers because their attention is more easily directed toward the most important sources of risk.

The method used here to identify key uncorrelated sources of risk within a large system is principal component analysis. Jamshidian and Zhu (1996) have shown how principal components may be used to improve computational efficiency for scenario-based risk measures in large multi-currency portfolios. This article extends these ideas to the efficient computation of the large positive semi-definite covariance matrices that are necessary for many internal models for measuring market risk.

The problem with multivariate GARCH

Univariate generalized autoregressive conditional heteroscedasticity (GARCH) models were introduced by Engle (1982) and Bollerslev (1986). They have been very successful for volatility forecasting in financial markets. The mathematical foundation of GARCH models compares favorably with some of the alternatives used by financial practitioners, and this mathematical coherency makes GARCH models easy to adapt to new financial applications.

There is evidence that GARCH models generate more realistic medium-term forecasts than equally or exponentially weighted moving averages. This is because the GARCH volatility and correlation term structure forecasts will converge to the long-term average level, which may be imposed on the model, whereas moving average models forecast volatility to be the same for all risk horizons (see Alexander, 1998). As for short-term volatility forecasts, statistical results are mixed – for example, see Andersen and Bollerslev (1998), Alexander and Leigh (1997), Brailsford and Faff (1996), Cumby, Figlewski and Hasbrouck (1993), Dimson and Marsh (1990), Figlewski (1997), Frennberg and Hansson (1996), and West and Cho (1995). This is not surprising since the whole area of statistical evaluation of volatility forecasts is fraught with difficulty (see Alexander, 2001, Chapter 5).

Another test of volatility forecasting models is in their hedging performance. There is much to be said for using the GARCH volatility framework for pricing and hedging options (see Duan 1995, 1996). Engle and Rosenberg (1995) provide an operational evaluation of GARCH models for option pricing and hedging, demonstrating a clear superiority to the Black-Scholes methods with an extensive empirical study.

Large covariance matrices that are based on GARCH models would, therefore, have clear advantages over those generated by exponentially or equally weighted moving averages. Previous research in this area has met with rather limited success. It is straightforward to generalize the univariate GARCH models to multivariate parameterizations, as in Engle and Kroner (1993). But the actual implementation of these models is extremely difficult. With so many parameters, the likelihood function becomes very flat, and so convergence problems are very common in the optimization routine.

Multivariate GARCH models have been the subject of extensive academic research. Bollerslev, Engle and Nelson (1994) provide a good review of most of the earlier literature; Alexander (2001) gives a review of the more recent work. Bivariate GARCH models are relatively simple to estimate and have some useful applications to the computation of time-varying hedge ratios – see Baillie and Myers (1991); Kroner and Claessens (1991); and Park and Switzer (1995) – and the pricing of options that are based on two correlated assets – see Duan and Wei (1999).

GARCH models on more than two variables have been less successful because substantial computational difficulties may be encountered when they are applied to the problems that actually arise in practice. There has been considerable research on different ways of parameterizing multivariate GARCH models so that the GARCH covariance matrices are positive definite, see Engle and Mezrich (1996). However, the computational aspects become more and more problematic as the dimension increases and at the moment there is no chance that multivariate GARCH models can be used to estimate directly the very large covariance matrices that are required to net all the risks in a large trading book.

This article introduces a new method for generating large, positive, semi-definite covariance matrices.[1] The method is computationally very simple, as it is based on the univariate GARCH volatilities of the first few principal components of a system of risk factors. For example, a full dimensional covariance matrix for a yield curve can be generated by simply combining two or three univariate GARCH volatilities with the factor weights matrix from the principal component analysis of the yield curve. The usual GARCH analytic formulae for computing the term structure of

---

[1] The orthogonal GARCH model is a generalization of the factor GARCH model introduced by Engle, Ng and Rothschild (1990) to a multi-factor model with orthogonal factors. The idea of using principal component analysis for multivariate GARCH modeling goes back to Ding (1994). However, in his PhD thesis, Ding used the full number of principle components in the representation and the results were not particularly good. The idea of using a reduced space of principal components was first introduced by Alexander and Chibumba (1996). Commercial software that generates large orthogonal GARCH matrices has been available since 1996 from S-Plus GARCH and since 1998 from www.algorithmics.com An Excel add-in for orthogonal GARCH model is available from cleigh@dial.pipex.com

volatility and correlation are applied so that the n-day covariance matrix converges to the long-term average as n increases. Other advantages of this method include the ability to tailor the amount of noise in the system so that correlation estimates are more stable. The method may also be used to obtain volatility and correlation forecasts of new issues, and it allows one to estimate volatilities and correlation even when markets are illiquid.

Given these considerable advantages for generating high dimensional covariance matrices, one would not necessarily expect orthogonal GARCH to perform as well as other multivariate GARCH models when the system has only a few dimensions. Indeed, some multivariate GARCH models are designed for the specific purposes of estimating single correlations, so they are based only on a bivariate GARCH specification. Nevertheless, Engle (2000) shows that the orthogonal GARCH model performs extremely well according to three out of the four diagnostics that he has chosen for assessing the accuracy of correlation forecasts.

The method can also be used with EWMA volatilities of the principal components. In orthogonal EWMA there is no need to impose the same value of the smoothing constant on all variables, as there is in the RiskMetrics data sets. In Orthogonal EWMA the persistence in volatilities and correlation will not be the same for all factors. Instead it will be determined by the correlation in the system.

Identification of the key risk factors: principal component analysis

Suppose a set of data with T observations on k asset or risk factor returns is summarized in a $T{\times}k$ matrix $\mathbf{Y}$. Principal component analysis will give up to k uncorrelated stationary variables, called the principal components of $\mathbf{Y}$, each component being a simple linear combination of the original returns as in (1) below. At the same time it is stated exactly how much of the total variation in the original system of risk factors is explained by each principal component, and the components are ordered according to the amount of variation they explain.

The first step in principal component analysis is to normalize the data in a $T{\times}k$ matrix $\mathbf{X}$ that represents the same variables as $\mathbf{Y}$, but in $\mathbf{X}$ each column is standardized to have mean zero and variance 1. So if the ith risk factor or asset return in the system is $\mathbf{y}_i$, then the normalized variables are $\mathbf{x}_i = (\mathbf{y}_i - \mu_i)/\sigma_i$ where μ_i and σ_i are the mean and standard deviation of $\mathbf{y}_i$ for $i = 1, \ldots k$. Now let $\mathbf{W}$ be the matrix of eigenvectors of $\mathbf{X}'\mathbf{X}$, and Λ be the associated diagonal matrix of eigenvalues, ordered according to decreasing magnitude of eigenvalue.[2] The principal components of $\mathbf{Y}$ are given by the $T{\times}k$ matrix

$$\mathbf{P} = \mathbf{XW} \tag{1}$$

Thus a linear transformation of the original risk factor returns has been made in such a way that the transformed risk factors are orthogonal, i.e., they have zero correlation.[3]

---

[2] Thus $\mathbf{X}'\mathbf{X}\,\mathbf{W} = \mathbf{W}\,\Lambda$.

[3] Note that $\mathbf{P}'\mathbf{P} = \mathbf{W}'\mathbf{X}'\mathbf{X}\mathbf{W} = \mathbf{W}'\mathbf{W}\Lambda$, but $\mathbf{W}$ is an orthogonal matrix so $\mathbf{P}'\mathbf{P} = \Lambda$, a diagonal matrix. This also shows that the variance of the ith principal component equals the ith eigenvalue of $\mathbf{X}'\mathbf{X}$.

The new risk factors are ordered by the amount of the variation they explain.[4] Hence only the first few, the most important factors, may be chosen to represent the system as follows: since $\mathbf{W}$ is orthogonal, (1) is equivalent to $\mathbf{X} = \mathbf{PW}'$, that is

$$\mathbf{x}_i = w_{i1}\, \mathbf{p}_1 + w_{i2}\, \mathbf{p}_2 + \ldots\ldots + w_{ik}\, \mathbf{p}_k \tag{2}$$

so the matrix $\mathbf{W}$ is called the matrix of "factor weights." In terms of the original variables $\mathbf{Y}$ the representation (2) is equivalent to

$$\mathbf{y}_i = \mu_i + \omega^*_{i1}\, \mathbf{p}_1 + \omega^*_{i2}\, \mathbf{p}_2 + \ldots\ldots + \omega^*_{im}\, \mathbf{p}_m + \boldsymbol{\epsilon}_i \tag{3}$$

where $\omega^*_{ij} = w_{ij}\sigma_i$ and the error term in (3) picks up the approximation from using only the first m of the k principal components. These m principal components are the "key" risk factors of the system, and the rest of the variation is ascribed to "noise" in the error term. The representation (3) indicates how, when covariance or scenario calculations are based only on the most important principal components, the effect may be easily translated back to the original system through a simple linear transformation.

Using PCA to generate positive semi-definite covariance matrices

Since principal components are orthogonal, their covariance matrix is simply the diagonal matrix of their variances. These variances can be transformed into a co-variance matrix of the original system using the factor weights as follows: Taking variances of (3) gives

$$\mathbf{V} = \mathbf{ADA}' + \mathbf{V}_\varepsilon \tag{4}$$

where $\mathbf{A} = (\omega^*_{ij})$ is the k×m matrix of normalized factor weights, $\mathbf{D} = \mathrm{diag}(V(\mathbf{p}_1), \ldots V(\mathbf{p}_m))$ is the diagonal matrix of variances of principal components, and $\mathbf{V}_\varepsilon$ is the covariance matrix of the errors. Ignoring $\mathbf{V}_\varepsilon$ gives the approximation

$$\mathbf{V} \approx \mathbf{ADA}' \tag{5}$$

with an accuracy that is controlled by choosing more or fewer components to represent the system. This shows how the full $k\times k$ covariance matrix of asset or risk factor returns $\mathbf{V}$ is obtained from just a few estimates of the variances of the principal components.

Note that $\mathbf{V}$ will be positive semi-definite, but it may not be strictly positive definite unless $m = k$.[5] Although $\mathbf{D}$ is positive definite because it is a diagonal matrix

---

[4] The proportion of the total variation in $\mathbf{X}$ that is explained by the mth principal component is λ_m/k, where the eigenvalue λ_m of $\mathbf{X'X}$ corresponds to the mth principal component and the column labeling in $\mathbf{W}$ has been chosen so that $\lambda_1 > \lambda_2 > \ldots\ldots > \lambda_k$.

[5] A symmetric matrix $\mathbf{A}$ is positive definite iff $\mathbf{x'Ax} > 0$ for all non-zero $\mathbf{x}$. If $\mathbf{w}$ is a vector of portfolio weights and $\mathbf{V}$ is the covariance matrix of asset returns, then the portfolio variance is $\mathbf{w'Vw}$. So covariance matrices must always be positive definite, otherwise some portfolios may have non-positive variance.

with positive elements, there is nothing to guarantee that $\mathbf{ADA'}$ will be positive definite when $m < k$. To see this write

$$\mathbf{x'ADA'x = y'Dy}$$

where $\mathbf{A'x = y}$. Since y can be zero for some non-zero $\mathbf{x}$, $\mathbf{x'ADA'x}$ will not be strictly positive for all non-zero x. It may be zero, and so $\mathbf{ADA'}$ is only positive semi-definite. When covariance matrices are based on (5) with $m < k$, they should be run through an eigenvalue check to ensure strict positive definiteness. However, it is reasonable to expect that the approximation (5) will give a strictly positive definite covariance matrix if the representation (3) is made with a high degree of accuracy.

The first advantage of using this type of orthogonal transformation to generate risk factor covariance matrices is now clear. There is a very high degree of computational efficiency in calculating only m variances instead of the $k(k+1)/2$ variances and covariances of the original system. For example, in a single yield curve with, say, 15 maturities, only the variances of the first two or three principal components need to be computed, instead of the 120 variances and covariances of the yields of 15 different maturities.[6]

Orthogonal EWMA

Exponentially weighted moving averages (EWMA) of the squares and cross products of returns are a standard method for generating covariance matrices. But a limitation of this type of direct application of EWMA is that the covariance matrix is only guaranteed to be positive semi-definite if the same smoothing constant is used for all the data.[7] That is, the reaction of volatility to market events and the persistence in volatility must be assumed to be the same in all the assets or risk factors that are represented in the covariance matrix.

A major advantage of the orthogonal factor method described here is that it allows EWMA methods to be used without this unrealistic constraint. Each principal component exponentially weighted moving average variance would normally be applied with a different smoothing constant. So the degree of smoothing in the variance of any particular asset or risk factor that is calculated by the orthogonal method will depend on the factor weights in the principal component representation. Since the factor weights of an asset are determined by its correlation with other variables in the system, so also is the degree of smoothing. That is, the market reaction and volatility persistence of a given asset will not be the same as the other assets in the system, but instead it will be related to its correlation with the other assets.

[6] In highly correlated systems the first principal component, which represents a common trend in the variables, will explain a large part of the variation. In term structures and other ordered systems, the second principal component represents a "tilt" from shorter to longer maturities. Often the majority of the variation in a term structure can be explained when the system is represented by these two components alone. It is common for more than 90 percent of the variation to be explained when a third component, the "curvature," is added, so the considerable dimension reduction achieved by using two or three principal components results in little loss of accuracy. More details about principal component analysis and examples may be found in Alexander (2001).

[7] See the RiskMetrics Technical Document, 4th Edition, 1996 (www.riskmetrics.com).

Orthogonal GARCH

A principal component representation is a multi-factor model. The idea of using factor models with GARCH is not new. Engle, Ng and Rothschild (1990) use the capital asset pricing model to show how the volatilities and correlations between individual equities can be generated from the univariate GARCH variance of the market risk factor. Their results have a straightforward extension to multi-factor models, but unless the factors are orthogonal, a multivariate GARCH model on the risk factors will still be required. The orthogonal GARCH model is a generalization of the factor GARCH model introduced by Engle, Ng and Rothschild (1990) to a multi-factor model with orthogonal factors.

The orthogonal GARCH model allows $k \times k$ GARCH covariance matrices to be generated from just m univariate GARCH models. It may be that m, the number of principal components, will be much less than k, the number of variables in the system – and quite often one would wish m to be less than k so that extraneous "noise" is excluded from the data. But since only univariate GARCH models are used, there are no dimensional restrictions as there are with the direct parameterizations of multivariate GARCH.

Of course, the principal components are only unconditionally uncorrelated, so a conditional covariance matrix of principal components is not necessarily diagonal. However, the assumption of zero conditional correlations has to be made in order to generate large GARCH covariance matrices from GARCH volatilities alone.

The degree of accuracy that is lost by making this assumption is investigated by a thorough calibration of the model, comparing the variances and covariances produced with those from other models such as exponentially weighted moving averages or, for small systems, with multivariate GARCH. Care needs to be taken with the initial calibration, in terms of the number of components used and the time period used to estimate them, but once calibrated the orthogonal GARCH model may be run very quickly and efficiently on a daily basis. The remainder of this article examines how to calibrate orthogonal GARCH(1,1) models to term structures and to large dimensional equity and FX systems.

Orthogonal GARCH of a futures term structure

The orthogonal method is ideally suited to highly correlated ordered systems such as a term structure. The first example will compare orthogonal EWMA with orthogonal GARCH(1,1) with just two principal components for the WTI crude oil futures from 1 month to 12 months, sampled daily between 4 February 1993 and 24 March 1999. The 1, 2, 3, 6, 9 and 12-month maturity futures prices are shown in Figure 1 and the results of a principal component analysis on daily returns are given in Table 1.[8]

Of course the factor weights show that, as with any term structure, the interpretations of the first three principal components are the trend, tilt and curvature components respectively. In fact, this particular system is so highly

---

[8] See Alexander (1999) for a fuller discussion of correlations in energy markets. Many thanks to Enron for supplying these data.

Figure 1: NYMEX sweet crude prices

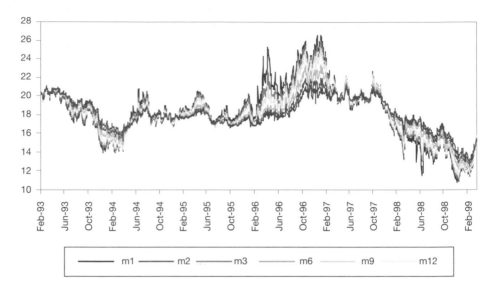

Table 1a: Eigenvalue analysis

Component	Eigenvalue	Cumulative R^2
P1	11.51	0.9592
P2	0.397	0.9923
P3	0.069	0.9981

Table 1b: Factor weights

	P1	P2	P3
1mth	0.89609	0.40495	0.18027
2mth	0.96522	0.24255	−0.063052
3mth	0.98275	0.15984	−0.085002
4mth	0.99252	0.087091	−0.080116
5mth	0.99676	0.026339	−0.065143
6mth	0.99783	−0.020895	−0.046369
7mth	0.99702	−0.062206	−0.023588
8mth	0.99451	−0.098582	0.000183
9mth	0.99061	−0.13183	0.020876
10mth	0.98567	−0.16123	0.040270
11mth	0.97699	−0.19269	0.064930
12mth	0.97241	−0.21399	0.075176

correlated that more than 99 percent of its variation may be explained by just two principal components and the first principal component alone explains almost 96 percent of the variation over the period.

The GARCH(1,1) model defines the conditional variance at time t as

Table 2: GARCH(1,1) models of the first two principal components

	1st principal component		2nd principal component	
	Coefficient	t-stat	Coefficient	t-stat
constant	0.650847E-02	0.304468	0.122938E-02	0.066431
ω	0.644458E-02	3.16614	0.110818	7.34255
α	0.037769	8.46392	0.224810	9.64432
β	0.957769	169.198	0.665654	21.5793

$$\sigma_t^2 = \omega + \alpha\,\varepsilon_{t-1}^2 + \beta\,\sigma_{t-1}^2 \tag{6}$$

where $\omega > 0$, α, $\beta \geq 0$. This simple GARCH model effectively captures volatility clustering and provides convergent term structure forecasts to the long-term average level of volatility $100\sqrt{250\omega/(1-\alpha-\beta)}$. The coefficient α measures the intensity of reaction of volatility to yesterday's unexpected market return ε_{t-1}^2, and the coefficient β measures the persistence in volatility.[9]

Applying (6) to the first two principal components of these data gives the parameter estimates shown in Table 2. Note that the first component has low market reaction but high persistence, and the opposite is true for the second component. This reflects much of what is already known about the data from the principal component analysis: the system is very highly correlated indeed, in fact price decoupling occurs for only very short periods of time. Now in the orthogonal model all the variation in correlations will come from the second or higher principal components because with only one component all variables are assumed to be perfectly correlated. The second component here has a "spiky" volatility, and this gives rise to orthogonal GARCH correlations that also have only temporary deviations from normal levels. Thus the orthogonal GARCH model will capture the true nature of the spot-future relationship. Unfortunately the exponentially or equally weighted moving average correlations that are in standard use will have a substantial bias following temporary price decoupling (see Alexander, 2001).

Figure 2 shows how closely the volatilities that are obtained using the orthogonal method compare with those obtained by the direct application of (a) exponentially weighted moving averages and (b) GARCH(1,1) models.[10] Of course there is no space here to graph all 78 volatilities and correlations from the 12×12 covariance matrix. Interested readers may use the programs provided with Alexander (2000) to verify that all volatilities, not just those shown in Figure 2, are very similar. However, there is a difference in correlations, depending not on whether a direct or an orthogonal approach is used but on whether exponentially weighted moving averages or GARCH(1,1) models are used. As mentioned above, the orthogonal

---

[9] Note that these are determined separately in the GARCH(1,1) model, subject only to the constraint that $\alpha + \beta < 1$. In the exponentially weighted moving average model these parameters are not independent because they always sum to 1. Also the constant is zero, so there is no long-term average level in the EWMA model and volatility term structures are constant.

[10] There is no optimal method for choosing a value for the smoothing in these exponentially weighted moving averages. A value of 0.95 has been used throughout.

Figure 2: Direct and orthogonal volatilities

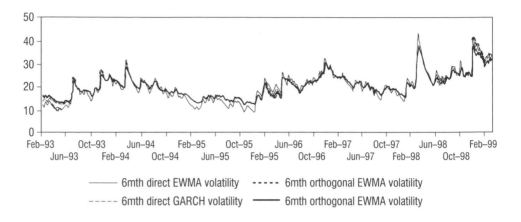

GARCH correlations more accurately reflect the true nature of the spot-future relationship.

The main disadvantage of the direct method is that it requires estimating 78 volatilities and correlations, using (a) the same value of the smoothing constant for the exponentially weighted moving average model, or (b) a 12-dimensional multivariate GARCH model. Both of these approaches have substantial limitations, as described above. However, using the orthogonal method, only two moving average variances, or two univariate GARCH(1,1) variances, of the trend and tilt principal components need to be generated. The entire 12×12 covariance matrix of the original system is simply a transformation of these two variances, as defined in (5) above, and it may be recovered in this way with negligible loss of precision.

Several good reasons to prefer GARCH models over exponentially weighted moving averages have already been mentioned. One of the most compelling reasons is that only the GARCH approach will give mean-reverting term structure forecasts. In the orthogonal GARCH model these forecasts, for volatilities and correlations of all maturities, are obtained from the simple transformations (5) where the diagonal matrix **D** contains the n-period GARCH(1,1) variance forecasts of the principal components.[11] Some of these are illustrated for volatilities of the 1mth oil future in Figure 3.

Using orthogonal GARCH with illiquid data

The orthogonal method, applied with either GARCH or exponentially weighted moving average variances, allows one to generate estimates for volatilities and correlations of variables in the system even when data are sparse and unreliable, such as in illiquid markets. For example, the direct estimation of a time-varying variance of a 12-year bond may be difficult, but the orthogonal method allows its

---

[11] The n-period GARCH(1,1) variance forecast is the sum of n forward variances for $j = 1, \ldots. $ n:
$\hat{\sigma}^2_{t+j} = \hat{\omega} + (\hat{\alpha} + \hat{\beta})\hat{\sigma}^2_{t+j-1}$.

Figure 3: Orthogonal GARCH term structure volatility forecasts for one-month crude oil futures

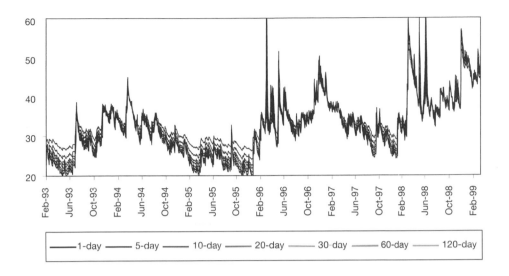

variance to be calculated from the variances of the key risk factors used in its representation.

The next example applies the orthogonal GARCH(1,1) model to another term structure, but a rather difficult one. Daily zero coupon yield data in the UK with 11 different maturities between 1 month and 10 years from 1 January 1992 to 24 March 1995 are shown in Figure 4. It is not an easy task to estimate univariate GARCH models on the first differences of these yields directly because the yields often remain the same for a number of days. Particularly on the more illiquid maturities, there is insufficient conditional heteroscedasticity for univariate

Figure 4: UK zero-coupon yields

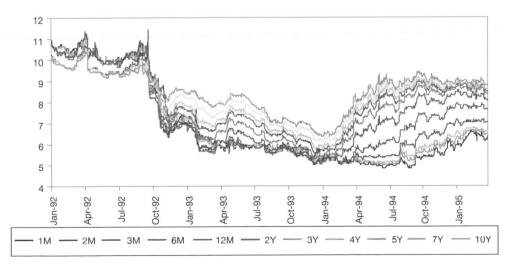

Table 3a: Eigenvalue analysis

Component	Eigenvalue	Cumulative R^2
P1	5.9284117	0.53894652
P2	1.9899323	0.71984946
P3	0.97903180	0.80885235

Table 3b: Factor weights

	P1	P2	P3
1mth	0.50916	0.60370	0.12757
2mth	0.63635	0.62136	−0.048183
3mth	0.68721	0.57266	−0.10112
6mth	0.67638	0.47617	−0.10112
12mth	0.83575	0.088099	−0.019350
2yr	0.88733	−0.21379	0.033486
3yr	0.87788	−0.30805	−0.033217
4yr	0.89648	−0.36430	0.054061
5yr	0.79420	−0.37981	0.14267
7yr	0.78346	−0.47448	0.069182
10yr	0.17250	−0.18508	−0.95497

GARCH models to converge well, so an 11-dimensional multivariate GARCH model is out of the question.

Again two principal components were used in the orthogonal GARCH, but the principal component analysis illustrated in Table 3 shows that these two components account for only 72 percent of the total variation. Also, the 10yr yield has a very low correlation with the rest of the system, as reflected by its factor weight on the first principal component; it is quite out of line with the rest of the factor weights on this component; so the fit of the orthogonal model could be improved if the 10yr bond were excluded from the system. Despite these difficulties, the volatilities obtained using the orthogonal GARCH model are very similar to those obtained by direct estimation of exponentially weighted moving averages.[12]

The GARCH (1,1) parameter estimates of the principal components are given in Table 4. This time both components have fairly persistent volatilities. Combine this

Table 4: GARCH(1,1) models of the first two principal components

	1st principal component		2nd principal component	
	Coefficient	t-stat	Coefficient	t-stat
constant	0.769758E-02	0.249734	0.033682	1.09064
ω	0.024124	4.50366	0.046368	6.46634
α	0.124735	6.46634	0.061022	9.64432
β	0.866025	135.440	0.895787	50.8779

[12] The smoothing constant for all exponentially weighted moving averages was again set at 0.95.

Figure 5: Orthogonal GARCH corretations, UK zero-coupon yields

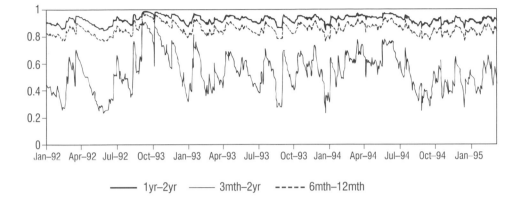

with the fact that almost 28 percent of the variation has been ascribed to "noise" by using only these first two principal components, and it is not unsurprising that the orthogonal GARCH model produces quite stable correlation estimates – more stable than those obtained by direct application of exponentially weighted moving averages.

Figure 5 shows some of the orthogonal GARCH correlations for the UK zero coupon yields. Not only does the orthogonal method provide a way of estimating GARCH volatilities and volatility term structures that may be difficult to obtain by direct univariate GARCH estimation, it also gives sensible GARCH correlations, which would be extremely difficult to estimate using direct multivariate GARCH. And all these are obtained from just two principal components, the key market risk factors that are representing the most important sources of information – all the rest of the variation is ascribed to "noise" and is not included in the model.

It is not only in illiquid markets that the orthogonal GARCH model can be used to overcome data problems. When there is a new equity issue, lack of historical data can present enormous difficulties, not just for risk management, where a minimum standard of one year of historical data is often imposed, but also in pricing long-term derivatives if the firm wishes to raise capital in this way. However, it is possible to obtain volatility forecasts using orthogonal GARCH (or orthogonal EWMA) if the price of the stock is related to the prices of several other stocks for which there is a reasonable amount of historical data. One must also wait a while after the issue, long enough for the price to have settled and for there to have been enough price quotations for a reasonable short-term analysis. Alexander (2001) shows that excellent results can be obtained not just for the volatility of the stock but for the simulation of an historic price series.

Generating a large covariance matrix across all risk factor categories

All risk factors, such as equity market indices, exchange rates, commodities, government bond and money market rates, and so on, must first be divided into reasonably highly correlated categories. These categories will normally be according to geographic locations and instrument types. Principal component analysis is then used to extract the key risk factors from each category and their variances obtained using GARCH or EWMA. Then the factor weights from the principal component analysis are used to "splice" together a large covariance matrix for the original system.

The method is explained for just two categories, then the generalization to any number of categories is straightforward. Suppose there are n variables in the first category, say it is European equity indices, and m variables in the second category, European exchange rates. It is not the dimensions that matter but that each category of risk factors is suitably codependent, so that it justifies the categorization as a separate and coherent sub-system. The first step is to find the principal components of each system, $\mathbf{P} = (\mathbf{p}_1 , \ldots \mathbf{p}_r)$, and separately $\mathbf{Q} = (\mathbf{q}_1 , \ldots \mathbf{q}_s)$ where r and s are the number of principal components that are used in the representation of each system. Denote by $\mathbf{A}$ $(n{\times}r)$ and $\mathbf{B}$ $(m{\times}s)$ the normalized factor weights matrices obtained in the principal component analysis of the European equity and exchange rate systems respectively. Then the "within factor" covariances, i.e., the covariance matrix for the equity system and for the exchange rate system separately, are given by $\mathbf{AD}_1\mathbf{A}'$ and $\mathbf{B}\,\mathbf{D}_2\mathbf{B}'$ respectively. Here $\mathbf{D}_1$ and $\mathbf{D}_2$ are the diagonal matrices of the variances of the principal components of each system. The cross-factor covariances are $\mathbf{ACB}'$ where $\mathbf{C}$ denotes the $r{\times}s$ matrix of covariances of principal components across the two systems, that is $\mathbf{C} = \{\mathrm{Cov}(\mathbf{p}_i, \mathbf{q}_j)\}$. Then the full covariance matrix of the system of European equity and exchange rate risk factors is:

$$\begin{pmatrix} \mathbf{AD}_1\mathbf{A}' & \mathbf{ACB}' \\ (\mathbf{ACB}')' & \mathbf{BD}_2\mathbf{B}' \end{pmatrix}$$

The within factor covariance matrices $\mathbf{AD}_1\mathbf{A}'$ and $\mathbf{BD}_2\mathbf{B}'$ will always be positive semi-definite. But it is not always possible to guarantee positive semi-definiteness of the full covariance matrix of the original system, unless the off diagonal blocks $\mathbf{ACB}'$ are set to zero. This is not necessarily a silly thing to do; in fact, it may be quite sensible in the light of the huge instabilities often observed in cross-factor covariances.[13]

The method is illustrated using four European equity indices and their associated sterling foreign exchange rates. The graphs in Figure 6 are based on daily return data from 1 April 1993 to 31 December 1996 on France (CAC40), Germany (DAX30), Holland (AEX), and the UK (FTSE100). In this seven-dimensional system of equity indices and foreign exchange rates there are 28 volatilities and correlations in total. Figure 6 shows just two of the correlations from an orthogonal GARCH(1,1) model of the system compared with those obtained from two different direct parameterizations of a multivariate GARCH(1,1) model: (a) the Vech model, and (b) the BEKK model. These multivariate GARCH models were only possible to estimate on each

---

[13] For non-zero cross-factor covariances it is possible to estimate the covariance between principal components of different risk factor sub-systems using exponentially weighted moving averages or orthogonal GARCH (again), giving the required estimate for $\mathbf{C}$.

Figure 6a: Equity correlation comparison (CAC-FTSE)

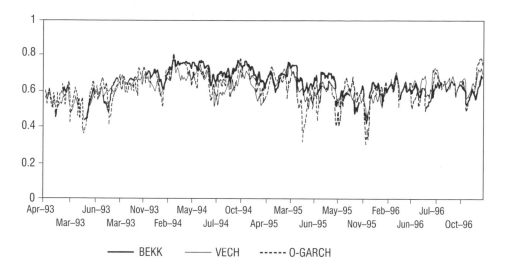

Figure 6b: FX correlation comparison

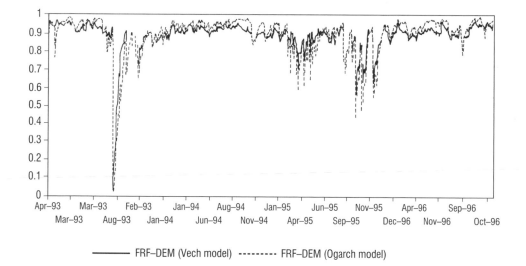

category separately. In fact, there were convergence problems with the BEKK model for the foreign exchange system, so only the Vech model correlations (which have severe cross-equation restrictions) are shown in Figure 6b.[14] These two graphs, which indicate a close similarity between the correlations, were chosen at random from the correlations for which multivariate GARCH models also produce results.

[14] In the Vech model all variances and covariances depend only on their own lag, and not on the lags of other variances and covariances in the system.

Principal component analysis and orthogonal GARCH, Vech and BEKK model parameter estimates are not reported here due to lack of space, but full details of these models and the results are given in Alexander (2000). The example has been mentioned here to illustrate the scope and flexibility of the approach to all types of asset class. It shows that it is possible to estimate these covariance matrices when direct methods are not possible, or require unrealistic restrictions. Provided the assets are first divided into reasonably highly correlated categories, principal component analysis provides a way to extract the important uncorrelated sources of information in each category. The covariance matrices for each category are generated from the variances of these key risk factors, and then a large covariance matrix that encompasses all categories is spliced together.

Conclusion

It is a common problem in risk management today that pricing models and risk measures are being applied to a very large set of scenarios based on movements in all possible risk factors. The dimensions are so large that the computations become extremely slow and cumbersome, so it is quite common that over-simplistic assumptions will be made. In particular, the large covariance matrices that are used in Value-at-Risk models can be generated only if some very strong constraints are imposed on the movements in volatility and correlations. For example, if exponentially weighted moving averages are used, the same smoothing constant must be used for every risk factor. And normally an assumption of constant volatility is made because it is extremely difficult to generate large covariance matrices with mean-reverting term structures.

In this chapter, orthogonal methods for generating covariance matrices have been applied to several different types of asset class: commodity futures prices, yield curves, equity indices, and foreign exchange rates. Large covariance matrices that are based on the volatility of a few, uncorrelated key market risk factors alone are calculated, and are shown to have many advantages over the other methods in standard use:

- positive semi-definiteness is assured, without severe constraints such as using the same model parameters for all assets and all markets;
- stochastic volatility models such as GARCH, that have many advantages but that are usually difficult to apply in higher dimensions, may be employed;
- correlations are more stable because the "noise" in the system may be measured and, if required, ignored;
- periods of sparse trading on some (but not all) assets do not present a problem because their current volatilities and correlations will be inferred from their historic relationship with the other variables in the system;
- the method conforms to the standard regulatory requirements on historic data if at least one year of data is used in the principal component analysis.

The method advocated in this chapter is computationally efficient because it allows an enormous reduction in the dimension of the scenario set while retaining a very high degree of accuracy in the risk measures and prices obtained. Since the key risk factors are uncorrelated, the method is computationally efficient even when many factors are used to represent the system. In most cases only a few key factors are necessary, and any movements that are not captured by these factors are ascribed to "noise" in the system. In fact, by cutting out this noise the model produces risk measures and prices that are more robust. Finally, it is straightforward to quantify how much risk is associated with each key factor, so risk managers will be able to focus their attention on the most important sources of risk.

Summary

Carol Alexander introduces a new method for generating large, positive semi-definite covariance matrices. These matrices have relatively few constraints imposed on the movements in volatility and correlation and the method produces covariance matrix term structures that are mean reverting. The method is computationally simple, as it is based on the univariate GARCH volatilities of the first few principal components of a system of risk factors.

Suggested further reading

Alexander, C.O. (1996) "Evaluating the use of RiskMetrics™ as a risk measurement tool for your operation: what are its advantages and limitations," *Derivatives Use, Trading and Regulation*, 2:3, pp. 277–285.

Alexander, C.O. (1998) "Volatility and correlation: methods, models and applications" in *Risk Management and Analysis: Measuring and Modelling Financial Risk* (C.O. Alexander, ed.), Wiley, Chichester, UK.

Alexander, C.O. (1999) "Correlation and cointegration in energy markets" in *Managing Energy Price Risk* (2nd Edition), RISK Publications, pp. 291–304.

Alexander, C.O. (2000) "A primer on the orthogonal GARCH model," pdf paper, data and programs available from www.ismacentre.reading.ac.uk

Alexander, C.O. (2001) *Market Models: A Guide to Financial Data Analysis*, Wiley, Chichester, UK.

Alexander, C.O. and Chibumba, A. (1996) "Multivariate orthogonal factor GARCH," *University of Sussex Discussion Papers in Mathematics*.

Alexander, C.O. and Leigh, C. (1997) "On the covariance matrices used in Value-at-Risk models," *Journal of Derivatives*, 4:3, pp. 50–62.

Andersen, T.G. and Bollerslev, T. (1998) "Answering the skeptics: yes, standard volatility models do provide accurate forecasts," *International Economic Review*, 39:4, pp. 885–905.

Baillie, R.T. and Myers, R.J. (1991) "Bivariate GARCH estimation of the optimal commodity futures hedge," *Journal of Applied Econometrics*, 6, pp. 109–24.

Basel Committee on Banking Supervision (1995) "An internal model-based approach to market risk capital requirements".

Bollerslev, T. (1986) "Generalized autoregressive conditional heteroskedasticity," *Journal of Econometrics*, 31, pp. 307–327.

Bollerslev, T., Engle, R.F. and Nelson, D.B. (1994) "ARCH models" in *Handbook of Econometrics*, Vol. 4, R.F. Engle and D.L. McFaddan (eds), North-Holland.

Brailsford, T.J. and Faff, R.W. (1996) "An evaluation of volatility forecasting techniques," *Journal of Banking and Finance*, 20:3, pp. 419–438.

Cumby, R., Figlewski, S. and Hasbrouk, J. (1993) "Forecasting volatility and correlations with EGARCH models," *Journal of Derivatives*, 1:3, pp. 51–63.

Dimson, E. and Marsh, P. (1990) "Volatility forecasting without data snooping," *Journal of Banking and Finance*, 14, pp. 399–421.

Ding, Z. (1994) *Time Series Analysis of Speculative Returns*, PhD Thesis, University of California, San Diego.

Duan, J-C (1995) "The GARCH option pricing model," *Mathematical Finance*, 5:1, pp. 13–32.

Duan, J-C (1996) "Cracking the smile," *RISK Magazine*, 9:12, pp. 55–59.

Duan, J-C and Wei, J.Z. (1999) "Pricing foreign currency and cross-currency options under GARCH," pdf available from www.rotman.utoronto.ca/~jcduan

Engle, R.F. (1982) "Autoregressive conditional heteroscedasticity with estimates of the variance of United Kingdom inflation," *Econometrica*, 50:4, pp. 987–1007.

Engle, R.F. (2000) "Dynamic conditional correlation – a simple class of multivariate GARCH models," pdf version available from http://weber.ucsd.edu/~mbacci/engle/cv.html

Engle, R.F. and Kroner, K.F. (1993) "Multivariate simultaneous generalized ARCH," *Econometric Theory*, 11, pp. 22–150.

Engle, R.F. and Mezrich, J. (1996) "GARCH for groups," *RISK Magazine*, 9:8, pp. 36–40.

Engle, R.F., Ng, V. and Rothschild, M. (1990) "Asset pricing with a factor ARCH covariance structure: empirical estimates for treasury bills," *Journal of Econometrics*, 45, pp. 213–238.

Engle, R.F. and Rosenberg, J. (1995) "GARCH gamma," *Journal of Derivatives*, 2, pp. 47–59.

Figlewski, S. (1997) "Forecasting volatility," *Financial Markets, Institutions and Instruments*, 6, pp. 1–88.

Frennberg, P. and Hansson, B. (1996) "An evaluation of alternative models for predicting stock volatility: evidence from a small stock market," *Journal of International Financial Markets, Institutions and Money*, 5, pp. 117–134.

Jamshidian, F. and Zhu, Y. (1996) "Scenario simulation: theory and methodology," *Finance and Stochastics*, 1:1, pp. 43–67.

Klaassen, F. (2000) "Have exchange rates become more closely tied? Evidence from a new multivariate GARCH Model." *University of Tilburg: Centre for Economic Research Discussion Paper.*

Kroner, K.F. and Claessens, S. (1991) "Optimal dynamic hedging portfolios and the currency composition of external debt," *Journal of International Money and Finance*, 10, pp. 131–48.

Palm, F.C. (1996) "GARCH models of volatility," in *Handbook of Statistics* (Vol. 14), *Statistical Methods in Finance*, G.S. Maddala and C.R. Rao (eds), Amsterdam: Elsevier, North Holland, pp. 209–240.

Park, T.H. and Switzer, L.N. (1995) "Bivariate GARCH estimation of the optimal hedge ratios for stock index futures: A note," *Journal of Futures Markets*, 15:1, February, pp. 61–7.

West, K.D. and Cho, D. (1995) "The predictive ability of several models of exchange rate volatility," *Journal of Econometrics*, 69, pp. 367–391.

Strike-adjusted spread: a new metric for estimating the value of equity options

by Joseph Zou and Emanuel Derman

Investors in equity options experience two problems that compound each other. In contrast to fixed-income and currency markets, there are thousands and tens of thousands of options, and each underlyer can have a potentially large volatility skew. How can an options investor gauge which option provides the best relative value?

In this chapter, we propose a method for estimating the fair volatility smile of any equity underlyer from information embedded in the time series of that underlyer's historical returns. We can then compute the relative richness or cheapness of any particular strike and expiration by examining the option's strike-adjusted spread, or SAS, the difference between its market implied volatility and its estimated historically fair volatility.

Our method obtains fair volatility smiles by estimating the appropriate risk-neutral distribution for valuing options on any equity underlyer from that underlyer's historical returns. The distribution includes the effect of both past price jumps and past shifts in realized volatility. Using this distribution, we can estimate the fair volatility skews for illiquid or thinly traded single-stock and basket options. We can also forecast changes in the skew from changes in a single options price.

The richness and cheapness of options

The equities world is a mass of data. Surrounded by fluctuating share prices, dividend yields, earnings forecasts, price/earnings (P/E) ratios, and hosts of more sophisticated measures, analysts and investors are in need of some gauge or metric with which to compare the relative attractiveness of different stocks. Into the breach, in newsletters, books and on websites, step countless economists, technical analysts, fundamental analysts, chartists, wave theorists, alpha-maximizers and other optimists, hoping to impose order and rationality, to tell you what to buy and sell.

Investors in equity options face an equally difficult task, with fewer resources. For each underlying stock, basket or index, many standard strikes and expirations are available. For a given underlyer, each strike and expiration trades at its own implied volatility, all of which, together, comprises an implied volatility surface (Derman, Kani and Zou, 1996) that moves continually. Each underlyer has its own idiosyncratic surface. In addition, underlyers can be grouped to create baskets, new underlyers with their own (never before observed) volatility surface.

For a given stock or index, how is an investor to know which strike and expiration provides the best value? What metric can options investors use to gauge their estimated excess return? What is the appropriate volatility surface for an illiquid basket? Help is sparse.

Current versus past implied volatilities

The most common gauge of options value has been the spread between current and past implied volatilities. This is the metric of options speculators, who hope to get in at historically low volatilities, hedge for a while, and get out high. When all options of a given expiration trade at the same implied volatility, it is not too hard to compare changes in implied volatility over time. Since the advent of the volatility smile, however, it has become harder to have a clear opinion of the relative richness of two complex volatility surfaces.

Implied versus historical volatilities

A second gauge is the spread between current implied and past realized volatilities. This is the metric of options replicators, who hope to lock in the difference between future realized and current implied volatilities by delta-hedging their options to expiration. This comparison becomes imprecise in the presence of a volatility skew when there is a range of implied volatilities, varying by strike, that must be compared with only a single historical realized volatility.

Strike-adjusted spread

The historical time series of a stock's returns contains much useful information. In this article we try to come to the aid of options investors by proposing a model for estimating the fair value of options based on the historical returns of their underlyers. This method leads us to the notion of strike-adjusted spread, a natural one-dimensional metric with which to rank the relative value of all standard equity options, irrespective of their particular strike or expiration. We propose to use SAS in roughly the same way that stock investors use "alpha" and mortgage investors use OAS (option-adjusted spread). To be specific, the SAS of an option is the spread between the current market implied volatility of that option and our model's estimate of its historically appropriate volatility. Our estimate includes both the effect of past price jumps and the influences of changes in volatility and correlations for basket options.

Theoretically, the historically appropriate implied volatility for a given option is determined by the cost of replicating that option throughout its lifetime. Not only is this replication cost difficult and time-consuming to simulate but, in our experience, the hedging errors due to inaccurate volatility forecasting and infrequent hedging make the resulting statistics inconclusive. Instead, our method for obtaining the appropriate implied volatility of a stock option involves the estimation of an appropriate *risk-neutral* distribution from the past *realized* return distribution of the stock. We will explain the method in more detail below, and describe its application to SAS. The same technique can be used to mark and hedge illiquid equity options whose market prices are unknown.

The strike-adjusted spread of an option depends on both its strike K and time to expiration T, and can be written more precisely as *SAS(K, T)*. SAS can be thought of as an extension of the commonly quoted implied-to-historical volatility spread, which is unique only in the absence of skew. In non-skewed worlds, both spreads become identical.

In brief, the SAS of a stock option is calculated as follows. First, choosing some historically relevant period, we obtain the distribution of stock returns over time T. This empirical return distribution characterizes the past behavior of the stock. Option theory dictates that options are valued as the discounted expected value of the option payoff over the risk-neutral distribution. We do not know the appropriate risk-neutral distribution. However, we use the empirical return distribution as a statistical prior to provide us with an estimate of the risk-neutral distribution by minimizing the entropy[1] associated with the difference between the distributions, subject to ensuring that the risk-neutral distribution is consistent with the current forward price of the stock. We call this risk-neutral distribution obtained in this way the risk-neutralized historical distribution, or RNHD. We then use the RNHD to calculate the expected values of standard options of all strikes for expiration T, and convert these values to Black-Scholes implied volatilities. We denote the Black-Scholes implied volatility of an option whose price is computed from this distribution as σ_H. This is our estimated fair option volatility.

For an option with strike K and expiration T, whose market implied volatility is $\sigma(K, T)$, the strike-adjusted spread in volatility is defined as

$$S(K, T) = \sigma(K, T) - \sigma_H(K, T).$$

[1] As we explain later, markets in equilibrium are characterized by maximum uncertainty or minimal information, and minimal entropy change is an expression of minimal information.

This spread is a measure of the current "richness" of the option based on historical returns. A positive SAS connotes richness only for standard options whose value is a monotonically increasing function of volatility. Exotic options may have values that decrease as volatility increases.

ATM strike-adjusted spread

The volatility skew, the relative gap between at-the-money and out-of-the-money implied volatilities for a given expiration, is more stable than the absolute level of at-the-money implied volatilities. Often, therefore, irrespective of historical return distributions, the current level of at-the-money implied volatility is the most believable estimate of future volatility. It is likely that historical distributions tell us more about the higher moments of future distributions than about their standard deviation.

Therefore, we will often use a modified version of SAS for which the risk-neutralized historical distribution is further constrained to reproduce the current market value of at-the-money options. We call this (additionally constrained) distribution the at-the-money adjusted, risk-neutralized historical distribution, or $RNHD_{ATM}$. The strike-adjusted spread computed using this distribution, denoted $SAS_{ATM}(K, T)$, is a measure of the relative value of different strikes, assuming that, by definition, at-the-money-forward implied volatility is fair.

We propose using $SAS_{ATM}(K, T)$ to rank options on the same underlyer, in order to determine which strikes provide the best value by historical standards. More radically, we can also use the same measure to compare options of different underlyers.

In the remainder of this chapter, we flesh out these concepts. The next section explains the relation between options prices and implied distributions. Then, we go on to compare implied distributions to historical return distributions. We then explain that markets in equilibrium are characterized by maximal investor uncertainty, and, introducing the notion of entropy, show that we can obtain an estimate of the risk-neutral distribution from the historical distribution by minimizing the entropy difference between the distributions. The main body of the chapter develops several applications of the risk-neutralized historical distribution, including SAS. For those readers interested in the mathematical appendices that go with this article, see Zou and Derman (1999).

Options prices and implied distributions

According to the theory of options valuation, stock option prices contain information about the market's collective expectation of the stock's future volatility and its return distribution. If no riskless arbitrage can occur, there exists a risk-neutral return probability distribution Q such that the value V of an option on a stock with price S at time t is given by the discounted expected value of the option's payoff, written as

$$V(S, t) = e^{-r(T-t)} E_Q[\text{ option pay-off at } T \mid S, t]$$

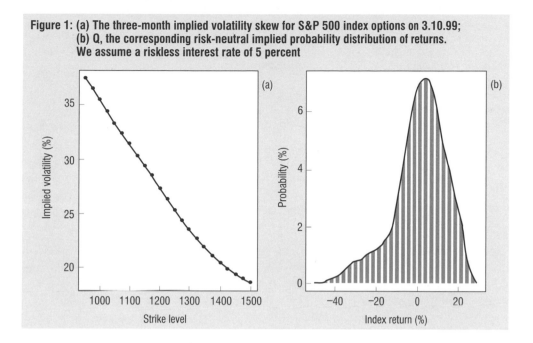

Figure 1: (a) The three-month implied volatility skew for S&P 500 index options on 3.10.99;
(b) Q, the corresponding risk-neutral implied probability distribution of returns.
We assume a riskless interest rate of 5 percent

where r is the risk-free interest rate and $E_Q[\ ]$ denotes the expected value of the future payoff at time T, given that the stock price at time t is S.

In the Black-Scholes theory, the risk-neutral implied probability distribution Q is the lognormal density function with a specified volatility. In implied tree models (Derman, Kani and Zou, 1996) Q is skewed relative to the Black-Scholes density, and can be estimated at any time from a set of traded European option prices. Figure 1a illustrates an implied volatility skew for S&P 500 index options, typically about five volatility points for a 10 percent change in strike level; Figure 1b shows the correspondingly skewed risk-neutral implied distribution Q. Whenever the shape of the skew changes, there is a corresponding change in the distribution. Knowing Q, you can calculate the fair value of any standard European option.

Stock returns and historical distributions

Stock options' prices determine the implied distribution of stock returns. Independently, we can also observe the actual distribution of stock. Consider the historical series S_i of daily closing prices of a stock or stock index. We can construct the rolling series of continuously compounded stock returns R_i from day i for a subsequent period of N trading days by calculating

$$R_i = ln(S_{i+N}) - ln(S_i).$$

Figure 2 shows the distribution of actual three-month S&P 500 returns for periods both before and after the 1987 stock market crash, where the latter period includes the crash. The pre-crash return distribution is approximately symmetric and normally distributed. In contrast, the post-crash distribution (1987 crash data included) has a higher mean return and a lower standard deviation, as well as an

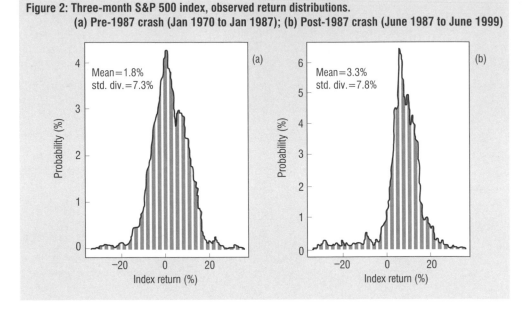

Figure 2: Three-month S&P 500 index, observed return distributions.
(a) Pre-1987 crash (Jan 1970 to Jan 1987); (b) Post-1987 crash (June 1987 to June 1999)

asymmetric secondary peak at its lower end. There is a rough similarity in shape between the implied distribution of Figure 1b, whose mean reflects the risk-free rate at which its options were priced, and the historical distribution of Figure 2b, whose (different) mean is the average historical return over the post-crash period.

Options theory does not enforce an unambiguous link between historical and implied distributions. Nevertheless, historical distributions, suitably interpreted, can provide plausible information about fair options prices. Our aim here is to develop a heuristic but logical link between the two distributions, utilizing the notions of market equilibrium and uncertainty.

Maximal uncertainty and market equilibrium

Markets are supposed to settle into equilibrium when supply equals demand, when there are equal numbers of buyers and sellers at some price. In an efficient market, the potential buyers of a stock must think the stock is cheap, and potential sellers must think it rich. This difference of opinion means that, in equilibrium, the distribution of expected returns displays great uncertainty. How do we quantify this simple intuition that equilibrium involves uncertainty in the expected return distribution?

Entropy as a measure of uncertainty

The probability of a single event is a measure of the uncertainty of its occurrence. Entropy is a mathematical function that measures the uncertainty of a probability distribution. The entropy of a random variable R, whose ith occurrence in the distribution has probability p_i, is defined to be

$$H(R) = -\Sigma p_i \, ln \, (p_i).$$

Since any probability p_i is less than or equal to 1, the entropy is always non-negative. If the distribution R collapses to one certain single event j, then H(R) = 0. Therefore, certainty corresponds to the lowest possible entropy. You can also show that the entropy takes its maximum value, ln(n), when all outcomes have an equal chance and uncertainty reigns. This is consistent with the notion that maximum entropy corresponds to maximum uncertainty and minimum information.

H(R) is the entropy of a single distribution R. We can also define the relative entropy S(P, Q) between an initial distribution P and a subsequent distribution Q. S measures the decrease in entropy (or the increase in information) between the initial distribution P and the final distribution Q, and is given by

$$S(P, Q) = E_Q[ln\ Q - ln\ P] = \sum_x Q(x)\ ln\left(\frac{Q(x)}{P(x)}\right).$$

The relative entropy is always non-negative, and is zero if and only if the two distributions P and Q are identical.[2] This agrees with our intuition that any change in a probability distribution conveys some new information. The relative entropy between two distributions measures the information gain (or reduction in uncertainty) after a distribution change. Thus, minimum relative entropy corresponds to the least increase in information.

The risk-neutralized historical distribution

Consider a stock option with time to expiration T on a stock whose spot price is S_0. To value the option, we need to average the option payoff over the risk-neutral probability density. In theory, Q is found by solving the differential equation that constrains the instantaneously hedged option to earn the instantaneously riskless return. In the Black-Scholes world, a stock's future probability distribution is assumed to be lognormal, and consequently, though not obviously, Q itself is a lognormally distributed probability density, and its options prices have no volatility skew.

This theoretical lack of skew conflicts with the data from markets, where stocks and indexes that have sufficiently liquid out-of-the-money strikes display clear, and often large, skews. How can we estimate a suitable risk-neutral probability density that is more consistent with market skews than the Black-Scholes lognormal distribution?

It is natural to turn for insight to the distribution of actual returns. The two distributions Q and P cannot be strictly identical, because the expected value of the stock price under the risk-neutral distribution Q at any time must be the stock's current forward price, as determined by the current risk-free rate, whereas the expected value of the stock price under P is the average historical forward price, which bears no relation to current risk-free rates.

The rigorous way to obtain Q from the past evolution of stock prices is to obtain fair historical options prices for a variety of strikes by simulating the

---

[2] See Appendix A of Zou and Derman (1999).

instantaneously riskless hedging strategy over the life of these options, and to then infer the risk-neutral density that matches these prices. This requires a detailed knowledge of every past instant of the stock price evolution, at all times and market levels, and is time-consuming, difficult, error-prone and ultimately impractical. Instead, we will estimate the current risk-neutral return distribution Q for a stock from its historical distribution P by assuming that the latter is a plausible estimate for the former, and then requiring that the relative entropy S(P, Q) between the distributions is minimized. We impose this criterion in order to avoid any spurious increase in apparent information in creating the risk-neutral distribution from the historical distribution. We perform the minimization subject to the risk-neutrality constraint, that is, that the expected value of the stock price under the risk-neutral distribution Q is consistent with the stock's current forward price.[3] We call Q found in this way the risk-neutralized historical distribution. It is our plausible guess for the distribution to use in options valuation, given our knowledge of the past. Our knowledge of a stock's historical volatility, the second moment of its distribution, is often used to estimate options values using the Black-Scholes formula. Here we go one step further by using the entire historical return distribution.

For a normal historical distribution of simply compounded returns, one can show that the risk-neutralized historical distribution obtained by entropy minimization is equivalent to a translation of the historical distribution to re-center it at the appropriate risk-neutral rate, without altering its shape. This translation invariance of the shape in moving from the historical to the risk-neutral distribution does not hold in general.

It is possible to impose further constraints on Q. If you believe that the current at-the-money volatility for some particular stock is fair, you can constrain the distribution Q to match not only the stock forward price but also the current at-the-money implied volatility. We denote this additionally constrained distribution by Q_{ATM} and refer to it as the at-the-money-consistent, risk-neutralized historical distribution, or $RNHD_{ATM}$. It can be used to compare the relative values of options with different strikes on one underlyer, assuming that at-the-money volatility is fair.

Having obtained our estimate of the risk-neutral distribution, we can estimate the fair price for any standard option as the discounted expected value of its payoff at expiration. We then extract the fair implied volatility as the volatility which equates the Black-Scholes option price to the estimated fair price. This procedure can be repeated for all strikes and maturities to yield an entire fair implied volatility surface.

Applications of the risk-neutralized historical distribution

The RNHD contains information which can be used to estimate the value of illiquid options whose prices are unobtainable, as well as to compare the relative value of options with known market prices. We present several representative examples below.

---

[3] Several authors have studied the relevance of entropy in financial economics and derivatives pricing. See Stutzer (1996), Derman et al. (1997), Buchen and Kelly (1996), and Gulko (1996).

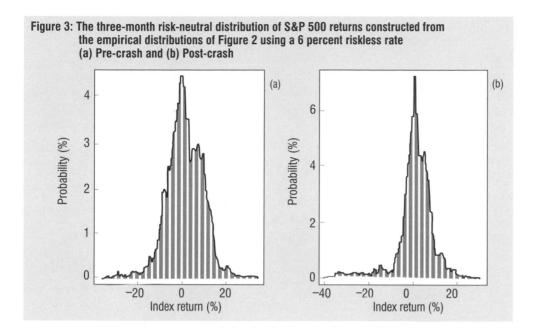

Figure 3: The three-month risk-neutral distribution of S&P 500 returns constructed from the empirical distributions of Figure 2 using a 6 percent riskless rate (a) Pre-crash and (b) Post-crash

Is the index implied volatility skew fair?

Since the 1987 crash, equity index markets have displayed a pronounced, persistent implied volatility skew. Is this skew fair? Are the options prices determined by the skew justified by historical returns? Figure 3a shows the risk-neutralized three-month S&P 500 return distribution for the pre-crash period corresponding to Figure 2a, constructed using our method of relative entropy minimization. Figure 3b shows the same distribution corresponding to the post-crash era of Figure 2b. The post-crash distribution has a substantially longer tail at low returns than the pre-crash distribution.

Skew slopes seem more stable than volatility levels. Therefore, we will focus here on the relation between the implied volatilities of different strikes that follows from these distributions, and pay little attention to the prevailing absolute level of implied volatility. We estimate the fair volatility skew by using the distributions of Figure 3 to calculate options prices, and by then converting these options prices to Black-Scholes implied volatilities.

The results are shown in Figure 4. The pre-crash skew is approximately flat, but the post-crash volatilities increase for low strikes, with a slope similar to actual index skews in stable markets. The observed degree of skew, about five to six volatility points per 10 percent change in strike level, seems approximately fair in the light of post-crash market behavior. Our fair post-crash skew is bilinear and more convex than the recent skew of Figure 1a, but index markets do sometimes display skews like that of Figure 4.

We find that estimated one-month skews tend to resemble a smile more than a skew: our fair implied volatilities of both out-of-the-money calls and puts for one-month expirations exceed at-the-money volatilities. Short-dated index options often

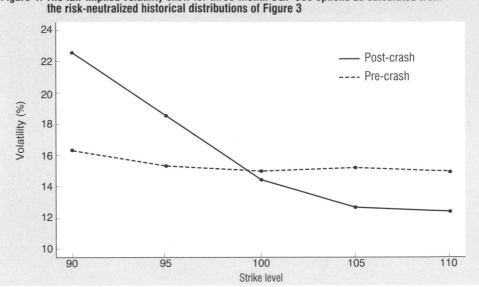

Figure 4: The fair implied volatility skew for three-month S&P 500 options as calculated from the risk-neutralized historical distributions of Figure 3

display this type of behavior. We have applied our method to several other major stock indexes and found that their fair volatility skews are roughly consistent with observed market skews during normal market periods, as shown in Table 1.

Strike-adjusted spread as a measure of options value

SAS_{ATM} is constrained to be consistent with the market's at-the-money-forward implied volatility for that particular underlyer and expiration, so that $SAS_{ATM}(S_F[T], T) = 0$, where $S_F[T]$ is the forward value of the underlyer at time T. Thus SAS_{ATM} is a measure of the current richness of an option, relative to history, assuming that at-the-money-forward options, usually the most liquid, are fairly valued.

Figure 5a shows a plot of fair and market skews for September 1999 S&P 500 options, on 18 May 1999, using the 12 years of historical returns from May 1987 to May 1999 to calculate. Figure 5b shows the SAS_{ATM} for the same options. The options

Table 1: Comparison of actual skews with estimated fair volatility skews for three major indexes. The spread shown is the difference in volatility points between a 25-delta put and a 25-delta call

Index	Normal spread [a]	Extreme spread [b]	Fair spread [c]
SPX	4–7%	14%	6.0%
DAX	3–6%	10%	3.5%
FTSE	2–6%	10%	4.0%

[a] Average during normal market conditions (excluding the periods of extreme volatility in late October 1997 and August–September 1998).
[b] Average during periods of extreme market volatility.
[c] Based on historical returns over the period June 1987 to June 1999.

Figure 5a: Fair and market skews for S&P 500 index options on 18 May 1999
Figure 5b: SAS$_{ATM}$ for the same options

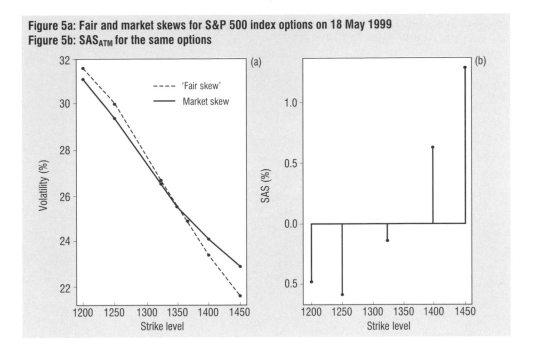

considered expire on 17 September 1999. Both fair and market implied volatilities are constrained to match at the money, forward. The RNHD is constructed using returns from May 1987 to May 1999, including the 1987 crash. For out-of-the-money puts, the entropy-adjusted volatilities slightly exceed the market volatilities, which

Figure 6: Re-evaluate SAS$_{ATM}$ on 21 June 1999 for 17 September 1999 S&P 500 options

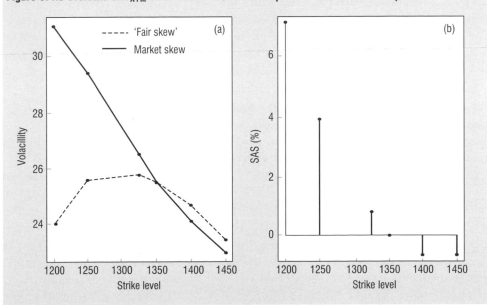

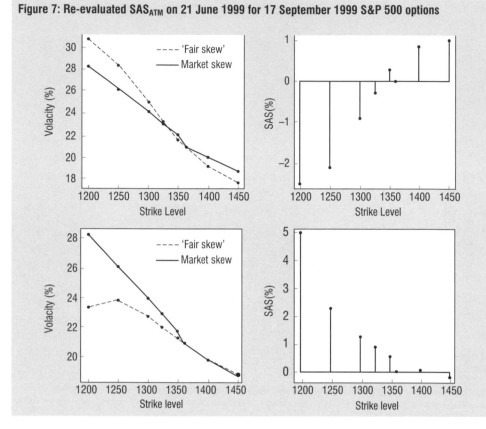

Figure 7: Re-evaluated SAS$_{ATM}$ on 21 June 1999 for 17 September 1999 S&P 500 options

suggests that out-of-the-money puts are slightly cheap. Conversely, out-of-the-money calls seem rich.

Figure 6 shows the same plots based on a historical return distribution taken from May 1988 through May 1999, thereby excluding the 1987 global stock market crash. The options considered expire on 17 September 1999. Both fair and market implied volatilities are constrained to match at the money, forward. In this case, out-of-the-money puts seem much too rich, while out-of-the-money calls are slightly cheap.

In our view, SAS is a quantitative tool for ranking the relative value of options, but this does not absolve the user from choosing the historical period relevant to the computation of the risk-neutralized distribution. There is no escaping the judgement necessary to decide which past period is most relevant to the current market from both a fundamental and a psychological point of view.

In Figure 7, we plot the skews and SAS$_{ATM}$ for the same set of options used in Figures 5 and 6, but evaluated one month later. The top two figures correspond to the crash-inclusive distributions of Figure 5; the bottom two correspond to the crash-exclusive distributions of Figure 6. Although at-the-money volatility has now fallen from 25.5 percent to 21 percent, the size of skews has remained relatively stable. Roughly irrespective of which historical distribution was used, the strike-adjusted spreads have changed so that out-of-the-money puts have become about two SAS points cheaper, whereas the SAS of out-of-the-money calls has changed less. If you had thought the relevant historical distribution was the crash-inclusive one of Figure 5 and had bought cheap puts, you would have lost SAS. If, on the other hand, you had thought that the relevant distribution was the crash-exclusive one of Figure 6 and had sold rich puts, you would have gained several points of SAS.

Valuing options on baskets of stocks

The value of an OTC option on a custom basket of stocks is difficult to estimate since there is no liquid options market from which to extract pricing information. Consider an investor interested in buying a collar on a basket of bank stocks he owns. Suppose he wants to buy a 10 percent out-of-the-money put and finance it by selling a 10 percent out-of-the-money call on the basket. What volatility spread or skew should one use to price the collar? Our method involves finding the risk-neutralized historical distribution of the basket of bank stocks.

To be specific, we consider an example in which the basket consists of an equal number of shares of five bank stocks: J.P. Morgan, Wells Fargo, Bank One, Bank America, and Chase. We first retrieve the historical data for all five stocks and aggregate them to form the time series of basket returns and their historical distribution. We use historical data from June 1987 to June 1999 in this example. By minimizing the relative entropy, we convert the historical distribution into an estimate of the risk-neutral distribution. Figure 8 displays the estimated three-month implied volatility skew for the bank basket calculated from the risk-neutral distribution. The volatility spread between the 10 percent OTM call and the 10 percent OTM put is approximately seven volatility points. In the absence of any market information on the price of options on this basket with a variety of strikes, this seems a useful method of obtaining some sense of the appropriate skew. We note that in using this approach, we managed to bypass the problem of predicting future correlations between the component stocks in the basket, a major hurdle in valuing basket options. It is well known that correlations between stocks can be highly unstable during large market movements. Our approach takes into account the changes in correlations embedded in the basket time series.

We have also applied our model to options on the BKX index (a basket of 24 large US banks with options listed on the Philadelphia exchange). We constructed a basket with the same weighting as the BKX index and calculated both its empirical return distribution and its estimated risk-neutral distribution. The resulting three-month volatility skew is close to the skew observed in the listed options market, even when the at-the-money volatility levels differ. This further demonstrates the reasonableness of our approach.

Forecasting the shape of the skew from a change in a single option price

Market makers in index options keep a steady eye on the skew. Suppose that for a given expiration there are n options, with strikes K_i and known implied volatilities, that characterize the skew. Suppose that implied volatilities and the skew have been relatively stable; then, one of the option's implied volatilities suddenly changes in response to new market sentiments or pressures. How should the market maker adjust the quotes for all other options given the sudden change in the price of one?

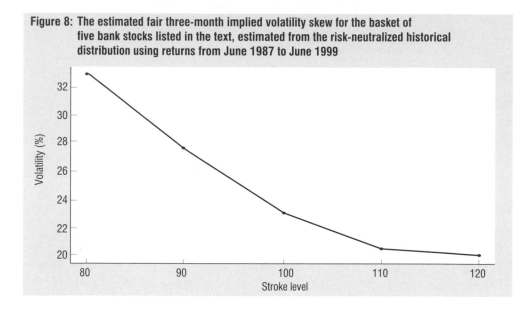

Figure 8: The estimated fair three-month implied volatility skew for the basket of five bank stocks listed in the text, estimated from the risk-neutralized historical distribution using returns from June 1987 to June 1999

This question is particularly relevant for automated electronic market-making systems. The maximum entropy method provides a possible answer.

We start with the implied distribution computed from the known implied volatilities $\sigma_i(K_i)$ – see Derman, Kani and Zou (1996). Now suppose the implied volatility of one option with strike level K_j has changed to a new value $\sigma^*(K_j, T)$. We would like to regard this one move in implied volatility as the visible tip of the iceberg, the observable segment of a new skew that will soon manifest. To identify this new skew, we seek to find the new risk-neutral distribution $Q^*(S_T, T \mid S_0, 0)$ that is consistent with the single new and known implied volatility, while minimizing the entropy change between the old and new distributions. Once the new risk-neutral distribution is obtained, we can update the quotes for the rest of the options by valuing them off the new distribution.

Figure 9 shows several examples where the volatility at one particular strike is shocked. Note that shifts in at-the-money volatility seem to lead to parallel shifts in the skew, whereas shifts in out-of-the-money volatility lead to changes in slope as well as level.

Now consider a hypothetical index whose current value is 100. Suppose the three-month, at-the-money volatility is 24 percent, and the three-month skew is linear in strike with a slope corresponding to a two-volatility-point increase per ten-strike-point decline, as displayed in Figure 10a. The heavy X in the figure shows the one newly observed implied volatility, assumed to rise by four implied volatility points, from 26 percent to 30 percent, for the 90-strike put. Figure 10b shows the change in the risk-neutral implied distribution obtained by minimizing the change in distributional entropy consistent with one new implied volatility. The increase in 90-strike implied volatility has led to a significant hump in the risk-neutral distribution below the 90 level. Finally, Figure 10c shows both the old and new skews, the latter computed from the new risk-neutral distribution. The new

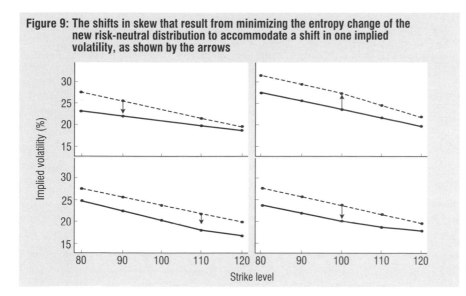

Figure 9: The shifts in skew that result from minimizing the entropy change of the new risk-neutral distribution to accommodate a shift in one implied volatility, as shown by the arrows

estimated skew differs from the old in a non-obvious way: it has not shifted parallel to accommodate the one new item of information but instead suggests that the skew slope will increase as a response to this shock.

End-of-day mark-to-market

At the end of a trading day, volatility traders need to re-mark all their options positions. Often, only the liquid strikes have traded close to the end of the day and, if the last traded option has undergone a significant change in implied volatility, one needs to estimate the appropriate skew for the remaining, less liquid options, based

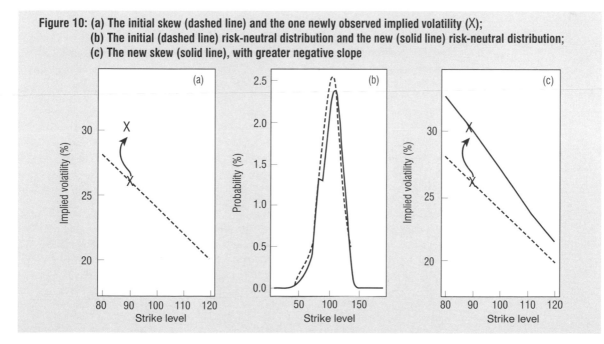

Figure 10: (a) The initial skew (dashed line) and the one newly observed implied volatility (X);
(b) The initial (dashed line) risk-neutral distribution and the new (solid line) risk-neutral distribution;
(c) The new skew (solid line), with greater negative slope

on the new information. Our model of minimizing the relative entropy provides a ready solution to the problem. In the examples shown in Figure 9, one could plausibly mark to market the rest of the options using the solid lines as our best guesses for closing volatilities.

Filling gaps in investors' market views

Risk arbitrageurs, speculators, and other situation-driven investors often have specific, but not necessarily complete, views on the market. For instance, risk arbitrageurs taking a position in the stocks of two companies involved in a merger or acquisition may estimate a 90 percent probability that the deal will be completed and the stock will move above a certain target level within three months. Suppose they would like to take positions in stock and options to implement this belief. Although the arbitrageurs have a firm opinion about only one segment of the probability distribution, a more complete distribution can be helpful in constructing strategies and determining reasonable prices. How can we fill the gap and extract the arbitrageurs' market distribution based on their specific prediction that the market has a 90 percent chance of moving above the target level? One good starting point is to use the option implied distribution, P, as a prior distribution, and then find a new distribution, Q, that satisfies the arbitrageur's 90 percent probability estimate

$$\int_{S_r}^{\infty} Q(S, T; S_0, 0)\, dS = 0.9$$

where S_T is the arbitrageur's target stock price. Again, the model of minimizing the relative entropy provides a natural solution to this problem.

Conclusion

Investors in equity options have two problems that compound each other: the many thousands of equity underlyers and the presence of a unique volatility skew for each of them. For many thinly traded single stock and basket options, it is difficult or impossible to get adequate information on the market skew.

In this article we have developed a systematic, semi-empirical method for estimating the risk-neutral distribution of any underlyer, stock or basket, whose historical returns are available. Our method involves the determination of a new, risk-neutralized historical distribution for an underlyer by minimizing the relative entropy between the historical distribution and the risk-neutral distribution.

Using the RNHD, we can compute the estimated fair implied volatilities of options of any strike and expiration. We can apply this method to illiquid or thinly traded derivatives where market prices are unavailable.

We have defined a new metric, the strike-adjusted spread, for gauging the value of options whose prices are known. SAS is the difference between an option's implied volatility and its fair volatility as estimated using the RNHD. This spread represents the richness in volatility points of an option, compared with the history of its underlyer. Most often, in liquid markets, we calibrate the SAS to be consistent with current at-the-money volatility, so that it becomes a measure of skew richness as compared with history. The SAS ranking cannot be used blindly; it depends on the user's selection of the historical period most relevant to the current market.

There are many other applications of the method of minimal relative entropy which we have illustrated here. One may choose as a prior an existing option's implied distribution, or any other distribution reflecting subjective market views. We hope that this practical method and its extensions will help investors make more rational decisions about value in volatility markets.

Summary

With thousands of underlyers and tens of thousands of options, and with each underlyer having a potentially large volatility skew, how can an options investor gauge which option provides the best relative value? **Joseph Zou** and **Emanuel Derman** propose a method for estimating the fair volatility smile of any equity underlyer from information embedded in the time series of that underlyer's historical returns. The relative value of any particular strike and expiration is calculated and used to estimate the fair volatility skews for illiquid or thinly traded single-stock and basket options. Changes in the skew are forecast from changes in a single option price.

Suggested further reading
Buchen, P.W. and Kelly, M. (1996) *Journal of Financial and Quantitative Analysis*, 31, pp. 143–159.
Constantinides, G.M. (1982) *The Journal of Business*, 55, No. 2.
Cover, T.M. and Thomas, J.A. (1991) *Elements of Information Theory*, New York, John Wiley & Sons.
Derman, E., Kani, I. and Zou, J. (1996) "The local volatility surface," *Financial Analysts Journal,* July/August, pp. 25–36.
Derman, E., Kamal, M., Kani, I. and Zou, J. (1997) "Is the volatility skew fair?," *Goldman, Sachs Quantitative Strategies Research Notes.*
Gulko, L. (1996) Yale University Working Paper.
Kullback, S. (1967) *Information Theory and Statistics*, New York, Dover Publications, Inc.
Stutzer, M. (1996) "A simple nonparametric approach to derivative security valuation," *Journal of Finance*, 51, pp. 1633–1652.
Zou, J. and Derman, E. (1999) "Strike-adjusted spread: a new metric for estimating the value of equity options," Goldman Sachs Quantitative Strategies Research Notes, July.

Recent advances in more realistic market risk management: the hyperbolic model

by Ernst Eberlein

The quantification of risk exposure has become a key issue for financial institutions. There are quite a number of reasons which lead to this need for a more accurate and efficient risk assessment, of which globalization and deregulation are among the first to be mentioned.

Not very long ago many financial markets were rather closed due to national laws and restrictions impeding foreign investments. Globalization and deregulation opened up investment opportunities and therefore chances which did not previously exist. On the other hand, from the point of view of risk exposure, a number of investors had to learn the hard lesson that higher returns and higher risk are just two sides of the same coin. Examples of this are the Asian and Russian crises at the end of the 20th century. In both cases the crisis came rather abruptly after a period of enthusiasm. In order to illustrate this over-optimism one should consider the following incident, which took place in connection with the Asian crisis, where not long before the problems in some emerging economies became evident, the management of some institutional funds had dismissed portfolio managers on the grounds that they had not invested enough capital in the Asian markets.

It is not only this change in the global environment that makes more accurate quantitative methods in risk management desirable. Trading volumes have reached levels compared to which the gross national product (GNP) of the corresponding economy is a negligible quantity. Volatilities hit values that had not previously been known for blue chip stocks. The VDAX, which measures the annualized volatility implied by options on the DAX index at the exchange in Frankfurt, jumped to 55 percent in October 1998 (see Figure 1). Its long-term average is in the low 20s. This record level had an enormous effect on risk exposure. The losses produced at Barings, Metallgesellschaft and UBS made clear that it is not difficult to endanger a company by taking positions in derivatives. The LTCM case went a step further, showing that leverage effects can produce a magnitude of risk that could destabilize the whole financial system.

A sound understanding of the risk resulting from financial derivatives and structured products depends crucially on how one models the underlying securities. It is through these new products that mathematics and statistics entered a field where science had not been appreciated before. The speed of innovation of financial products is impressive, as is the increased complexity of each following generation of products.

As a main driving force for better risk measurement it is necessary to mention the enforced legislation. National laws, based on the recommendations of the Basel

Figure 1: VDAX (DAX volatility index)

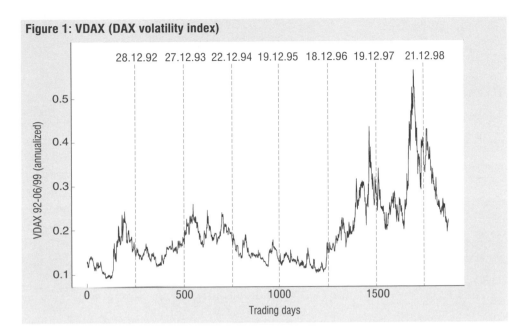

Committee on Banking Supervision, force financial institutions to establish sophisticated risk management systems handling both market and credit risk. The imposed capital requirements are derived directly from the numbers produced by these systems.

Finally, the technical innovations achieved during the past decades have had a major impact on risk management. The speed at which trades and transactions can be executed demands an appropriate response in risk assessment. The possibilities offered by internet technologies will accentuate this aspect even more in the years to come. There is no doubt that financial institutions will have to invest a lot of their energy and money into sound risk management if they do not want to be excluded from this higher chances-higher risk world. The most advanced mathematical-statistical methods and IT technologies are the clue to mastering this.

How can one quantify risk?

The entire stochastic uncertainty associated with a particular book or portfolio and a set time horizon is encapsulated within its profit and loss (P&L-) distribution F. This function $F(x)$ gives the probability of obtaining no greater profit than x over the time horizon. Losses are negative profits in this sense. The standard risk measures used in practice such as value at risk (VaR), volatility, or shortfall measures are simple functions of the P&L-distribution. This also holds for chance measures such as the expected return. The upside half of the distribution F is the one needed for optimization of portfolios. Thus, forecasting the entire P&L-distribution and not only a simple statistic prepares the ground for both risk assessment and portfolio management.

A poor approximation of the true P&L-distribution as it is used in the classical normal model will lead to wrong decisions. In this situation risk managers and traders do not see the true risk of their positions. This underlines the importance of realistic modeling, i.e., the use of models which can be empirically justified.

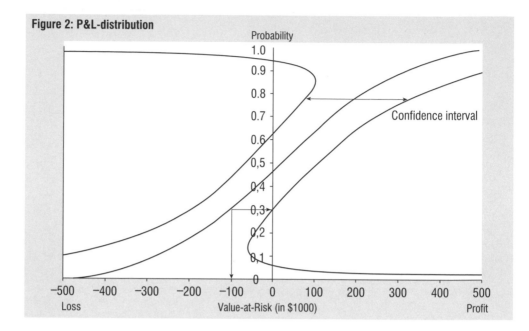

Figure 2: P&L-distribution

Backtesting against the whole P&L-distribution as described later will reveal whether the forecast is sufficiently close to reality or not. In order to get the proper P&L-distribution, it is necessary to start with an empirical analysis of financial data.

Financial data is typically provided in the form of a discrete time series S_1, S_2, S_3, ..., where S_n denotes the price (e.g., closing price or settlement price) of a certain security at time point n. As one of the consequences of the present transition from traditional floor trading to electronic markets, large data sets are produced every

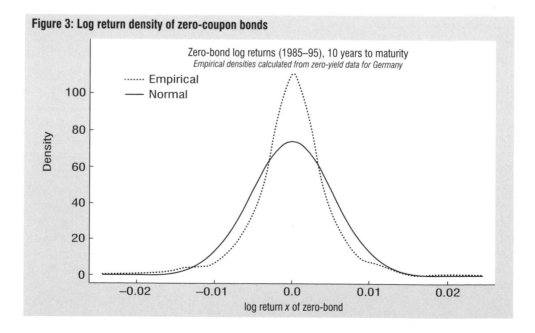

Figure 3: Log return density of zero-coupon bonds

Figure 4: USD/DEM six-hour log returns

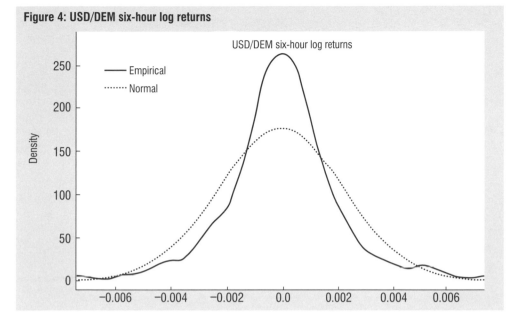

day at the exchanges on an intraday level. These intraday records collect price quotes (bid and ask) as well as prices at which trades actually took place together with the corresponding time stamp. Time series corresponding to equidistant time points can easily be extracted from these intraday data sets.

In order to allow the comparison of investments in different securities it would be natural to look at relative price changes

$$Y_n = (S_n - S_{n-1})/S_{n-1}.$$

For a number of reasons most authors in the financial literature prefer a rate of return defined by *ln* returns instead

$$Z_n = ln \ S_n - ln \ S_{n-1}.$$

The difference between Y_n and Z_n is negligible since the functions *ln x* and *x*–1 have almost identical values for *x* close to 1. For visual presentations we prefer density plots instead of those of distribution functions. Integrating the density from minus infinity to *x* will produce the value of the corresponding distribution function $F(x)$.

Looking at empirical densities of log returns from financial data one observes the following stylized features: compared with the normal distribution, which is used in classical models, there is more mass near the origin, less in the flanks, and considerably more mass in the tails. This means that tiny price movements occur with higher frequency, small and middle-sized movements with lower frequency, and large changes are much more frequent than predicted by the normal law. Figure 3 shows a typical example. The points represent the kernel-smoothed density of *ln* returns of zero-coupon bonds with ten years to maturity. Given the rather small numerical values in the tails, the strong deviation there would only be visible if one looked at the same graph with the *y*-axis in logarithmic scale. Figures 4 and 5 provide other examples of this phenomenon. Returns of exchange rates along daily

Figure 5: DAX log returns

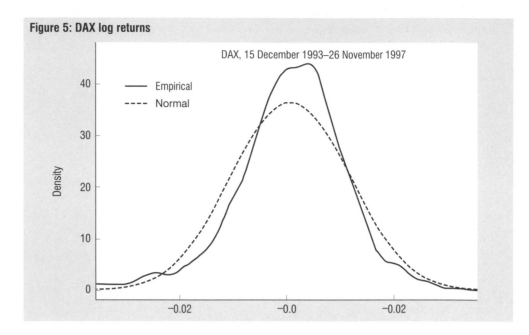

Figure 6: Zero-bond log returns

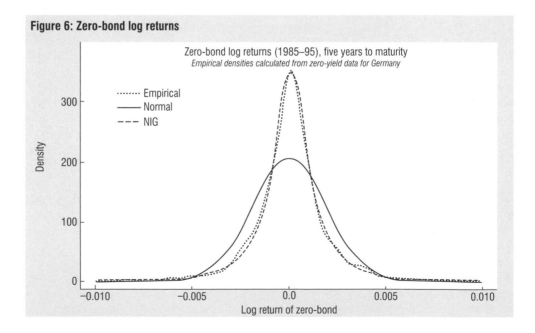

or shorter time grids deviate clearly from normality. It is often said that the returns of portfolios of many instruments are normally distributed due to aggregation effects. Again this cannot be confirmed. The DAX data used in Figure 5 in addition shows a skewed distribution. Symmetric distributions like the normal distribution cannot catch this effect. It is the class of generalized hyperbolic distributions, which will now be introduced, that is flexible enough to allow an almost perfect statistical fit to the empirical distributions in finance. To illustrate this we have shown the fit for the zero-bond returns with five years to maturity (Figure 6).

Generalized hyperbolic distributions

Generalized hyperbolic distributions were introduced by Barndorff-Nielsen (1977) in connection with the "sand project," where in cooperation with geologists the physics of wind-blown sand was investigated. Their densities are given by:

$$d_{GH}(x; \lambda, \alpha, \beta, \delta, \mu) = a(\lambda, \alpha, \beta, \delta)(\delta^2 + (x-\mu)^2)^{(\lambda-\frac{1}{2})/2}$$
$$\times K_{\lambda-\frac{1}{2}}(\alpha\sqrt{\delta^2 + (x-\mu)^2}) \exp(\beta(x-\mu)) \tag{1}$$

where

$$a(\lambda, \alpha, \beta, \delta) = \frac{(\alpha^2 - \beta^2)^{\lambda/2}}{\sqrt{2\pi}\alpha^{\lambda-\frac{1}{2}}\delta^\lambda K_\lambda(\delta\sqrt{\alpha^2-\beta^2})}$$

is the normalizing constant and K_ν denotes the modified Bessel function of the third kind with index ν. An integral representation of K_ν is given by

$$K_\nu(z) = \frac{1}{2}\int_0^\infty y^{\nu-1} \exp\left(-\frac{1}{2} z(y + y^{-1})\right)dy.$$

The densities above depend on five parameters: $\alpha > 0$ determines the shape, β with $0 \leq |\beta| < \alpha$ the skewness, and $\mu \in \mathbb{R}$ the location. $\delta > 0$ is a scaling parameter comparable to σ in the normal distribution. Finally $\lambda \in \mathbb{R}$ characterizes certain sub-classes. It is essentially the heaviness of the tails which can be modified by changing λ. Compared with the normal density with only two parameters μ and σ, the class described by (1) is very flexible and therefore enables us to fit the empirical densities appearing in finance in an optimal way.

Various special cases are of interest. For $\lambda = 1$ one gets the sub-class of hyperbolic distributions. Since $K_{1/2}(z) = (\pi/2z)^{\frac{1}{2}} e^{-z}$, the density (1) simplifies considerably. The density is then

$$d_H(x) = \frac{\sqrt{\alpha^2 - \beta^2}}{2\alpha\delta\, K_1(\delta\sqrt{\alpha^2-\beta^2})} \exp\left(-\alpha\sqrt{\delta^2 + (x-\mu)^2} + \beta(x-\mu)\right). \tag{2}$$

The name "hyperbolic" is explained by this density. If we take the logarithm of d_H we get a hyperbola from the term $\sqrt{\delta^2 + (x-\mu)^2}$, instead of the parabola which results from the normal distribution. It is the hyperbolic case which was first used in finance (Eberlein and Keller, 1995; see also Eberlein, Keller, and Prause, 1998). Figure 7 shows the effect of varying the shape parameter in the case of the hyperbolic distribution. All other parameters are kept fixed. The shape parameter ζ used in this graph is given by $\zeta = \delta\sqrt{\alpha^2 - \beta^2}$ and is a different parameterization than the one above. As Figure 7 shows, the normal distribution appears as a limiting case if the shape parameter ζ increases to infinity.

Another special case is the normal inverse Gaussian distribution, which results when $\lambda = -1/2$. It was introduced to finance in Barndorff-Nielsen (1998) and has the density

$$d_{NIG}(x) = \frac{\alpha}{\pi} \exp\left(\delta\sqrt{\alpha^2 - \beta^2} + \beta(x-\mu)\right) \frac{K_1\left(\alpha\delta\sqrt{1 + \left(\frac{x-\mu}{\delta}\right)^2}\right)}{\sqrt{1 + \left(\frac{x-\mu}{\delta}\right)^2}}. \tag{3}$$

Figure 7: Hyperbolic densities

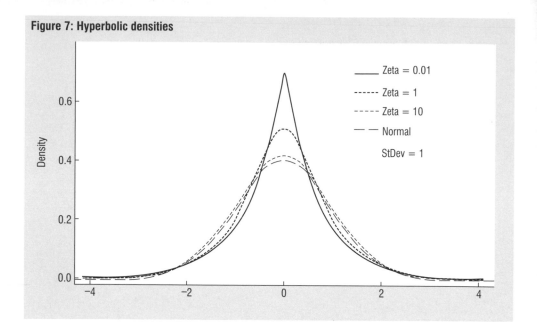

Normal inverse Gaussian distributions have a property similar to the normal distribution, where means and variances of independent random variables add up. This property simplifies the numerics of the option pricing formula which will be derived later and speeds up simulations of paths of processes constructed from it.

Let us mention that generalized hyperbolic distributions are intimately related to the normal distribution, in addition to the fact that the latter appears as a limit, as can be seen from Figure 7. They are variance-mean mixtures of normal distributions in the sense that

$$d_{GH}(x; \lambda, \alpha, \beta, \delta, \mu) = \int_{0}^{\infty} d_{N(\mu + \beta y, y)}(x)\, d_{GIG}(y; \lambda, \delta, \sqrt{\alpha^2 - \beta^2})dy. \qquad (4)$$

Here $N(\mu + \beta y, y)$ denotes the normal distribution with mean $\mu + \beta y$ and variance y whereas $d_{GIG}(x; \lambda, \delta, \gamma)$ denotes the density of the generalized inverse Gaussian distribution with parameters λ, δ and γ.

How much data is required for fitting generalized hyperbolic distributions? In order to get a sufficiently smooth empirical density, one should have at least one year of daily price changes for each security in the corresponding portfolio. One year means roughly 250 trading days. Nevertheless, Figure 8 shows that even with fewer data points – 100 trading days are used here – reasonable results can be obtained. The empirical density is still very crude compared with the one plotted in Figure 3, where data from ten years was available. Note that a portfolio containing derivatives such as call options in this example characteristically produces asymmetric return distributions.

Figure 8: Returns of a portfolio including options

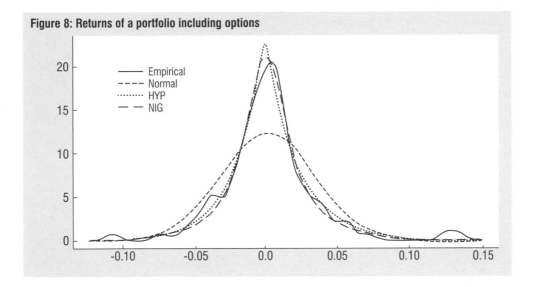

The dynamic asset price model

Fitting the empirical return distribution by a generalized hyperbolic distribution is already half way to a more realistic asset price model. The classical geometric Brownian motion model is given by

$$S_t = S_0 \exp(\sigma B_t + (\mu - \sigma^2/2)t)$$

where $(B_t)_{t \geq 0}$ denotes a standard Brownian motion and μ, σ the drift and volatility parameters. In its differential form this model is given by

$$dS_t = S_t(\mu dt + \sigma dB_t)$$

The basic assumption entering this model is that returns along any time interval are normally distributed. We have seen from empirical investigations that this assumption cannot be justified. If one goes from daily to intraday returns, for example, to one-hour returns, it is clear that the deviation from normality increases further (Figure 9).

A return process which reflects this effect is the Lévy process associated with a generalized hyperbolic distribution. This Lévy process $(X_t)_{t \geq 0}$ is generated by the generalized hyperbolic distribution with parameters λ, α, β, δ, μ in exactly the same way as the standard normal distribution generates the Brownian motion process $(B_t)_{t \geq 0}$ (see, for example, Breiman, Prop. 14.19, 1968). It has stationary, independent increments, such that increments along time intervals of length 1 are distributed according to the generalized hyperbolic distribution. We call this process the *generalized hyperbolic Lévy motion*. It is characterized by the five parameters λ, α, β, δ, μ. One should note that Brownian motion is also a Lévy process. Contrary to Brownian motion this process has the nice property that if one looks at increments along shorter time intervals such as .1 or .3, one gets distributions which are much closer to the corresponding empirical intraday return distributions than the normal distributions from Brownian motion.

The natural asset price model based on this return process $(X_t)_{t \geq 0}$ is

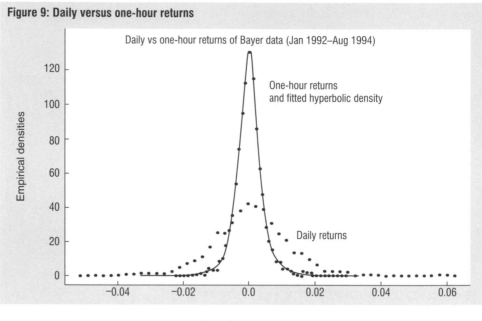

Figure 9: Daily versus one-hour returns

$$S_t = S_0 \exp(X_t).$$

We consider this as "natural" because taking the *ln* returns of $(S_t)_{t\geq0}$ one gets the increments of $(X_t)_{t\geq0}$. In particular $X_t - X_{t-1}$, an increment of time length 1, has the distribution which was fitted to the empirical return distribution. Thus, our model reflects rather accurately what one observes in the data.

Of course, one could also write $(X_t)_{t\geq0}$ in the form $(\sigma X_t' + \mu t)_{t\geq0}$, by using a standardized generalized hyperbolic Lévy motion $(X_t')_{t\geq0}$. This would make the new model formally more compatible with the classical Brownian model above. By Itô's formula, the stochastic differential equation with solution $S_t = S_0 \exp(X_t)$ is given by

$$dS_t = S_{t\text{-}}(dX_t + e^{\Delta X}t - 1 - \Delta X_t).$$

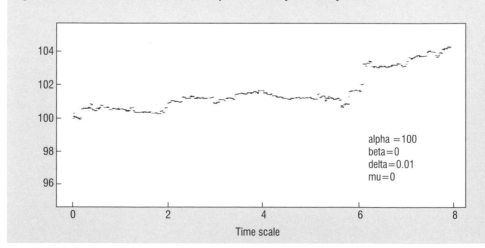

Figure 10: Pathwise simulation of an asset price driven by a GH Lévy motion

Figure 11: Intraday prices, Deutsche Bank, 9 December 1998

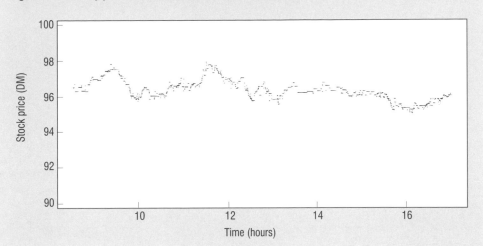

Here S_{t^-} denotes left limits and ΔX_t the jump at time t. This equation indicates that the paths of $(X_t)_{t \geq 0}$ as well as of $(S_t)_{t \geq 0}$ have jumps. Going deeper into the analysis of these processes, one sees that $(X_t)_{t \geq 0}$ and consequently $(S_t)_{t \geq 0}$ change their values only by jumps. Whereas Brownian motion $(B_t)_{t \geq 0}$ has continuous paths, our return process $(X_t)_{t \geq 0}$ here is (up to the drift part) purely discontinuous. It is exactly this that one sees when observing intraday price changes. Compare the simulation of a path driven by a generalized hyperbolic Lévy motion (Figure 10) with the intraday price path of Deutsche Bank, 9 December 1998 (Figure 11). Thus, the hyperbolic asset price model is not only much more accurate as far as distributional assumptions are concerned, it is also able to catch the microstructure of price fluctuations.

The model above allows the risk-neutral valuation of derivatives. From the set of risk-neutral probabilities we choose the so-called Esscher transform. If $H(S_T)$ is the payoff of a derivative depending on the price of the underlying at time T, the value of the derivative is the discounted expectation of $H(S_T)$ with respect to the risk-neutral probability P^θ, i.e.

$$e^{-rT} E^\theta [H(S_T)],$$

where r denotes the interest rate. For a European call option with strike K, the payoff at expiration is $H(S_T) = (S_T - K)^+$. The following explicit expression can be obtained for the expectation. It has the same structure as the Black-Scholes formula

$$S_0 \int_\gamma^\infty d_{GH}^{*T}(x;\, \theta + 1)dx - e^{-rT} K \int_\gamma^\infty d_{GH}^{*T}(x;\, \theta)dx. \tag{5}$$

Here $\gamma = ln(K/S_0)$ and $d_{GH}^{*t}(x;\theta)$ is the density of X_t under the risk-neutral probability.

Figure 12 shows the difference of the classical Black-Scholes price and the generalized hyperbolic price in the case $\lambda = 1$ for various maturities. We see the typical W-shape. At the money, where most of the volume is traded, the Black-

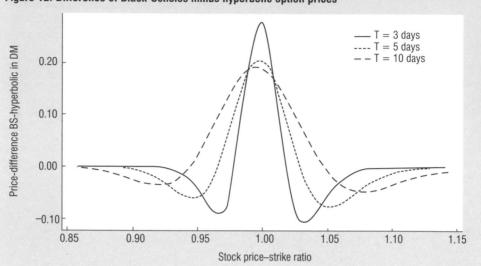

Figure 12: Difference of Black-Scholes minus hyperbolic option prices

Scholes price is too high. On the contrary, in the money and out of the money, the Black-Scholes price is too low. This is clear if one is aware of the fact that the Black-Scholes model does not see the risk of larger price movements. Note that very deep in the money and very deep out of the money the option price is essentially model independent. This follows from the fact that in these cases the integrals in the option pricing formula are close to 0 and 1.

There are various ways of looking at the performance of this new option pricing formula. An inconsistency of the classical Black-Scholes valuation is the so-called smile effect. This is the dependence of implicit volatilities on the moneyness, i.e., the stock price–strike ratio S_0/K, of the option. For a fixed time to maturity the resulting curve looks like a smiling mouth. As shown in Eberlein, Keller, and Prause (1998) for the hyperbolic model, and in Eberlein and Prause (1998) for the generalized hyperbolic model, the new formula leads to a reduction of the smile. The reduction is stronger for the generalized hyperbolic model than for the hyperbolic or the normal inverse Gaussian model.

Another approach to pricing performance is to compare theoretical and observed prices directly. If we compare only implicit volatilities, this will not give a complete picture since the same change in volatility has a larger effect on the price for an option with a longer time to maturity. This analysis was also done in the two papers mentioned above. Mispricing is somewhat reduced by the new formula.

For the purpose of portfolio management one might be interested in a multivariate asset price process due to the fact that it is necessary to model a large universe of instruments simultaneously. Using the representation as a mixture of normal distributions (4), it is straightforward to introduce multivariate generalized hyperbolic distributions. One only has to replace the normal density in (4) by a multivariate normal density with the right parameters. Of course, the number of parameters increases rapidly with dimensions. Based on this multivariate distribution one can now construct a multivariate asset price process in exactly the same way as for univariate distributions.

Figure 13: Interest rate fluctuations

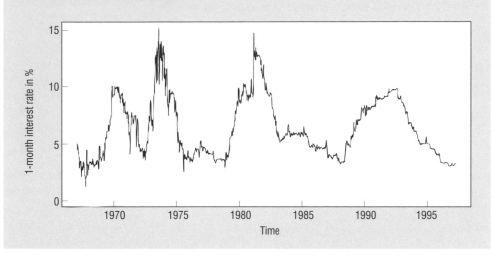

Modeling term structures

The shape of the distribution of returns is a key assumption in modeling financial time series. In the case of stock returns the deviation from normality is widely known, although the various modifications and generalizations of classical models do not really take this into account. The deviation is much less known for returns from the bond market. It is for this reason that we chose interest rate data for Figures 3 and 6. Generalized hyperbolic distributions provide a perfect fit. The theory that we shall sketch briefly is for Lévy processes in general under some mild assumptions.

Historically, it was always the short rate that was modeled as the basic process. Most of the models in the literature are so-called δ-root models

$$dr_t = (\theta(t) - ar_t)dt + \sigma r_t^{\delta} dB_t.$$

As Figure 13 shows, interest rates fluctuate around a long-term mean $\theta(t)$. This behavior can be modeled through a proper choice of the drift term. $\theta(t) - ar_t$ has a mean reverting effect.

The exponent δ in the random term forces the solution r_t to stay positive if $\delta \geq 1/2$. The case $\delta = 1/2$ is the widely used Cox-Ingersoll-Ross model (Cox, Ingersoll, and Ross, 1985), which was further extended by Hull and White (1990).

However, interest rates are not a one-dimensional object. On the US market there are bonds with maturities of between 0 and 30 years. The interest received depends on the time to maturity. Under normal conditions the interest paid for a bond with many years to maturity is higher than that for a bond which is close to maturity. Thus, we have to consider a vector- or function-valued process. One assumes that there is a complete set of bonds with maturities T in the time interval $[0, T^*]$. T^* can be 30 years, for example. Mathematically it is simpler to consider zero-coupon bonds.

Let $P(t, T)$ denote the price at time $t \in [0, T]$ of a zero-coupon bond with maturity $T \in [0, T^*]$. We define

$$f(t, T) = -\frac{\partial}{\partial T} \ln P(t, T). \tag{6}$$

$f(t, T)$ is called the forward rate. Since

$$P(t, T) = \exp\left(-\int_t^T f(t, s)ds\right) \tag{7}$$

zero-coupon bond prices and forward rates represent equivalent information. Note that the short rate $r(t)$ is contained in the forward rate since $r(t) = f(t, t)$. In 1992, Heath, Jarrow, and Morton introduced a model for the forward rate dynamics

$$df(t, T) = \alpha(t, T) \, dt + v(t, T) \, dB_t. \tag{8}$$

As explained above this is equivalent to modeling zero-coupon bond prices in the form

$$dP(t, T) = P(t, T)(m(t, T) \, dt + \sigma(t, T) \, dB_t). \tag{9}$$

Under a risk-neutral measure the drift coefficient $m(t, T)$ is replaced by $r(t)$. Therefore the starting point for our generalization is the Heath-Jarrow-Morton model in the form

$$dP(t, T) = P(t, T)(r(t) \, dt + \sigma(t, T) \, dB_t). \tag{10}$$

Here $\sigma(t, T)$ denotes a volatility structure. Often the Vasicek structure is used, which is given by

$$\sigma(t, T) = \frac{\hat{\sigma}}{a}(1 - \exp(-a(T - t))) \tag{10}$$

for parameters $\hat{\sigma}$ and a.

Let $(X_t)_{t \geq 0}$ be a Lévy process such as the generalized hyperbolic Lévy motion, for example. The natural generalization of the Heath-Jarrow-Morton bond price model is then in the integral form

$$P(t, T) = P(0, T) \exp\left[\int_0^t r(s)ds - \int_0^t \theta(\sigma(s, T))ds + \int_0^t \sigma(s, T)dX_s\right].$$

Here $\theta(u) = \ln E[\exp(uX_1)]$ denotes the logarithm of the moment generating function of the distribution of X_1. One can also derive the corresponding forward rate process, which is given by

$$f(t, T) = f(0, T) + \int_0^t \theta'(\sigma(s, T))\sigma_2(s, T) \, ds - \int_0^t \sigma_2(s, T) \, dX_s.$$

θ' in this formula denotes derivative and σ_2 the partial derivative with respect to the second variable. Based on this bond price model one can derive pricing formulas for interest rate-sensitive derivatives, e.g., for European call options on bonds.

Figure 14: Functional value-at-risk

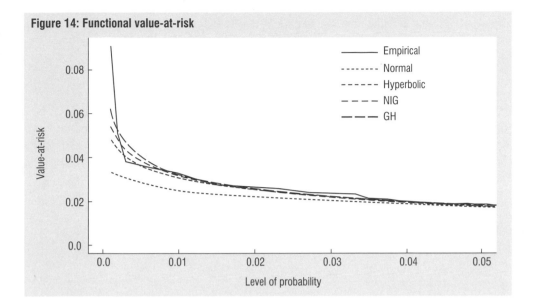

Measuring market risk

The risk measure which has become the standard in recent years is the Value-at-Risk or VaR. By definition, VaR(α) is the potential loss of a portfolio given a level of probability α and a time horizon t. Thus, VaR is essentially a quantile. Define u_α by

$$P[X_t < u_\alpha] = \alpha$$

where X_t is the return process defined above. As introduced earlier, the value of the portfolio at time t is $S_t = S_0 \exp(X_t)$. Therefore the Value-at-Risk expressed in currency units (USD or DM, for example) is

$$\mathrm{VaR}(\alpha) = S_0 (1 - \exp(u_\alpha)).$$

The holding period t which is normally considered is one day or ten days. The probability α is chosen as .01 or .05, which means that the safety level is 99 percent or 95 percent accordingly. Since the whole P&L-distribution is at our disposal, there is no reason to restrict ourselves to a particular α. We get much more information by considering VaR as a function of α (Figure 14). Any particular VaR value, such as VaR(.01), can be read from this graph. Figure 14 clearly indicates that the classical normal model underestimates VaR in a systematic way at levels which are smaller than .05.

The intersection of the empirical density with the fitted normal density in the left tail occurs typically at a point which corresponds roughly to $\alpha = 0.05$ (see Figures 3, 4, and 5). Therefore by pure chance VaR(.05) is often close to the correct value if one uses the normal model.

VaR itself, even if it is the standard risk measure, can be deficient. Artzner, Delbaen, Eber, and Heath (1998), in studying general properties a risk measure should satisfy, realized that VaR is not sub-additive. Sub-additivity means that the risk of a portfolio should be smaller than the sum of the risks associated with its

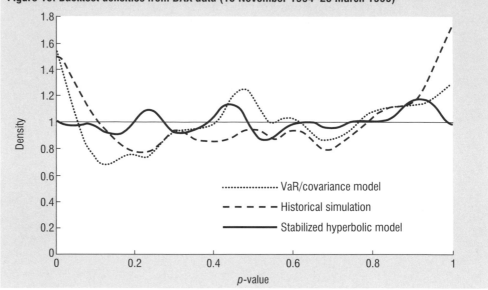

Figure 15: Backtest densities from DAX data (16 November 1994–25 March 1999)

sub-portfolios. Another way to look at this is that it should not be possible to reduce the risk taken by a bank by splitting up its portfolio into sub-portfolios.

Therefore, there are good reasons to consider other risk measures. An excellent candidate is the following shortfall measure

$$\text{Shortfall}(\alpha, t) = E\left[S_0\left(1 - \exp(X_t)\right) \mid X_t < u_\alpha\right].$$

This is the expectation of the loss given that the return is less than u_α. It tells the management *how bad* bad is, i.e., what could happen beyond the estimated VaR(α) value see Artzner et al. (1999). It is evident that the shortfall derived from the variance–covariance (normal) model systematically underestimates the true risk. Note that any other reasonable risk measure such as volatility is a specific function of the P&L-distribution. Therefore the approach presented here allows numerous variations.

In order to test how well the model depicts reality, the Basel Committee on Banking Supervision recommends backtesting. Backtesting means that for the given period one estimates VaR(.01) for every day using data from at least 250 trading days (i.e., one year) and then one counts the number of exceptions – exceptions are those days where the losses which occurred on the day following the estimation exceed the estimated VaR value. Since VaR is a quantile estimate, the percentage of exceeding values should correspond to the level of probability, i.e., 1 percent. Since we estimate the whole P&L-distribution in our approach, assessment of the model can be done through a more sophisticated backtesting procedure. We use the fact that given any random variable X and the corresponding distribution function F, $F(X)$ is a random variable which is uniformly distributed on the interval [0,1]. Thus, if we denote by F_t the P&L-distribution estimated on day t and by X_{t+1} the outcome of profit/loss on day $t + 1$, the values $F_t(X_{t+1})$ collected for a certain period $t = 1, ..., n$ should produce a histogram with the constant value 1 along all p-values between 0 and 1. Figure 15 shows the outcome for a portfolio of instruments corresponding to the DAX. The poor result obtained with the classical variance–covariance model is evident. There is a systematic deviation in both tails and in the center.

The hyperbolic model provides instead an excellent backtesting result with only some random fluctuations left. Figure 15 is taken from Breckling, Eberlein, and Kokic (2000), where the methodology is exposed further. The corresponding software for managing risk of financial institutions is developed at INSIDERS, Financial Solutions GmbH, Mainz.

We should emphasize that this approach provides a consistent way for managing market *and* credit risk. The P&L-distributions which arise from portfolios of bonds and loans are highly skewed because of the rare occurrence of defaults. It would not make any sense to fit a normal distribution for those portfolios. Generalized hyperbolic distributions are flexible enough to suit this situation as well.

In most cases one does not have the complete price series $(P_{jt})_{t=0,1,...}$ for loan portfolios that one has for equity portfolios. A loan is priced explicitly only at the time when it is issued, thereafter its market price must be imputed. This can be done via the yield-to-price relationship

$$P_{jt} = \sum_k \frac{c_j(\tau_{jk})}{(1 + \gamma_j(\tau_{jk}))^{t_{jk}}},$$

where $c_j(\tau_{jk})$ denotes the cash flow for loan j at forward time τ_{jk} and $\gamma_j(\tau)$ the interest rate of a zero-coupon version of loan j maturing at time τ. Based on a rating system that categorizes borrowers, a stochastic mechanism that models transitions from one category to another, and the yield curve for risk-free investments, we can determine the yield curve for each category. The price series can be derived from this. Once we have the P&L-distribution, any risk measure can be determined, as described before.

Conclusion

The need for sound risk management is not only a consequence of enforced legislation, it has become a competitive factor for financial institutions. The article surveys a new approach, the hyperbolic model, which results in a considerable increase in accuracy in risk measurement. The model is based on Lévy processes generated by generalized hyperbolic distributions as driving processes. This class, which replaces classical Brownian motion, is flexible enough to fit almost perfectly empirical distributions from financial time series.

Due to the properties of Lévy processes, the excellent fit of empirical distributions is not only obtained for a fixed time scale, it is consistent on various time scales such as daily, hourly, or weekly data. We discuss statistical estimation, derivative pricing, term structure modelling, and market and credit risk measurement in this new model world.

Summary

More accurate quantitative methods are the key to improving risk management in financial institutions. Based on empirical investigations of equity, foreign exchange, interest rate term structure, and credit data **Ernst Eberlein** shows the systematic bias in classical approaches. The hyperbolic model is introduced instead. It uses a flexible class, the generalized hyperbolic distributions, as a key input. The approach allows market and credit risk to be managed in a consistent way.

Acknowledgement: I would like to thank Deutsche Börse AG, Frankfurt, and Karlsruher Kapitalmarktdatenbank, Universität Karlsruhe, for a number of data sets concerning stock and option prices. In particular I would like to thank Annette Ehret, Fehmi Özkan, Karsten Prause, Sebastian Raible, and Michael Wiesendorfer Zahn for contributing the graphs.

Suggested further reading

Artzner, P., Delbaen, F., Eber, J.-M., and Heath, D. (1999) "Coherent measures of risk," *Mathematical Finance*, 9, pp. 203–228.

Barndorff-Nielsen, O.E. (1977) "Exponentially decreasing distributions for the logarithm of particle size," *Proceedings of the Royal Society London A*, 353, pp. 401–419.

Barndorff-Nielsen, O.E. (1998) "Processes of normal inverse Gaussian type," *Finance & Stochastics*, 2, pp. 41–68.

Breckling, J., Eberlein, E., and Kokic, P. (2000) "A tailored suit for risk management: the hyperbolic model," in Franke, J., Härdle, W., and Stahl, G. (eds) "Measuring risk in complex stochastic systems," *Springer Lecture Notes in Statistics*, 147, pp. 189–202.

Breiman, L. (1968) *Probability*, Addison Wesley.

Cox, J.C., Ingersoll, J.E., and Ross, S.A. (1985) "A theory of the term structure of interest rates," *Econometrica*, 53, pp. 385–408.

Eberlein, E. (2001) "Application of generalized hyperbolic Lévy motions to finance," in Barndorff-Nielsen, O.E., Mikosch, T., and Resnick, S. (eds) "Lévy processes: Theory and Applications," Birkhäuser Verlag.

Eberlein, E. and Keller, U., (1995) "Hyperbolic distributions in finance," *Bernoulli*, 1, pp. 281–299.

Eberlein, E., Keller, U., and Prause, K. (1998) "New insights into smile, mispricing and value at risk: the hyperbolic model," *Journal of Business*, 71, pp. 371–406.

Eberlein, E. and Prause, K. (1998) "The generalized hyperbolic model: financial derivatives and risk measures," *FDM-Preprint*, 56.

Eberlein, E. and Raible, S. (1999) "Term structure models driven by general Lévy processes," *Mathematical Finance*, 9, pp. 31–53.

Heath, D., Jarrow, R., and Morton, A. (1992) "Bond pricing and term structure of interest rates: a new methodology for contingent claims valuation," *Econometrica*, 60, pp. 77–105.

Hull, J. and White, A. (1990) "Pricing interest rate derivative securities," *The Review of Financial Studies*, 3, pp. 573–592.

Kokic, P., Breckling, J., and Eberlein, E. (2000) "A new framework for the evaluation of market and credit risk" in Bol, G., Nakhaeizadeh, G., and Vollmer, K.-H. (eds) "Datamining und computational finance," Wirtschaftswissenschaftliche Beiträge, 174 Physica-Verlag, pp. 51–67.

Cointegration: the new risk relationship

by Jin-Chuan Duan

U nderstanding the relationships among multiple sources of risk is a key step in constructing any market risk management model. Financial data series are typically records of price history on some assets. These price series are in many instances non-stationary (or having a unit root in the jargon of time series analysis) in the sense that mean and/or variance are exploding with time. Non-stationarity is a feature that is both theoretically expected due to market efficiency and empirically verified in many studies. This type of data series is sometimes referred to as a random walk.

To circumvent non-stationarity, changes (or returns) on the price series are often used in practice. As a result, risk relationships are simply modeled by a correlation structure of price changes. This shortcut approach ignores potential long-run relations existing among price series and may give rise to seriously misleading conclusions. Long-run relationships among many price series are not only intuitively plausible but also empirically justifiable. In the econometrics literature, long-run relationships are typically modeled using the cointegration model. Cointegration implies that the model for changes must contain an error-correction term to account for the long-run relationship. Failure to do so, for example, leads to over-differencing and hence incorrect statistical inferences.

The cointegration concept is actually easy to grasp. Let us consider a drunken man who is out walking with his sober dog. It is obvious that this drunken man will be taking a random walk down the street with his dog tagging along. Although his dog may occasionally lead or trail, it will not travel too far away from him, however. As observers, we see that the man takes a random walk and the dog does so as well, but the distance between them is reasonable (or stationary). We cannot be certain where the drunken man will end up after a certain period of time elapses. Neither can we be sure where the dog will be then. But one thing is certain: they will always be reasonably close to each other. In terms of our technical jargon, the drunken man and his dog are cointegrated.

Figures 1 and 2 provide graphical illustration of cointegrated random walks. In Figure 1, two unrelated random walks are plotted. Clearly each series takes its own random walk. Cointegrated random walks, on the other hand, behave quite differently. Two series using a simple cointegration model to be described later are plotted in Figure 2, in which two series are trailing each other closely. If examined separately, they are random walks individually. Taken together, however, a clear relationship exists between them.

Economic examples of cointegration abound. In some cases, there is powerful intuition as to why series should be cointegrated; for example, soy beans and their crushed components (soy bean meal and soy bean oil) are expected to be cointegrated. If not, one can simply adjust crushing capacities to profit from their price discrepancies. The same logic applies to crude oil and its refined products. The purchasing power parity argument, on the other hand, suggests that general price

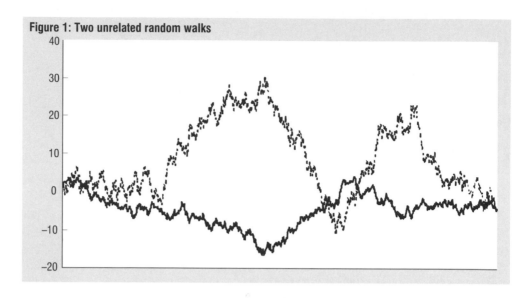

Figure 1: Two unrelated random walks

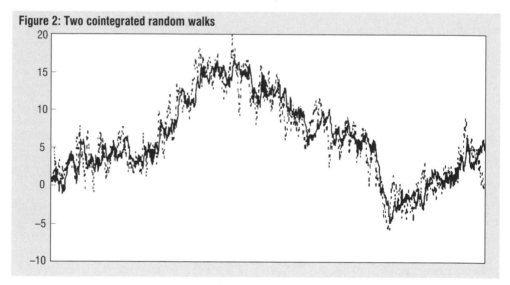

Figure 2: Two cointegrated random walks

indices in two countries and their nominal currency exchange rate should be cointegrated. Due to the potential of arbitrage, futures and spot prices are expected to be cointegrated (Brenner and Kroner, 1995), and statistical evidence appears to be supportive of this theoretical prediction (Ng and Pirrong, 1993a and b). Based purely on statistical evidence, cointegration has also been found in foreign exchange rates (Baillie and Bollerslev, 1989, Kroner and Sultan, 1993, and Alexander and Johnson, 1992 and 1994), in country stock indices (Taylor and Tonks, 1989, Alexander and Johnson, 1994), in stock prices within an industry (Cerchi and Havenner, 1988, Alexander, 1999), and in interest rates (Engle and Granger, 1987, Hall, Anderson, and Granger, 1992, and Alexander and Johnson, 1994).

In this article, we first introduce a simple illustrative model to zero in on the important difference between short-run and long-run relationships. We then relate it to the seemingly peculiar finding by Morris, Neal and Rolph (1999) in which credit spread is positively related to Treasury yield but change in credit spread is negatively related to change in Treasury yield. This particular finding highlights the critical importance of the distinction between long-run and short-run relationships. Cointegration can also have important implications on the pricing and hedging of derivative securities contingent upon multiple underlying assets. We will discuss the recent theoretical advances established in Duan and Pliska (1999) for cointegrated asset prices.

Cointegration vs correlation

In order to understand cointegration more precisely it is imperative to first grasp the concept of unit-root time series. A unit-root time series refers to the data series that is non-stationary but becomes stationary after the series is differenced once or several times. For simplicity, we will confine our discussion to the situation that requires only one differencing operation. Unit-root simply refers to the fact that the root of the differencing operator equals one. Unit-root series are sometimes referred to as random walks to describe the feature of independent increments exhibited by these series. It has been a long tradition in the finance literature arguing for market efficiency. In a nutshell, supporters of market efficiency think that market price changes are unpredictable and must therefore be random walks (or unit-root series). The unit-root series can be formally modeled as follows:

$$
\begin{aligned}
\Delta X_t &= X_t - X_{t-1} \\
&= \mu_x + \delta_x Z_{t-1} + \varepsilon_t
\end{aligned}
\tag{1}
$$

where ε_t is a mean 0 and variance σ^2 random variable independent of the time-$(t-1)$ information set; Z_{t-1} is some state variable that is stationary and measurable with respect to the time-$(t-1)$ information set.

For two unit-root series or more, we need to describe the relationship among them. For simplicity, we will confine our discussion to the case of two series. Let the second unit-root series be denoted by Y_t; that is,

$$
\begin{aligned}
\Delta Y_t &= Y_t - Y_{t-1} \\
&= \mu_y + \delta_y Z_{t-1} + \xi_t
\end{aligned}
\tag{2}
$$

where ξ_t is a mean 0 and variance v^2 random variable independent of the time-$(t-1)$ information set. For simplicity, we assume that ε_t and ξ_t are bivariate normal random variables with correlation coefficient ρ. It is tempting to describe the relationship solely by a constant correlation between ΔX_t and ΔY_t, but it would be hasty to do so due to the presence of Z_{t-1}.

For the two non-stationary variables – X_t and Y_t – there may exist a long-run relationship that is reflected in Z_t. One interesting way of describing their long-run relationship is the cointegration concept proposed and formalized by Granger (1983) and Engle and Granger (1987). If the two unit-root series can be linearly combined in a non-trivial way to yield a stationary process, then the two series are cointegrated. Let this particular linear transformation give rise to a stationary series Z_t. Specifically, we let

$$
Z_t = a + bt + cX_t + Y_t.
\tag{3}
$$

There are two facts deserving some explanation. First, the coefficient before Y_t is restricted to one because scale multiplication of a stationary series continues to be stationary. In other words, this restriction is used to remove indeterminacy. Second, we have allowed for a deterministic time trend variable bt, which can be used to offset potential difference in growth rates of the two series.

The system defined by equations (1), (2) and (3) is a simple error-correction model. Its name reflects that the nature of the change in both X_t and Y_t depends on how far apart they are from each other, which is captured by the term Z_t. Although Granger's representation theorem implies that two cointegrated series can always be expressed as an error-correction model, they may not be the same as the specific error-correction form defined in equations (1), (2) and (3). The question is therefore whether our simple error-correction model still constitutes a cointegrated system. The answer turns out to be positive as long as $-2 < c\delta_x + \delta_y < 0$, a condition that is a special case of Duan and Pliska (1999). In fact, it is easy to verify directly in our simple case.

$$
\begin{aligned}
\Delta Z_t &= b + c\Delta X_t + \Delta Y_t \\
&= b + c(\mu_x + \delta_x Z_{t-1} + \varepsilon_t) + (\mu_y + \delta_y Z_{t-1} + \xi_t) \\
&= -(c\delta_x + \delta_y)\left(-\frac{b + c\mu_x + \mu_y}{c\delta_x + \delta_y} - Z_{t-1}\right) + c\,\varepsilon_t + \xi_t.
\end{aligned}
\tag{4}
$$

It is clear that Z_t is stationary if $-2 < c\delta_x + \delta_y < 0$. Moreover,

$$
E(Z_t) = -\frac{b + c\mu_x + \mu_y}{c\delta_x + \delta_y}
$$

and

$$
\mathrm{VaR}(Z_t) = \frac{c^2\sigma^2 + 2c\rho\sigma\upsilon + \upsilon^2}{1 - (1 + c\delta_x + \delta_y)^2}
$$

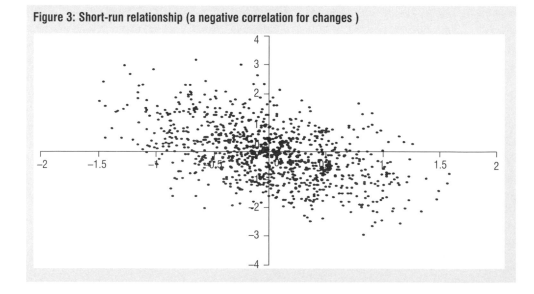

Figure 3: Short-run relationship (a negative correlation for changes)

Figure 4: Long-run relationship (a positive cointegration for levels)

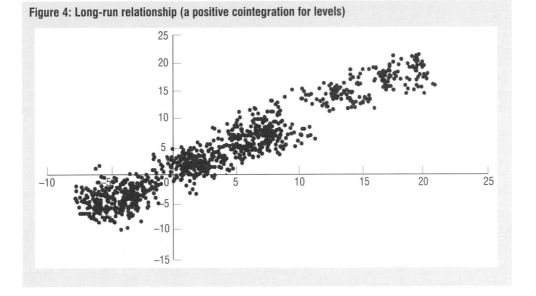

Taken together, X_t and Y_t are individually unit-root series and some linear combination of them yields a stationary series. In other words, the simple error-correction model is indeed a cointegrated system.

The simple error-correction model can be used to better understand the difference between long-run and short-run risk relationships. We use the following set of parameter values to simulate two cointegrated series:

$$\mu_x = \mu_y = 0,\ \delta_x = 0.1,\ \delta_y = -0.1,\ a = b = 0,\ c = -1,\ \sigma = 0.5,\ \upsilon = 1,\ \rho = -0.5.$$

We then plot the changes of these two series in relation to each other (short-run relationship) in Figure 3. It exhibits a clear negative relationship between changes. Their levels are plotted out in Figure 4, which shows a positive long-run relationship. The long-run and short-run relationships of these two series are distinctly different. The short-run relationship is captured by correlation, which is negative, and the long-run relationship is captured by cointegration, which is positive.

In a 1999 paper, Morris, Neal, and Rolph showed that credit spread is positively related to Treasury yield but changes in these two series have a negative relationship. This finding is troubling in the sense that traditional credit spread models cannot reconcile these two findings simultaneously. But they also appear exceedingly simple if one views the issue from the cointegration perspective. Although it would be naïve to think that the true structure is as simple as our illustrative model, a structure bearing the essence of our simple error-correction model may hold the key to our eventual understanding of the working of credit risk markets.

Continuous time cointegration

Continuous time models, particularly diffusion models, are commonly used in financial modeling. Can cointegration be incorporated into diffusion models? Duan and Pliska (1999) have shown that this is possible. In fact, we have developed a stochastic volatility cointegrated diffusion system using the weak convergence argument similar to my approach for the GARCH model in Duan (1997). Here we use the simplest version of cointegrated diffusion to convey the essence of the idea. The following diffusion system is a continuous-time version of the simple error-correction model described earlier:

$$
\begin{aligned}
dX_t &= (\mu_x + \delta_x Z_t)dt + \sigma dB_t \\
dY_t &= (\mu_y + \delta_y Z_t)dt + \upsilon dW_t \\
Z_t &= a + bt + cX_t + Y_t
\end{aligned}
\tag{5}
$$

where B_t and W_t are two correlated standard Brownian motions with ρ as the correlation coefficient.

If we can show that Z_t is stationary, then X_t and Y_t will meet the requirements of being two cointegrated processes. Recall that the conditions are (1) X_t and Y_t are individually random walks, and (2) some linear combination of them is stationary.

Applying the standard stochastic calculus to Z_t gives rise to

$$
\begin{aligned}
dZ_t &= b\,dt + c\,dX_t + d\,Y_t \\
&= [b + c\mu_x + \mu_y + (c\delta_x + \delta_y)Z_t]dt + c\sigma dB_t + \upsilon dW_t \\
&= -(c\delta_x + \delta_y) - \left[\frac{b + c\mu_x + \mu_y}{c\delta_x + \delta_y} - Z_t\right]dt + c\sigma dB_t + \upsilon dW_t.
\end{aligned}
\tag{6}
$$

It follows that Z_t is a stationary Ornstein-Uhlenbeck process if $c\delta_x + \delta_y < 0$. This stationarity condition is weaker than the one given earlier for the discrete-time error-correction model because this one has no lower bound. The lower bound is needed for discrete-time models to prevent an overcorrection. Since diffusion models have continuous sample paths, overcorrection will not happen.

It is clear that we have produced a cointegrated constant-volatility diffusion model. This simple model suggests that it is fairly easy to incorporate cointegration into diffusion models. If the construction of cointegrated diffusion models is for purposes of derivatives pricing, it is unlikely to gain anything of substance, however. This point will be elaborated later. For now, let us recall the standard martingale pricing theory. It stipulates that an option's value should have nothing to do with the specific functional form for the drift terms. In other words, cointegration should have no theoretical significance for option valuation in such diffusion models.

Option valuation under cointegration

In the literature, valuation of derivative contracts on multiple assets is typically conducted using multivariate geometric Brownian motions or the Black-Scholes approach. This approach clearly fails to consider the potential role of cointegration. This problem is particularly acute because derivatives of this type are naturally structured on the assets that are related in some way. In other words, they are not accidental combinations; rather, they are put together purposely to address particular market needs. If these assets are related, their prices are most likely to be cointegrated.

Another important deficiency is the constant volatility assumption of the standard approach. It is well documented in the empirical literature that asset volatilities are time-varying and stochastic. In fact, the GARCH family of models has been found very successful in capturing this phenomenon. Duan (1995) developed a theory of option pricing based on the GARCH model. Its multivariate generalization has been developed for cross-currency options in Duan and Wei (1999) without considering cointegration. In fact, the option pricing literature was completely silent on the issue of cointegration until our work in Duan and Pliska (1999). We took a discrete-time error-correction model with the GARCH effect as the basis for developing the pricing theory under cointegration and went on to derive a diffusion limit of the model. Interestingly, this work demonstrates for the first time how a simple cointegrated diffusion system can be constructed, such as that described in the preceding section.

The theory of option pricing under cointegration that was developed in Duan and Pliska (1999) is now described and its significance for pricing and hedging involving derivatives on multiple assets is discussed. A two-asset version of the model is used for illustration purposes.

$$
\begin{aligned}
\Delta \ln S_{1,t} &= r + \lambda_1 \sigma_{1,t} - \tfrac{1}{2}\sigma_{1,t}^2 + \delta_1 Z_{t-1} + \sigma_{1,t}\varepsilon_{1,t} \\
\Delta \ln S_{2,t} &= r + \lambda_2 \sigma_{2,t} - \tfrac{1}{2}\sigma_{2,t}^2 + \delta_2 Z_{t-1} + \sigma_{2,t}\varepsilon_{2,t} \\
Z_t &= a + bt + \ln S_{1,t} + c \ln S_{2,t}
\end{aligned}
\tag{7}
$$

where

$$
\begin{aligned}
\sigma_{1,t}^2 &= \beta_{10} + \beta_{11}\sigma_{1,t-1}^2 + \beta_{12}\sigma_{1,t-1}^2(\varepsilon_{1,t-1} - \theta_1)^2 \\
\sigma_{2,t}^2 &= \beta_{20} + \beta_{21}\sigma_{2,t-1}^2 + \beta_{22}\sigma_{2,t-1}^2(\varepsilon_{2,t-1} - \theta_2)^2 \\
\begin{bmatrix} \varepsilon_{1,t} \\ \varepsilon_{2,t} \end{bmatrix} \Big| F_{t-1} &\overset{P}{\sim} N\left(0, \begin{bmatrix} 1 & \rho \\ \rho & 1 \end{bmatrix}\right).
\end{aligned}
\tag{8}
$$

The error-correction part of the model is more complex than the simple error-correction model described earlier. The complexity comes from treating time-varying volatility and risk premium. The risk-free rate (continuously compounded) is denoted by r. The factor, $-\tfrac{1}{2}\sigma_{i,t}^2$ arises from logarithmic transformation. Parameter λ_i is the risk premium per unit of risk, whereas $\delta_i Z_{t-1}$ is interpreted as the cointegration risk premium. The GARCH part of the model is the constant correlation version of the multivariate GARCH specification of Bollerslev (1988) except that an asymmetric volatility response to positive and negative price innovations is allowed through parameter θ_i. This particular way of dealing with asymmetry is the nonlinear asymmetric GARCH specification of Engle and Ng (1993). This particular stochastic volatility error-correction model is a cointegrated system if the GARCH parameters satisfy the usual stationarity condition (see Duan, 1997) and $|1 + \delta_1 + c\delta_2| < 1$.

Relying on Duan's (1995) local risk-neutralization principle, Duan and Pliska (1999) obtained the following system for option valuation:

$$
\begin{aligned}
\Delta \ln S_{1,t} &= r - \tfrac{1}{2}\sigma_{1,t}^2 + \sigma_{1,t}\xi_{1,t} \\
\Delta \ln S_{2,t} &= r - \tfrac{1}{2}\sigma_{2,t}^2 + \sigma_{2,t}\xi_{2,t} \\
Z_t &= a + bt + \ln S_{1,t} + c \ln S_{2,t}
\end{aligned}
\tag{9}
$$

where

$$\sigma_{1,t}^2 = \beta_{10} + \beta_{11}\sigma_{1,t-1}^2 + \beta_{12}\sigma_{1,t-1}^2 (\xi_{1,t-1} - \theta_1 - \lambda_1 - \delta_1 \frac{Z_{t-2}}{\sigma_{1,t-1}})^2$$

$$\sigma_{2,t}^2 = \beta_{20} + \beta_{21}\sigma_{2,t-1}^2 + \beta_{22}\sigma_{2,t-1}^2 (\xi_{2,t-1} - \theta_2 - \lambda_2 - \delta_2 \frac{Z_{t-2}}{\sigma_{2,t-1}})^2 \qquad (10)$$

$$\begin{bmatrix} \xi_{1,t} \\ \xi_{2,t} \end{bmatrix} \mid F_{t-1} \overset{Q}{\sim} N \left(0, \begin{bmatrix} 1 & \rho \\ \rho & 1 \end{bmatrix} \right).$$

Note that Q in the above system refers to the locally risk-neutral pricing measure, whereas P in the earlier system refers to the data-generating probability measure. With the system under measure Q, valuation of derivatives follows the standard practice of taking the expected value of the contingent payoff and then discounts the expected value at the risk-free rate.

This valuation system has a distinct feature. Valuation of an option depends theoretically on the underlying asset's risk premiums and the cointegration premiums unless the asset volatilities are constant, i.e., $\beta_{12} = \beta_{22} = 0$. The theoretical reason for this feature is identical to that of Duan (1995), in which the asset's risk premium plays a role in the valuation equation under the GARCH volatility structure. With cointegration, additional terms related to cointegration risk premiums surface in the valuation system, suggesting that the relative position of the two underlying asset prices will determine how their paths will evolve. This result also implies that cointegration is important in a theoretical sense only if volatilities are stochastic. Under a constant volatility assumption, cointegration will impact option values only through its effects on parameter estimation.

In Duan and Pliska (1999) we have employed this valuation theory to examine spread options' pricing and hedging implications using the parameter estimates for the S&P 500 and NASDAQ 100 indices. Under the constant volatility assumption, we found that the statistical effects of cointegration on spread option values were negligible. However, with stochastic volatility, we found that the cointegration term can have an effect of 10 percent or more by switching the error-correction term's value from positive to negative. In other words, the relative position of the two underlying asset prices is important in determining a spread option's values.

Spread options' deltas and vegas are also affected by the consideration of cointegration. The difference in deltas is rather striking. The deltas with cointegration can be as high as 30 times the corresponding deltas without cointegration. The intuition behind this dramatic difference is that changing one asset price while keeping the other fixed alters the magnitude of the error-correction term, and thus affects the dynamics of volatilities under the local risk-neutral measure. This interesting feature is absent in the traditional option pricing models.

Conclusion

This chapter has introduced cointegration and shown how it should be applied in continuous time diffusion models for option pricing. It appears that cointegration is a factor of primary importance for the pricing and hedging of spread options when volatility is stochastic.

Summary

Many economic/financial data series are known to be individually non-stationary but have a long-run relationship among them. The cointegration model lends itself naturally to describing such a phenomenon. Simply applying correlation to the changes in these series may give rise to grossly misleading conclusions, however, because short-run and long-run behaviors are very different and should be dealt with carefully. **Jin-Chuan Duan** illustrates the important difference by employing a simple error-correction model, and relates it to recent findings on credit spread behavior and the theoretical advances in option pricing theory.

© Jin-Chuan Duan

Suggested further reading

Alexander, C. and Johnson, A. (1992) "Are foreign exchange markets really efficient?" *Economics Letters*, 40, pp. 449–453.

Alexander, C. and Johnson, A. (1994) "Dynamic links," *RISK*, 7:2, pp. 57–60.

Alexander, C.O. (1999) "Optional hedging using cointegration," *Philosophical Transactions of the Royal Society*, London, Series A 357, pp. 2039–2058.

Baillie, R. and Bollerslev, T. (1989) "Common stochastic trends in a system of exchange rates," *Journal of Finance*, 44, pp. 137–151.

Bollerslev, T. (1988) "On the correlation structure on the generalized autoregressive conditional heteroskedastic process," *Journal of Time Series Analysis*, 9, pp. 121–131.

Brenner, R. and Kroner, K. (1995) "Arbitrage, cointegration, and testing the unbiasedness hypothesis in financial markets," *Journal of Financial and Quantitative Analysis*, 30, pp. 23–42.

Cerchi, M. and Havenner, A. (1988) "Cointegration and stock prices: the random walk on Wall Street revisited," *Journal of Economic Dynamics and Control*, 12, pp. 333–346.

Duan, J.-C. (1995) "The GARCH option pricing model," *Mathematical Finance*, 5, pp. 13–32.

Duan, J.-C. (1997) "Augmented GARCH(p,q) process and its diffusion limit," *Journal of Econometrics*, 79, pp. 97–127.

Duan, J.-C. and Pliska, S. (1999) "Option valuation with cointegrated asset prices," Unpublished Manuscript, Hong Kong University of Science and Technology.

Duan, J.-C. and Wei, J. (1999) "Pricing foreign currency and cross-currency options under GARCH," *Journal of Derivatives*, 7:1, pp. 51–63.

Engle, R. and Granger, C. (1987) "Cointegration and error correction: representation, estimation, and testing," *Econometrica*, 55, pp. 251–276.

Engle, R. and Ng, V. (1993) "Measuring and testing the impact of news on volatility," *Journal of Finance*, 48, pp. 1749–1778.

Granger, C. (1983) "Cointegration and error-correction models," Unpublished Manuscript, University of California, San Diego.

Hall, A., Anderson, H. and Granger, C. (1992) "A cointegration analysis of treasury bill yields," *Review of Economics and Statistics*, 74, pp. 116–126.

Kroner, K. and Sultan, J. (1993) "Time varying distributions and dynamic hedging with foreign currency futures," *Journal of Financial and Quantitative Analysis*, 28, pp. 535–551.

Morris, C., Neal, R. and Rolph, D. (1999) "Credit spreads and interest rates," Unpublished Manuscript, Federal Reserve Bank, Kansas City.

Ng, V. and Pirrong, C. (1993a) "Price dynamics in physical commodity spot and futures markets: spreads, spillovers, volatility, and convergence in refined petroleum products," Unpublished Manuscript, University of Michigan.

Ng, V. and Pirrong, C. (1993b) "Fundamentals and volatility: storage, spreads, and the dynamics of metals prices," Unpublished Manuscript, University of Michigan.

Taylor, M. and Tonks, I. (1989) "The internationalisation of stock markets and the abolition of U.K. exchange control," *Review of Economics and Statistics*, 71, pp. 332–336.

Managing model risk

by Riccardo Rebonato

Model risk is arguably one of the least understood concepts in risk management. The term is used in such different contexts, and with such different connotations, that its meaning has become so diluted as to be of little practical use. The most "catholic" usage of the term includes the valuation – under any accountancy regime – of any product for which a "model" is used at some point in the valuation process in order to arrive at the book value. At the other extreme, some risk managers might hold the view that if, say, the FX smile surface used by their institution's finance department is perfectly corroborated by *today's* brokers' quotes, then the plain-vanilla options in the trading books present no model risk. This latter understanding of model risk therefore focusses all the attention on the congruence of *today's* mark-to-model and market prices.

I maintain that the first definition is too inclusive and the second too restrictive to be of practical use. I will argue that a risk manager should be concerned not only with the possibility of a mispricing today but also with *future* distributions of profit and losses over a suitably chosen holding period. I will make the point that this notional holding period, in the case of model risk, can be significantly greater than the one- or ten-day interval normally used for market risk purposes.

Furthermore, I will concur with the "modern" view that in order to account for model risk convincingly, the risk management function must possess tools and market understanding of similar quality and sophistication as the front office. I will also argue, however, that the approach, methodology, philosophy, and models used by the front and middle offices need not and *should not* be the same. In particular, I will make the point that the model validation unit of a bank will not necessarily be best served by having at its fingertips the same trading model used by the front desk, or even the most sophisticated model available in the market.

Given the variety of meanings attached to the term "model risk," and the very specific and precise sense in which I intend to analyze the concept, I begin by proposing a somewhat awkward but operationally useful definition:

> *Model risk is the risk of occurrence at a given point in time (today or in the future) of a significant difference between the mark-to-model value of a complex and/or illiquid instrument held on or off the balance sheet of a financial institution and the price at which the same instrument is revealed to have traded in the market – by brokers' quotes or reliable intelligence of third-party market transactions – after the appropriate provisions have been taken into account.*

There are several points worth noticing in this definition:

1. The instrument is often, but need not be, complex. I will argue that if we accept the definition above, a deeply out-of-the money plain-vanilla FX call/put, caplet, or European swaption can all present significant model risk.
2. The term "mark-to-model" refers to the practice of using in a specific and agreed-upon way a given model in order to obtain the value of the illiquid/complex

product. As discussed at length below, this agreed-upon procedure consists of several distinct phases: the first step in the valuation of the product consists of the observation of transparent ("screen-observable") variables of liquid prices/rates; the second is the employment of a specific methodology to transform these transparent market inputs and combine them with static ("opaque") input data – such as correlations – to produce the inputs needed by the chosen model; the last phase is the evaluation of the model price using the chosen model, the inputs obtained as above, and a well-defined numerical procedure.

3. Model risk is often associated with exotic OTC *off-balance sheet* instruments. This need not be the case: mortgage-backed securities, IOs, POs, inverse IOs, etc. are on-balance sheet instruments, but can present substantial model risk.

4. The given point in time referred to in the definition can be today or some time in the future. Unlike the case of general market risk, in fact, a non-zero model risk will, in general, exist even if the valuation point is today. As I will discuss later, the relevant probabilistic "clock" measures the time between reliable discovery of the prices and levels of market transactions (see Figure 1).

5. From the definition above, it follows that the instruments for which the concept of model risk applies must belong to the trading-book universe. This does not mean that banking-book products might not need complex models to value them (fixed-rate mortgages are a good example). The dynamics between book value, value discovery and price adjustment, however, can be fundamentally different in the trading and banking book worlds (or in investment portfolios or, again, wherever embedded-value accounting is employed). The boundary can sometimes be fuzzy, but for the purposes of the present discussion I shall assume that the distinction can always be unambiguously made, and I shall restrict my comments to the trading-book world.

6. The emphasis is on market price discovery, i.e., on the discovery of the "true" price via direct market transactions or reliable brokers' quotes. Mark-to-model is the practice (or the art) to "guess" at what price a transaction would go through in the *market* in normal *market* size, given a set of prevailing *market* conditions.

7. From the definition above, if reliable price observations were always available for all instruments, model risk would not exist, and the techniques used to estimate general market risk would suffice. As discussed in greater detail below, however, even if a risk manager knew perfectly *today's* prices of all the illiquid/complex instruments on the trading book, and had a series of calibrated models capable of reproducing those prices exactly, model risk would still exist over any finite holding period. In practice, model price uncertainty exists in the future but also today.

Having clarified these important points regarding the definition of model risk, a few observations are in order. The first is that market transactions and brokers' quotes are revealed to a financial institution with a frequency that depends on the nature and liquidity of the product. The interval between reliable quotes ranges from a few days to several weeks, or perhaps even a few months. Marking to model is therefore an extrapolation exercise by means of which the latest information about market transactions is projected forward out to the (unknown) point in time when a new transaction will be revealed.

Even if one knew the future market value of all the plain-vanilla (i.e., in this context, perfectly transparent) instruments and rates, this extrapolation exercise

Figure 1: Evolution of model risk

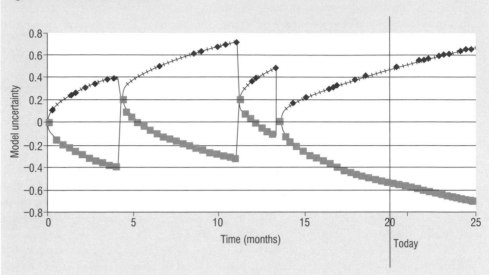

Schematic representation of the evolution of model uncertainty: in the example depicted, there have been four reliable price observations for the product for which model risk is being analyzed in the past 20 months. The thin line and the arrow represent the location in time of "today" with respect to these transactions. The last piece of reliable market information about the price of the product occurred approximately seven months before today. The lines that fan out after each price discovery represent the uncertainty about the price of the complex security. After each observation of a market transaction the uncertainty disappears, and the true value becomes what the market reveals it to be. Notice that the price discovery restarts the stochastic clock and repositions the center of the fan. If the position of the center of the new fan is within the uncertainty band that had been widening since the latest transaction it means that the new price information is within the model uncertainty band. This has always been the case for the (fictitious) example depicted in the figure. Note, however, that the latest price discovery was a "close call" and revealed a price almost outside the model uncertainty band. The risk manager will, in general, be interested in estimating the magnitude of model risk at a future point in time, so that this information can be combined with the general market risk to produce an overall (general + model) market risk picture. Since it is not known when the next transaction will take place, or the price at which it will occur, the uncertainty fan keeps on widening out beyond "today" to the chosen holding period (five months in this case).

would not, in general, produce a single projected value for the complex/illiquid product. In fact, the market consensus about the "best" model to be used for its valuation can change over time. The market risk aversion to some economic factors might increase or decrease, changes in the prevailing regulatory regime can alter the supply/demand balance, and so on. The best result the extrapolation exercise can hope to achieve is therefore the production of a *distribution* of possible future conditional[1] mark-to-model values, not unlike the renowned "uncertainty fans" produced by the Bank of England in its inflation bulletins (see Figure 1).

As mentioned above, however, there is an important difference. In the prediction of economic or financial quantities one always assumes that today's current value

---

[1] These values are conditional because they depend on the future realizations of the prices of the plain-vanilla instruments.

(say, today's inflation) is perfectly known. Therefore for these variables, the uncertainty fans out from an infinitely narrow distribution centered around today's known value. The case of model risk is fundamentally different, in that the uncertainty clock had already begun ticking when the last "visible" market transaction occurred (perhaps a few weeks ago). As a consequence, as of "today" the distribution of model risk will, in general, already have a finite width (see again Figure 1).

Model risk is therefore adequately captured not by a single number but only by the full distribution of differences between the *conditional* mark-to-future[2] values obtainable *using the current valuation methodology* for a set of instruments and the possible values that the market might choose to assign to the *same* instruments at the *same* point in time in the future, given a set of plain-vanilla market variables. Note carefully that model risk does *not* cover the changes in value of a complex/illiquid instrument simply due to the future variations in the plain-vanilla market prices and rates; rather, it focusses on the differences in the valuation methodology that transforms these rates and prices into the value for a given complex/illiquid product.

Just as in the case of general market risk, for practical purposes one might then want to collapse the full information contained in the distribution in a single representative number. The model risk can for instance be quantified, if one so desires, by specifying a suitable percentile, or some other descriptive statistic of its distribution. This choice of a percentile as a useful representative statistic, however, should not obscure the fact that only a whole distribution, and no single number, can adequately describe model risk.

I would like to conclude these preliminary remarks by stressing two important points: first, as mentioned above, the spread of the distribution will depend not just on how far out in the future we are projecting the valuation (the traditional "holding period") but also on when the last reliable market observation has taken place; and second, that given the illiquid nature of the products for which substantial market risk exists, it might not always be possible to distinguish neatly between mid price and bid/offer spread. This is particularly true when a complex product is embedded in a popular customer structure, and the books of the professional market players end up being all "the same way around." Long-dated equity derivatives embedded in principal-protected retail products are a good example. In these cases, seeing a two-way flow of market transactions can sometimes become very difficult, and the only observable becomes the (unknown) mid price plus or minus the (unknown) bid or offer spread, as appropriate. The importance of this observation will become apparent later on.

Model risk and market incompleteness: a trading perspective

It should not come as a surprise, given the preliminary observations just made, that model risk should be intimately linked to asset pricing in incomplete markets. In very abstract terms, one can say that if markets are complete, there exists a single

---

[2] The term mark-to-future, introduced in the risk management literature and practice by the work of Ron Dembo and colleagues (Algorithmics), indicates a hypothetical (conditional) mark-to-market valuation of a portfolio carried out in a future state of the world and with the portfolio itself suitably "aged" (those options which have expired by the end of the time horizon are, for instance, no longer included).

pricing measure that precludes arbitrage. In the case of incomplete markets, however, there exists an infinity of arbitrage-free possible pricing measures. I shall argue below that market completeness can be a good first approximation for trading purposes, but in reality market incompleteness is the norm rather than the exception. If this premise is accepted, model risk can be seen as the possibility that today's chosen pricing measure might change in the future. While correct, this abstract view provides little guidance as to how model risk can be captured in practice. In the following sections I intend both to justify the statement above and to indicate how it can be used to estimate model risk.

In order to understand more precisely why asset pricing in incomplete markets is central to model risk, I present here a stylized account of how the price of a complex instrument is arrived at in the market, both from the perspective of a trader and from the point of view of a risk manager.

In order to make the discussion concrete I will focus on a specific instrument, i.e., the case of the model risk associated with zero-coupon Bermudan swaptions. I will not dwell on any of the specific features of this product, and what I will say could be applied to several, much simpler, instruments. I have nonetheless chosen this example because it contains in almost paradigmatic form a wide variety of features that make the estimation of model risk challenging and because it highlights very clearly the different perspectives of a trader and of a risk manager. The features of the product I am interested in are:

- multi-call zero-coupon swaptions enjoyed enormous popularity among issuers for a limited period (approximately six months in late 1997/early 1998) and mainly in currencies (Deutschmark, Italian lira, French franc) which have now disappeared;
- the transaction volumes were very high, and therefore the residual risk sitting today in the trading books of several investment banks is significant;
- the deals tended to have very long maturities (up to, and sometimes beyond, 30 years), and the problems raised by their fair valuation are therefore not likely to disappear soon (and this example will retain topicality for at least a couple of decades);
- there was, and still is, no market consensus on how to price this product;
- there is virtually no customer demand for the product. As a consequence there are very few, if any, customer transactions to benchmark the price; those transactions that do go through the market tend to have significantly different terms (typically, much shorter maturities), and are not necessarily transacted in the same currency as the original ones.

Let us assume that a financial institution already has several of these products on its books. A request arrives via a broker to submit a bid for another zero-coupon swaption. If the trade went through, the new trade would therefore be added to the existing positions, and no hedging of existing risk can be expected. How would a trader requested to provide a quote today make a bid?

Her first consideration would be how, given the current market conditions, she expects to make money from the transaction, e.g., by off-loading it in the market to the professional community after a relatively short period of time, by finding a customer on the other side of the transaction, or by dynamically hedging the product out to its expiry. Given today's low customer demand for the product, no reliance can be made on executing the transaction via a customer-driven market trade. If the trader wanted to dispose of the transaction quickly, the most likely counterparty, therefore, would be a market professional, whose books, however, are likely to be already long similar products. Therefore the expected profit would have to be crystallized by means of a dynamic hedging strategy that would have to be conducted for the best part of 30 years, and the quoted price would have to reflect the cost of this exercise.

If the trader decides to go ahead with the quote, the second step in the price-making exercise would be to calibrate her favorite model to the specific trade. Calibration in this context is the process by means of which the "free parameters" of the model are chosen so as to ensure that the model-implied prices of the plain-vanilla instruments that will be used to hedge the zero-coupon swaption will be as close as possible to their corresponding market values. In this example, the plain-vanilla hedging instruments are, first of all, co-terminal European swaptions; the model prices that will have to be made as close as possible to the corresponding market values are therefore the prices of these European swaptions.

In order to inject further concreteness into the example, I shall assume that a modern BGM interest-rate model is used for the valuation (see, for example, Jamshidian, 1997). Once again, there is nothing in the following discussion that crucially depends on this particular choice, and, needless to say, *mutatis mutandis*, any other model would do. A reader more familiar with tree-based models might mentally substitute, say, "mean reversion of the short rate" for "instantaneous volatility" and the gist of the discussion would remain valid. Choosing a specific modeling approach, however, has the advantage of allowing me to provide a more precise and concrete description of the pricing process.

Focussing therefore on the BGM model, its practical use requires that specific choices should be made for its inputs, such as the instantaneous volatilities of the underlying forward rates. The market does provide (via the prices of caplets and European swaptions) some information about these quantities,[3] but this information is far from sufficient to pin down these input functions in a unique way. Actually, one can show that it is possible to calibrate the model (i.e., to choose the instantaneous volatilities) so as to recover exactly the prices of the underlying hedging instruments (the European swaptions) in an infinity of ways (see Rebonato, 2000). To each of these possible calibrations there will correspond a different price for the zero-coupon Bermudan swaption. Furthermore, for each possible choice for the instantaneous volatility function, the model will create a different future world. The trader will have to make a judgement as to which of these future universes is more likely to come true.

If some other instruments were available and liquidly traded (for example if serial options traded out to 30 years!) the market for instantaneous volatilities would be complete and this uncertainty would be resolved – assuming for a moment that the chosen model were indeed the correct one, and that no other input were required, in a frictionless market there would be only one price for the zero-coupon swaption, and this price would be given by the set-up cost of the replicating portfolio. If the market were perfect and complete, the trader would therefore not have to ask herself whether she concurs with the market's view regarding the implied future

---

[3] More precisely, the market provides information about the root mean squared instantaneous volatility of a given forward rate from today to its expiry.

behavior of the instantaneous volatilities; she would not even have to ask herself whether she finds this market-implied future behavior plausible. All that the trader would require would be the ability, today and in the future, to trade in the instruments necessary to eliminate *all* the sources of uncertainty.

In reality, however, and even without invoking market frictions and imperfections, the trader will never be in such an enviable position. There will never be sufficient instruments to ensure truly perfect replication: volatility might be stochastic; jumps might affect the path of the underlying; the volatility might itself display discontinuous behavior; etc. Faced with the task of making a price, the trader will therefore have to begin by making an educated guess about the "truest" (most likely) future realization of the financial universe: in practical terms, she will have to guess what the imperfectly hedgeable chosen inputs (in this case the instantaneous volatilities) will be like in the future. In the following I shall call "subjective (or risk-neutral) probability distribution" the set of probabilities that the trader associates with the possible future states of the world.[4] If and only if the trader were endowed with a crystal ball, and her "guess" therefore were exactly correct, i.e., if the instantaneous volatilities behaved in the future exactly as the trader had assumed, would a model such as BGM give her the price for the complex product.

Since this foresight is not possible, as a second step in the pricing process the trader will typically begin to explore how the price for the zero-coupon swaption is affected by possible errors in her guesses about the instantaneous volatilities. Re-running the model with these different volatility inputs (to each of which the trader attaches a subjective probability) will produce a distribution of prices. Loosely speaking we can, as a first approximation, identify the spread in these prices with the distribution of hedging errors that are likely to be incurred (excluding frictions) solely because of the possible mis-specification of the instantaneous volatility.

If the trader were risk-neutral, she would simply average these possible prices over her subjective probabilities to come up with a bid; in reality, she will be far from risk-neutral and she will skew the odds (her subjective pricing measure) in such a way as to be sufficiently compensated – given her risk aversion – for the amount of uncertainty left after the best possible hedge is put in place (see Figure 2).

Once the deal is struck, she will then proceed to hedge dynamically the product for the remaining 30 years, following the model suggestions obtained using as inputs her best (risk-neutral!) guesses, naturally updated as time goes by, about the unobservable instantaneous volatilities. For the purpose of future discussion it is essential to stress that the "value" that the trader will attempt to track by this hedging strategy is not the bid price that she has come up with by using her risk-adjusted distribution, but, roughly speaking, the value obtained by averaging over her risk-neutral (subjective) distribution. She will know that this hedge is necessarily imperfect, since the future input values for the instantaneous volatilities will, in general, turn out to be different from her continuously updated guesses. She will, however, hope that she has been sufficiently compensated for the hedging

---

[4] I am avoiding here any mention of the conditions that require that the subjective probability measures held by different traders should be probabilistically equivalent. The argument can be made more precise, although at the expense of some added mathematical complexity. See, for instance, Bingham and Kiesel (1998).

uncertainty that will accompany her trading career for the next 30 years by having adequately lowered her bid below the "subjective-expectation" value.[5]

Since perfect hedging is not possible (the market for instantaneous volatilities is incomplete), for her dynamic hedging strategy she will therefore have no choice but to enter transactions based on her best guess of what the real-world (as opposed to risk-adjusted) will be like. My colleague Peter Jaeckel has neatly encapsulated this state of affairs in the elegant statement: "If you can't hedge perfectly, you better guess well."

Let us assume for a moment that the counterparty to this transaction is not a *bona fide* customer[6] but another similar market professional. If both parties are risk averse, the bidder will willingly transact at a lower price than the average taken over her subjective probability distribution, and the seller at a correspondingly higher price. The only way both parties (i.e., the trader and "the market") will be happy to enter the transaction is therefore if the market's central estimate (i.e., the mean of its subjective distribution) of the realization of the unobservable quantities (the instantaneous volatilities) is sufficiently different from the trader's central estimate. Sufficiently in this context means that the difference should be large enough to more than compensate for risk aversion, transaction costs, etc.

In this process lies the fundamental and irreconcilable difference between the perspective of a trader and of a risk manager. Given the dynamics outlined above, for the trader to enter a transaction against the market she must believe that the market is "wrong." As pointed out above, in fact, she will attempt to crystallize this difference by engaging in a dynamic trading strategy, based on *her* (not the market's) beliefs about the future. By the maturity of the zero-coupon swaption she will have been proved right or wrong. Fortunately for the trader, the typical OTC transaction often takes place not against a market of identical professionals but against a different universe of customers who, for a variety of reasons, might perceive value in a different way. In fact, these customers might be subject to different accounting rules; they might be forced by regulatory constraints to hedge certain exposures even if they believe that self-insurance would be more economical; they might have a different tax treatment; they might have performance incentives that place different emphasis on under- or over-performance of a benchmark; etc. For all these reasons, and others, the risk-adjusted measure that can be indirectly imputed from the prices where they are ready to transact can be substantially different than the professional traders'. This state of affairs is schematically depicted in Figure 2.

This has important implications for model risk: to the extent that this customer flow will continue in the future (for 30 years), the market quotes will always be found at customer level, i.e., will continue to be based on the right-shifted risk-adjusted pricing measure of the customers. (See the arrow labeled Customer buys here in Figure 3.) If customer demand for the product were to disappear, however, as it has virtually in the case of the zero-coupon swaptions, the only way for the trader to ascertain a market price is to engage in a transaction with a market professional. Looking at Figure 3, it is easy to see that now the trader will not find a

---

[5] The "subjective-expectation value" could be described as the hypothetical price she would have rationally made if she had been forced to enter a transaction *without knowing whether she would be a buyer or a seller*.

[6] Who might perceive "value," perhaps because of accounting rules or regulatory constraints, differently from a mark-to-market trader.

Figure 2: Subjective and risk-adjusted distributions for trader and market

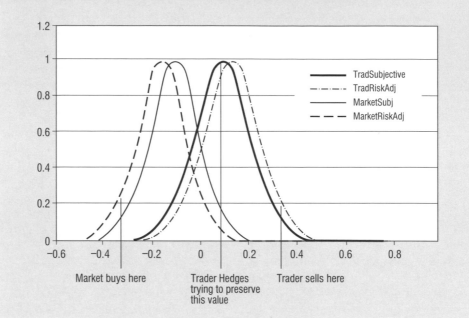

Schematic description of various distributions of P&L after the best hedge is put in place: from these distributions one can obtain the conditions for a trade to take place at the level suggested by the trader's model: given a choice of model and an approximate but imperfect, input-dependent hedging strategy the trader perceives a possible distribution of wealth at the end of the hedging period given by the line labeled TradSubjective (trader subjective). Let us assume that in order to establish a mark, the trader wants to sell the instrument. Given her risk aversion, she will shift the distribution of P&Ls to the curve TradRiskAdj (trader risk adjusted). If one assumes for simplicity that the trader's risk aversion can be expressed by a suitable loss percentile, the right-most arrow indicates where the trader would be happy to sell. The market's representative agent, however, believes in a different distribution of P&Ls, shown in MarketSubj (market subjective), and adjusts this subjective distribution to the left when submitting a bid to the curve labeled MarketRiskAdj. The left-most arrow indicates where the market is ready to buy. The central arrow gives the trader's expectation of the most likely outcome in terms of P&L of her hedging exercise. In these conditions no trade can take place at the level indicated by the trader's model. If the trader is long the option, the finance department needs a model that produces the level marked as "Market buys here." This price (see the caveat on page 85) will include the bid/offer spread. The trader, in order to hedge, needs a model that gives as mid the level indicated by the middle arrow.

level at which she would be happy to bid. According to the trader, the market is "wrong." The trader might well be smarter, better informed, more "right" than the market. Nonetheless, the only way for the finance department of the trader's investment house to ascertain where the zero-coupon swaptions held by the trader could be sold is to find via brokers' quotes the *market's* bid. This is the meaning of Björk's (1998) aphorism about pricing in incomplete markets: "Who chooses the pricing measure? The market!"

Even if the trader is right, she will be able to realize her theoretical (i.e., model-implied) PV only by the maturity of the zero-coupon swaption (in 30 years' time), or by the time the market "sees the light." In the meantime she might have to suffer severe mark-to-market storms.

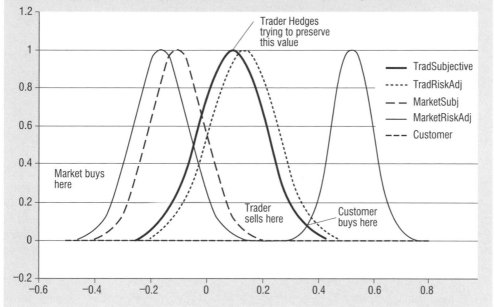

Figure 3: Subjective and risk-adjusted distributions for trader and market, plus customer

A similar graph to Figure 2, but now including the presence of a customer. The customer does not perceive value in the same mark-to-market way (perhaps because of different accounting rules, or because of regulatory restrictions in entering certain transactions). Furthermore, typically, the customer will not enter a hedging strategy, and therefore a similar distribution of P&Ls is not appropriate. Nonetheless, the trader and market interpret the customer dealing level with the appropriate percentile of a risk-adjusted distribution. (Incidentally, as long as the customer trades are forthcoming, the market risk-adjusted curve would no longer remain on the left.) When customer demand is present, the trader's and the customer's curves overlap, and intelligence of market transactions will corroborate the marking level of the trader. If the customer flow were to disappear, however, the trader would suddenly have to resort to other market professionals (who perceive value in the same mark-to-market terms and do not suffer from the institutional constraints), and the relevant curves are those on the left of the graph. The product is now mis-marked-to-model. The length of the segment between Customer buys here and Market buys here is one point in the model risk distribution. Note that this example is extremely simplified, and does not describe an equilibrium situation: in real life, as long as customer flow remains forthcoming, increasing competition between traders will shift the implied distribution of the customer more and more to the left (the customer obtains increasingly better terms). Incidentally, this is what happened in the case of the zero-coupon swaption trades: despite the fact that investment houses were accumulating more and more long-dated and illiquid volatility risk, and their risk aversion should therefore have pushed their risk-adjusted distributions to the left, they improved their trade terms dramatically over a period of six months The events in Russia and their aftermath put a sudden stop to the game.

Notice how, in this stylized account of complex derivatives trading, a model-independent event, i.e., the drying up of customer demand for a particular product, completely changes the level at which the trader can transact with the market, i.e., the price that the finance department will (with great difficulty!) discover. Nonetheless the trader will still need her most trusted model to continue her dynamic hedge. This is the first important reason why the model needed by the trader and the model needed by the risk manager are intrinsically different.

Model risk and market incompleteness: a risk management perspective

Let us now place ourselves in the risk manager's shoes. Well aware of the price-making dynamics just outlined, the risk manager will reason that if only he could discover, via today's trading prices, the market's risk-adjusted probability distribution (i.e., the curves labeled Market in Figures 2 and 3), he could deduce at what level the trades on the bank's books would be absorbed by the market. The risk manager, therefore, will want to have at his disposal a model capable of reproducing the market's observed trading prices. By using this model, the risk manager's obvious desire would then be to distill the market risk-adjusted distribution (measure) once and for all by using today's prices. The market's risk-neutral distribution (i.e., the distribution labeled MarketSubj in Figure 2) might well be inaccessible from the traded prices, but, after all, it is by itself of no interest to him. What the risk manager would like to obtain are the market's risk-adjusted parameters of the processes for the variables needed to price complex or illiquid instruments. In a way, the task for the risk manager seems simpler than the task for the trader, since there is no need to obtain a risk-adjusted distribution to make a price and a subjective probability to hedge. His task, however, is still fraught with difficulties.

To begin with, the risk manager must reverse-engineer from a collection of traded prices (for different strikes, maturities, etc.) what the market's chosen model is likely to be. Let us assume that the risk manager is interested in the "fair" valuation of a book of FX options, and that the market quotes obtained, say, a couple of weeks ago for FX plain-vanilla options can be well accounted for by a simple jump/diffusion model. The market will indicate, via a handful of genuine quotes, the (possibly time-dependent) parameters that specify the model, i.e., in this case, the volatility of the diffusive part, the jump amplitude ratio and the jump frequency, both adjusted for risk according to the market's risk aversion.

To make the argument concrete let us focus on the risk-adjusted jump frequency. One could be tempted to compare it with the corresponding econometric quantity, to assume that the latter coincides with the market unbiased (subjective) estimate, and to deduce from the observed prices how much the frequency is altered in moving from the risk-neutral to the risk-adjusted world. On the basis of the market quotes obtained, in this example, two weeks ago, the result might be that, after correcting for risk aversion, the jump frequency becomes, say, 50 percent higher. Since this piece of information about the market risk aversion is independent of the specific option, the next logical step would be to use the prescription: "increase the econometric jump frequency by 50 percent." This procedure should produce the mark-to-model value today for *all* the plain-vanilla options in the FX book. It would produce a single and certain number for the mark-to-model today. It would also produce a single value at any point in the future, conditional on a given state of the world being realized.

This procedure is conceptually appealing, and has been analyzed, in one form or another, in a large body of literature (see, for example, Jackwerth, 1997). For model risk management purposes, however, it is unfortunately of very little use. The problem is that there is no guarantee that the market risk aversion (in this particular example to jumps) will not change over time. Actually, observation and *ex-post-facto* rationalization of market dynamics suggests that this implied risk aversion can change dramatically over a relatively short period of time. For the example discussed above, where the quotes were collected two weeks ago, probably the market consensus has not had the time to change significantly; but what about those (still plain-vanilla) very out-of-the-money long-dated options that were traded two years ago? When did the finance department actually manage to see a real market transaction for such low delta levels? How can we know that the market risk aversion to those factors most affecting out-of-the-money options (e.g., jump amplitudes) has not changed in the meantime?

This change in risk aversion could have a number of causes. It could reflect the market's reaction to unanticipated events, such as the devaluations of the south-east Asian currencies in 1997, or the Russia crisis. In particular, the market dislocations that occurred in the summer and autumn of 1998 changed market perceptions of risk for a variety of risk factors in a fundamental way. Swap spread risk in the good old pre-Russia days was often taken to be little more than a second-order effect and, as a consequence, the practice of hedging long positions in corporate bonds by shorting government paper was much more prevalent than today. Trading the CMS/CMT spread was a seriously unexciting activity; in the case of interest-rate options, implied volatilities as a function of strike and for a fixed maturity used to show at most a monotonically decreasing shape, quite different from the current hockey-stick pattern. And the implied volatility of equity options has also changed shape in a noticeable way: liquidity risk and counterparty credit risk have moved much more to the forefront of the market's attention.

In addition to market events, changes in supply and demand can also shift the implied market risk-adjusted distribution in dramatic ways. As we saw above, for instance, the *apparent* risk aversion of a generic counterparty might change because a class of players (the *bona fide* customers) disappear from the market. More precisely, one should say that, with the disappearance of a set of players, the market shifts from being priced on the basis of the implied risk-adjusted probability measure of the customers to being priced using the risk-adjusted measure of the market professionals.

This state of affairs is captured by the words of a colleague of mine: "The market is always right, but it is also fickle." This statement, which, after all, should be quite obvious, is very often forgotten, or swept under the carpet. As an example let me quote a (perfectly correct) statement from one of the best books in asset pricing (Duffie, 1996) in the context of pricing with stochastic volatility:

> "[In the case of stochastic volatility], it follows from Ito's lemma that one can develop a stochastic differential equation (**under Q**) [*my emphasis*] for the price process (S,Y), where Y is the price of a given European call or put option. Given a second option, one can then proceed [...] to compute a self-financing trading strategy that replicates the second option."

The impression that the inattentive reader gets from this statement is that in the presence of stochastic volatility, the market can be completed simply by including another option in the set of the hedging instruments. The consequence of this would be that, by including the option Y in the hedging basket, we could arrive at a *single* price the market will always have to agree upon for any non-Y option. If this were true, model risk due to the presence of stochastic volatility would be dramatically reduced. This, however, is correct as long as one assumes that the market knows not just today's price for Y but *the full process* for this hedging option.

The important qualifier in the above quotation is the expression in parentheses ("under Q"): the price process for the hedging option Y can be obtained if we assume that we know the pricing measure Q today and in the future. But the latter, as we have discussed, is subject to constant revisions from the fickle market. From today's price for Y, from econometric information about the real world, and from an assumed knowledge of the *process* for the stock S, we can indeed attempt to recover the time-dependent market price of jump risk, λ (or equivalently, the future conditional measure pricing $Q_\lambda(\omega)$), *but only after making assumptions about the future behavior of λ or of Q_λ.*

In particular, the task would be simplified if we assumed, for instance, that the market risk aversion were not to change in the future. Sometimes, in a trading context, this can be a useful starting point or zeroth-order approximation – this was, after all, the approach implicitly taken by Vasicek and CIR in their pioneering work. In the context of model risk, however, enforcing this assumption is equivalent to pretending that the problem we are trying to solve (i.e., finding how our mark-to-model might change in the future due to the market's fickle nature) does not exist.

The example of risk aversion generated by the presence of unhedgeable jump risk is important because identical or similar considerations can be repeated in all those situations where, supposedly, the market can be completed by adding one or more derivatives to the set of hedging instruments (stochastic volatility and jump/ diffusions with a finite possible number of jump amplitude ratios are other good examples). In all these cases, the usual claim that there should exist a single price for instruments outside the hedging basket is true only if one assumes knowledge not only of today's prices for the hedging instruments but also of their prices in all the possible future states of the world.

As soon as one moves away from a Black universe, market incompleteness, and the accompanying dependence of market prices on the time-varying perceptions of risk, becomes virtually ubiquitous. The best that the risk manager can do therefore is to attempt to estimate, on the basis of analysis of past data, how much the risk-adjusted parameters that enter a model as inputs are likely to change over time. In order to see how this can be accomplished in practice, and how this estimation can be brought to bear on the assessment of model risk, a more detailed examination of how a model can be used in real-life situations is needed.

Practical applications

As we have said, the task of the risk manager, as far as model risk is concerned, is to estimate the conditional distribution of differences between future mark-to-model values (obtained using the "best" model chosen by the market today) and the prices at which a future actual market transaction will take place. It is essential to stress again that the expression "best model" designates the model and the calibration procedure that can best account for the most recent available observed market price. For risk management purposes, it should not be confused with what the trader, the risk manager, or the latest article in *Risk* magazine believe the best model to be. Having clarified this point, let us analyze in detail the inter-relationships between these two components, i.e., between the mark-to-model estimate and the future market price.

To begin with, the future value of the mark-to-model price is obviously not known today, dependent as it is on the realization of a future state of the world. As we have discussed, however, the mark-to-model procedure relies on an agreed-upon methodology to transform future liquid, transparent ("screen-visible") prices and rates into the (often unobservable) inputs of a chosen model, and on an also agreed-upon methodology which specifies how to transform these inputs via a chosen model into the price for a complex/illiquid product. To give concrete examples, the unobservable inputs could be the volatility of the short rate, or its risk-adjusted reversion speed and reversion level for old-fashioned short-rate-based models; the risk-adjusted jump frequency or jump amplitude ratio for FX or equity jump diffusion-models; the volatility of the variance of the short rate in the Longstaff-Schwartz model; the risk-adjusted pre-payment speed of a mortgage-backed security; the instantaneous volatilities and correlations in the BGM model; etc.

The liquid and screen-visible market prices and rates from which these unobservable inputs are distilled can be in-, at-, and out-of-the-money prices[7] for plain-vanilla calls and puts for equities and FX; caplets and European swaption implied volatilities; prices of benchmark mortgage-backed securities; prices of liquid government bonds; swap spreads at selected maturities; etc. The complex set of procedures for transforming a collection of plain-vanilla prices and rates into the price of a complex product should reflect the risk manager's best understanding of the correspondent methodologies followed by the market.

Note that there is far more in this process than the choice of a model, and that the choice of how the transparent prices are transformed into the model inputs is just as important, if not more, than the choice of model itself. Let me stress again that the risk manager's job, unlike the trader's, is not to choose the model that affords the most convincing description of financial reality, and its most convincing parameterization. His job is to reverse-engineer from the observation of prices for illiquid/complex products what the current market consensus is.

As mentioned in the introductory section, estimating market risk requires the evaluation of the distribution of *changes* in the mark-to-model valuation. It is therefore essential to explore carefully what can drive the variations in the model values. Given the knowledge of the current state of the world (as expressed by today's transparent prices and rates), and given a chosen pricing procedure, the mark-to-model process will produce a single number. Looking at the mark-to-model valuation at a future point in time, however, the model price will in general be different from today's value for four main reasons (see also Figure 4):

1. First, today's truly visible benchmark prices of plain-vanilla products will change when moving over a given holding period. If the approach used to capture market risk is, for instance, historical simulation, the set of future prices and rates (the risk factors) will be obtained by adding to today's values the corresponding observed historical changes experienced in the past over the chosen holding period. Similar considerations apply to parametric approaches such as the variance-covariance normal-VaR model. The crucial point is that, in practice, the risk manager will have at his disposal time series for a relatively small number of benchmark prices/rates: in the cases of volatilities, for instance, he will probably have time series for the at-the-money implied volatilities for a handful of

[7] It is market practice to quote implied volatilities rather than prices. These, however, are not truly volatilities but simply a conventionally agreed-upon way of expressing a price. They are "the wrong number to put in the wrong formula to get the right price" (Rebonato, 1999).

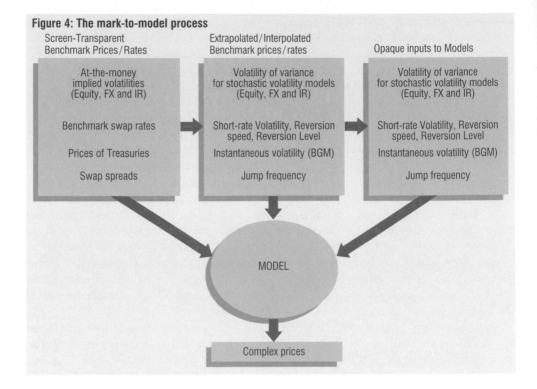

Figure 4: The mark-to-model process

A schematic description of the mark-to-model process: the risk manager has at his disposal time series of changes for a relatively small number of transparent reference rates/prices, e.g., benchmark swap rates for a handful of maturities; implied volatilities for several maturities and a few strikes; swap spreads at a few selected points on the yield curve; etc. The risk manager is then faced with the task of interpolating or extrapolating these benchmark quantities to obtain other still plain-vanilla, but not directly observable, quantities. The construction of the yield curve from the deposit rates, the futures prices, and the swap rates is an example of this procedure. Other pertinent examples are the construction of the smile surface for a continuum of strikes and maturities, and the extraction of caplet prices from cap quotes. Once these pseudo-prices of plain-vanilla instruments are obtained, the unobservable (opaque) inputs for the chosen model can be obtained: the instantaneous volatilities of the BGM model, the reversion speed and level of short-rate-based approaches, the risk-adjusted jump frequency for jump-diffusion processes are examples of these opaque inputs. The latter are then fed into the chosen model as required. Occasionally the model might take in as inputs either the extrapolated/interpolated plain-vanilla prices or, very occasionally, the benchmark prices/rates themselves.

maturities. Occasionally he might have historical information about two further strikes to enable him to make the roughest estimate of straddle and risk reversal risk.

In order to price complex products, however, he will in general need the changes in a much larger number of (still plain-vanilla) prices/rates for which no directly observable time series is available. This additional possible source of changes in the mark-to-model value is analyzed below. However, note that these changes *do not* constitute model risk, despite the fact that the changes in the benchmark risk factors do ultimately alter the price of illiquid/complex instruments. Rather, these changes simply define the state of the world in which the conditional mark-to-model valuation is carried out. The three possible sources of price variations for complex/illiquid products examined below, on the other hand, do contribute to model risk.

2. The next possible reason for a variation in the mark-to-model price (again see Figure 4) is a change in the transformation from the few really screen-transparent prices and rates to prices of still plain-vanilla, but not directly observable, quantities. The importance of this step is often overlooked: today there might well be market consensus about how this extrapolation/interpolation exercise should be accomplished. However, this transformation in the future might be carried out in a different manner. At the time of writing, excellent agreement could be obtained, for instance, for the FTSE index smile over approximately 20 strikes of same-expiry plain-vanilla option prices with as few as three parameters per maturity. It seems to me that the most likely explanation for this uncanny agreement is that the market has (momentarily) settled on a given methodology to obtain implied volatilities using the ATM straddle and the 25-delta calls and puts. This agreement is, however, not immutable and, in general, if today's transformation process changes, the mutual relationships between the plain-vanilla prices that serve as inputs to a model will also change: the skewness or steepness of the implied volatility surface for equity or FX options may be different from today's; the term structure of volatilities (i.e., the at-the-money volatilities as a function of expiry) might change; the relative levels of caplet and swaption volatilities might be altered; swap spreads might widen or tighten in an uneven manner across maturities; etc.

   The risk manager should not be lulled into complacency by speculating that the possible variations in opaque plain-vanilla prices should, after all, be rather small if the benchmark liquid prices/rates are to be recovered – an extrapolation procedure which is not in line with the market will in fact allow the trader to book at a profit plain-vanilla transactions that could only be unwound in the market at a loss. In recent history this has proven to be a powerful incentive to build very large positions in unprofitable (and actually loss-making) relative-value trades. It is also important to note that these variations in the extrapolation procedure will not only change the future prevailing market conditions but could also make a model incapable of accounting for market prices: once implied volatility smiles began to appear, for instance, the Black and Scholes model could no longer produce agreement with market prices of plain-vanilla options across all strikes. Similarly, the BGM model can be modified easily (using, for instance, displaced diffusions) to account for monotonically decreasing implied volatility smiles, but cannot explain the more recent hockey-stick shape of the swaption implied volatilities.

3. The mark-to-model price might change because the way these plain-vanilla, but not directly observable, quantities are translated into unobservable model inputs has changed. One example of such an opaque input are the instantaneous volatilities needed in the BGM model. In the early days of the BGM implementations implied volatilities of caplets (the plain-vanilla derived "prices") used to be directly equated to the instantaneous volatilities of the corresponding forward rates (the opaque inputs); imposing an identical time dependence to the volatilities of all the forward rates then acquired popularity; obtaining the shape of the instantaneous volatilities functions by requiring that the evolution of the term structure of volatilities should be as time-homogeneous as possible is now

more widespread (see Rebonato, 2000). Similarly, the consensus about how the FX and equity smiles should be accounted for is still oscillating between stochastic volatility models, jump-diffusion processes, or a combination of the two.

4. Finally, the engine by which the semi-observable inputs are translated into prices of complex instruments might change – as far as interest-rate products are concerned, for instance, the market's "best modeling practice" has evolved over time from the early Vasicek/CIR approaches, to Ho and Lee, BDT, Hull and White, HJM, BGM... Stochastic volatility variations on the BGM theme are now beginning to attract some serious interest. For equities and FX products, jump processes have become more widely accepted, while local-volatility-function approaches, à la Dupire (1993), (1994), Derman, Kani and Zou (1996) and Rubinstein (1994) – DDKR in the following – after a few years of popularity are rapidly losing favor.

Distinguishing as carefully as I have just done among these possible causes of market risk can seem either somewhat abstract, or unnecessarily detailed. A simple example can help to clarify these different components to model risk, and to show the practical relevance of separating the different possible sources of model uncertainty. So let us focus on the risk associated with a single complex product, and let me define, first of all, *the trade time*, which is the date when the last reliable market information about the product was available; *the current time*, i.e., today; and the *evaluation time*, which is the time at the end of the holding period when model risk has to be estimated. Occasionally, the evaluation time could coincide with the current time, but in a Value-at-Risk context, we generally would like to know what the model risk will be at the end of the same holding period (ten days, one month, one year...) when general market risk is estimated. Only by doing so can the two distributions (i.e., the distributions of price changes originating from exposure to general market risk factors and from model risk) be suitably combined to provide a description of the overall market risk.

For the purpose of this example I shall assume that the complex instrument in question is a barrier option whose fair price depends on, among other factors, an out-of-the-money implied volatility with maturity of 3.35 years, and that the barrier option also displays sensitivity to risk reversal and straddle risk. On the trade date, the risk manager had access to the volatilities for the at-the-money strikes and the 25-delta calls and puts with expiries in three and four years. As a first step, he therefore constructed an interpolated/extrapolated smile surface using these six benchmark prices as reference points. He used a particular method for doing so, which had been proposed by the front office and tested by the model validation team, and which had proved to be reliable and robust. This procedure corresponds to step 2 in the account given above, and to the transition from the first to the second box in Figure 4.

With this "synthetic" plain-vanilla information, the risk manager then calibrated the chosen model (a jump-diffusion model), and estimated the opaque inputs (e.g., the risk-adjusted jump frequency and the volatility of the diffusive part) required for its inputs. This is step 3 in the description above, and is schematically shown in Figure 4 as the transition from the second to the third box.

With the chosen model, and its opaque inputs calibrated to produce correctly the prices of the synthetic plain-vanilla options, a price was then produced on the trade date for the barrier option. Much to the risk manager's relief, the price obtained by following this procedure exactly matched the then-observed market price. On the trade date itself, therefore, for an evaluation time identical to the current time (i.e., for a holding period of zero), and barring fortuitous cancellation of errors in the various steps, the risk manager could say that his model risk for that particular product was zero. *This conjunction of trade time, current time and evaluation time is the only combination that can give zero model risk* (i.e., an infinitely sharp delta distribution of differences between the mark-to-model and the market values).

A couple of months have now elapsed and no other market prices for the same type of barrier option have been observed. The risk manager can observe today the prices of the same-maturity benchmark plain-vanilla options as he could two months ago and so repeats the procedure of interpolation, extrapolation, calibration, and use of the model. He cannot compare the price he obtains by doing so with a current market price for the complex product, and he must therefore entertain the possibility that the best market practice to carry out the inter-extrapolation (step 2) might have changed; that the market's risk aversion to jumps might have changed and that, as a consequence, the market's implied jump frequency might today be different (step 3); and that the market consensus about the best model to use (step 4) might have changed (perhaps stochastic volatility models are now the flavor of the month). All these sources of uncertainty produce a distribution of possible prices for the barrier option; the distribution of the differences between these possible prices and today's mark-to-model value, obtained using the same procedure that proved successful two months ago, constitutes model risk today (i.e., for a holding period of zero).

The risk manager, however, will in general also want to know what the model risk will be at the end of a holding period of, say, one month's time. He obviously does not know what world state will prevail at the end of the chosen holding period, but his database of historical changes in risk factors allows him to construct a large number of possible market conditions (this is step 1 above). In each of these world states he can apply the same procedure he would apply today to obtain a conditional mark-to-model value. He must also estimate, in the same world states, how the market agreement about the extrapolation/interpolation procedure, and about the way to obtain the opaque inputs and about the model itself, might have changed (steps 2, 3 and 4 again). All these changes will produce a series of conditional distributions (one for each world state) of differences between his mark-to-model value obtained using today's chosen procedure and the mark-to-model obtained if any of the possible changes have actually taken place. These will then have to be combined with the distribution of profit and losses over the same holding period attributable to general market risk, to obtain an overall distribution of market risk.

This example clearly indicates that the most difficult task the risk manager faces is the estimation of how the fickle market might change its way of choosing the pricing measure. Given the variety of factors that can give rise to this instability, the quantitative estimation of the possible changes in mark-to-model seems to be a hopelessly complex task. Without underplaying the complexity of the task, I intend to show in the following that it can be made considerably simpler by tackling the various steps in turn. I will also try to provide concrete suggestions on how to carry out the different estimations in practice. Since, as explained above, step 1 does not produce model risk but simply defines the conditional state of the world, my analysis will begin with step 2.

Step 2 – from transparent prices/rates to opaque plain-vanilla inputs

It is difficult to give general prescriptions on how to account for changes in the mark-to-model values due to changes in the interpolation/extrapolation process because of the degree of variability in the final output that different procedures afford depending on the specific instruments: the transformation from the cash/deposit rates, futures prices, and equilibrium swap rates to a LIBOR discount curve offers relatively little scope for creative variations on a well-rehearsed theme.[8] Already much more variability can be observed in the way a continuous par-coupon curve is distilled out of the prices of traded bonds. Greater variations are then encountered in moving to the construction of an equity or FX implied volatility surface for a continuum of strikes and maturities. An even greater degree of variability is found in the distillation of the (smiley) caplet prices from the brokers' quotes of cap implied volatilities at a few maturities and strikes.

To give concrete examples of how these synthetic plain-vanilla prices can be used in further stages of the mark-to-model procedure, one can mention the DDKR approach, which requires knowledge of prices of plain-vanilla calls and puts for as many strikes and maturities as nodes in their computational tree (typically thousands); the BGM methodology, which requires the volatilities of caplets or European swaptions expiring on the dates of all the price-sensitive events; virtually all interest-rate models assume that the user knows the prices of a continuum of discount bonds; credit derivatives extend the same requirement to defaultable bonds; pricing inflation-linked derivatives similarly assumes that the prices of a continuum of pure discount inflation-linked bonds should be available; etc.

One might be tempted to speculate that the room for reasonable variation in the production of the opaque plain-vanilla prices is, in most cases, rather limited, and that, therefore, variations in this construction methodology should have a comparatively modest pricing impact. This line of thought, however, neglects the fact that often the *raison d'être* of relative-value trades is exactly the attempt to exploit second-order differences between similar, relatively plain-vanilla instruments. Trades involving the wings of the smile surface, butterfly positions along the yield curve, many bond basis trades, etc. all fall into this category. Furthermore, in order to benefit in a meaningful way from the perceived mispricings, the offsetting positions tend to be very large. Therefore future variations in the transformation procedure from the benchmark prices or rates to the not-directly-observable quantities can produce significant model risk.

In the context of model risk, the risk manager's first task is therefore to explore the possible effect of changes in extrapolation/interpolation procedures. The common crucial *caveat* in exploring the possible ways in which future plain-vanilla market prices might stand in relation to each other is to ensure that no *model-independent* arbitrage should be allowed. So, negative forward rates should never occur, no matter how the procedure to build the discount curve has been modified; more out-of-the-money options should never be worth more than more in-the-money

---

[8] Even in the rather "tame" area of discount curve building, the attempt to produce smooth forward rates by using, for instance, cubic splines can give rise to surprisingly different discount curves.

ones;[9] credit-risky instruments should always yield more than the corresponding risk-free products (apart, possibly, from liquidity considerations); etc.

If one were to vary the possible future prices in an arbitrary way, it would not be difficult to violate these conditions. In this respect, by far the most demanding constraint lies in the avoidance of inter-option arbitrage when a possible future implied volatility smile surface is created. Note carefully that, unlike the trader, the risk manager need not, and *should not*, confine himself to those future volatilities that are implied by today's prices (see Schonbucher, 1999, on the future implied volatility surfaces compatible with a stochastic volatility process for the underlying). To what extent spot option prices constrain in a model-independent fashion future possible volatilities is a delicate and complex topic, discussed in detail in Jaeckel and Rebonato (2000). The crucial point in the context of model risk is that the risk manager must "simply" ensure that *some* process exists such that, given today's implied volatility curves, a particular future smile surface can indeed be attained. This important point is discussed in detail later on in the context of weak static replication.

This requirement is just as important in the case of FX and equities as it is in the case of interest rate products. The procedure by means of which one can ensure that this condition is satisfied is, however, substantially different in the case of interest rate products, on the one hand, and of FX and equity derivatives on the other. In both cases, the name of the game is to produce future admissible implied volatility surfaces (more specifically, term structures of volatilities for caplets, swaption matrices for European swaptions, and smile surfaces for equities and FX). The procedure is sufficiently different, however, to warrant separate treatment.

Starting with the case of interest-rate products, a BGM implementation provides the most flexible framework within which the most general deterministic volatility structures can be explored. (A restricted but, in the interest-rate context, important type of smile can also be easily accounted for in the BGM framework using displaced diffusions, see, for example, Marris, 1999.) Once the instantaneous volatility of each forward rate has been specified, the future (time-τ) implied volatility of a forward rate of generic maturity T can be easily obtained by integration:

$$\sigma_{Black}(\tau,\,T)^2 \, T = \int_{\tau}^{T+\tau} \sigma_{inst}(u,T)^2 \, du \tag{1}$$

where $\sigma_{Black}(\tau,T)$ is the implied volatility at time τ of the forward rate expiring T years thereafter, and $\sigma_{inst}(u,T)$ its instantaneous volatility at time u. If the instantaneous volatility function is then described by a simple but flexible functional form, the integration in (1) can be carried out analytically. Elsewhere (Rebonato, 1999 and Rebonato, 2001) I have recommended the simple function

$$\sigma_T(t) = k_T [a + b \, (T - t)] \exp [- c(T - t)] + d \tag{2}$$
$$\sigma_T(\tau) = k_T [a + b\tau] \exp [- c\tau] + d, \qquad\qquad \tau = T - t$$

that can produce, for instance, the shapes shown in Figure 5. The factor k_T is

---

[9] Also, the second derivative of a call with respect to the strike should always be positive and, for zero dividend and interest rates, a longer-maturity option should always be worth more than a shorter-maturity one. All these conditions together make an implied volatility surface "admissible" (see Jaeckel and Rebonato, 2000).

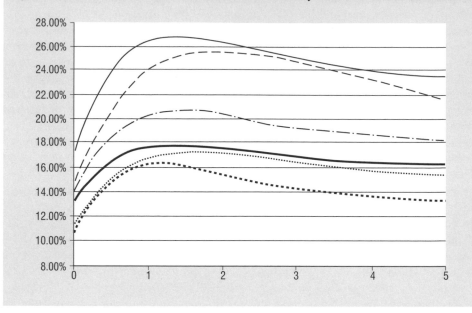

Figure 5: The stochastic evolution of the instantaneous volatility of forward rate in BGM framework

The central thick line without markers indicates the estimate of the market's belief *today* about how the volatility of a given forward rate will evolve over time as imputed from the prices of liquid plain-vanilla options (caplets and European swaptions). This estimate is obtained by taking into account (cross-sectionally) today's market prices for caplets and European swaptions. The instantaneous volatility function thus obtained is then parameterized in terms of a suitable $f(t, T, \{a^i\})$, where $\{a_i\}$ is a set of parameters. The lines with markers are obtained by allowing for a stochastic behavior for the $\{a_i\}$. The parameters of the processes for the $\{a_i\}$ (simple Ornstein-Uhlenbeck mean-reverting diffusions) are estimated from the time-series analysis of the fitted parameters. By constructing the future (stochastic) term structure of volatilities from the processes for the instantaneous volatilities obtained in this manner, one can rest assured that the future implied volatility surfaces will always be admissible (i.e., that model-independent arbitrage will not be possible).

introduced to ensure correct pricing of all the caplets.

In order to obtain the instantaneous volatility curves identified by markers in the same figure, a stochastic behavior has then been postulated for the coefficients $\{a, b, c, d\}$ – more precisely, a simple Ornstein-Uhlenbeck process either for the coefficient itself or for its logarithm, as appropriate, in order to preserve a positive instantaneous volatility curve. For the first coefficient, for instance, which is of indeterminate sign, the postulated process is of the form:

$$da = k_a [\text{Rev}_a - a] \, dt + \sigma_a \, dz \qquad (3)$$

with k_a the reversion speed of a, Rev_a its reversion level, and σ_a its absolute volatility. Realistic estimates of these quantities can be obtained by fitting each day the instantaneous volatility parameters to the existing caplet market prices, and then analyzing the time series of the changes in the coefficient thus obtained.

By following this procedure the risk manager can obtain plausible future instantaneous volatility curves, and, using (1) and (2), future admissible term structure of volatilities. Thus he can ensure that the resulting volatility curves can explore a sufficiently wide range of possible shapes, while at the same time preserving their desired qualitative behavior. More precisely, thanks to the specific choice of the Ornstein-Uhlenbeck process, which admits closed-form explicit solution, the joint realizations of the four coefficients at a chosen future point in time (the required holding period) can then be obtained with just four random (possibly correlated) draws and a single "long jump," without the need for a stepped Monte Carlo simulation. Once the future realization of the instantaneous volatility curve has been obtained, the integration in (1) directly produces a future caplet term structure of volatilities which is guaranteed to be admissible. Simple, fast and accurate semi-analytic techniques (Rebonato and Jaeckel, 2000) also allow the creation of a whole swaption matrix from a given forward-rate instantaneous volatility curve.

Note that the instantaneous volatility functions have simply been used as a device to obtain future admissible prices of plain-vanilla options (the caplets) in this procedure. Despite the fact that instantaneous volatility functions also play the role of the unobservable inputs to the model, the task which has been tackled in this first step is just the transformation from a handful of visible benchmark prices to a large number of opaque plain-vanilla implied volatilities.

In the case of equities and FX the problem is somewhat different, since to the whole smile surface of each equity price or foreign exchange rate there corresponds a single underlying (this should be contrasted with the case of interest rates, where each forward rate is a correlated but independent variable). A possible procedure in order to ensure a realistic variety of possible smile surfaces is to start from a parameterized description of today's risk-adjusted price densities for different maturities. Mirfendereski and Rebonato (2000) have shown how this can be efficiently accomplished by modeling the density function directly using the four-parameter Generalized Beta 2 (GB2) distribution. The nice features of this choice are the ability to recover accurately a wide variety of skew and smile shapes, the availability of simple closed-form solutions for calls, puts and their deltas and gammas, and the fact that the familiar Black log-normal (no smile) density can be obtained as a special case of the GB2 family.

With this approach, given a series of GB2 coefficients $\{\alpha_i\}$ chosen so as to describe in an optimal way today's price densities at a series of maturities T_i, the risk managers can apply the same approach described in the case of interest rates, and postulate a suitable stochastic correlated behavior for the $4 \times i$ coefficients. The stochastic parameters for the evolution of these coefficients can again be obtained from an analysis of the time series of the cross-sectionally fitted coefficients.

There is, however, one important difference: in the case of interest rates, once the coefficients have been evolved to a future point in time, the integration (1) automatically ensures that the future caplet prices are admissible. In particular, if it so happens that $\sigma_{Black}(\tau, T_2)^2 T_2 < \sigma_{Black}(\tau, T_1)^2 T_1$ for $T_2 > T_1$, no model-independent arbitrage condition has been violated (this "inverted" relationship between the variance of forward rates of different maturities is actually often observed in the market, and simply describes a lack of time homogeneity in the evolution of the term structure of volatilities). In the case of equities and FX, however, different forward rates are all linked to the same underlying. Therefore "market uncertainty" should always increase with time, i.e., the total variance of distributions at different maturities should always be an increasing function of the maturity itself. If the coefficients of the GB2 distributions obtained today for different option maturities were allowed to change stochastically over different time horizons in an arbitrary way, however, there would be no guarantee that the variance condition would in general be satisfied. Fortunately, the availability of closed-form expressions for the second moment of the distribution is of help in this respect, by allowing the rejection of the financially impossible densities.

The two solutions to the problem of the creation of admissible future implied volatility surfaces proposed above do not exhaust the problem of how to estimate the model risk connected with the extrapolation/interpolation exercise mentioned. However, they should provide some valuable help in two of the most challenging applications. More generally, extending the same type of reasoning, a prescription of sufficiently wide applicability to be of use in a variety of situations can be extracted from the two examples above:

- choose a financially satisfactory functional description of the prices of the plain-vanilla instruments (prices of zero-coupon bonds, swap spreads, etc.) to be extrapolated or interpolated. Typically this will mean choosing a suitably flexible functional form expressed in terms of a number of parameters. Approaches where at least some of the parameters can be given a transparent financial meaning (as is the case for the instantaneous volatility parameters in (2)) are to be preferred to pure fitting approaches (e.g., cubic splines);
- assume a simple and analytically tractable stochastic behavior for the parameters so as to produce future possible values for the continuum of plain-vanilla instruments. A diffusion with mean-reverting drift is often useful to provide sufficient flexibility, and to ensure that the parameters themselves do not stray too much from plausible values;
- ensure that no model-independent arbitrage is possible (volatility surfaces are admissible, forward rates are never negative), etc.

Having highlighted the general ideas, problems, and possible solutions connected with the production of admissible future prices for synthetic plain-vanilla instruments, we are now in a position to tackle the task of transforming these quantities into the opaque inputs a model typically requires. This topic is addressed below.

Step 3 – from plain-vanilla prices to opaque model inputs

We can assume at this point that we are in a position where the future conditional plain-vanilla prices of all maturities (and, in the case of options, of all strikes) are available. This information can be used in two distinct ways. First, it can be used to construct the opaque model inputs to the chosen models. Alternatively, I show below how the model stage can sometimes be bypassed and the plain-vanilla information used directly for pricing purposes.

If the traditional, and more general, route of determining the "opaque" inputs that specify the models is chosen, step 2 above is almost always necessary, because most models require the notional availability of a very large number (if not a continuum) of plain-vanilla prices in order to determine their inputs. Given these synthetic

Case study: model risk associated with CMS caps – static replication

A CMS (constant maturity swap) cap of tenor α is a contract that resets at time T and pays at time $T+\alpha$ the positive difference between the then prevailing X-year LIBOR swap rate, SR_T, and a chosen strike, K:

$$\text{Payoff (CMScap)} = \text{Max}\,[SR_T - K, 0]\,\alpha \qquad (4)$$

This contract shares many similarities with a plain-vanilla $T \times X$ European swaption,[10] whose payoff at time T is given by

$$\text{Payoff (EuroSwaption)} = \text{Max}\,[SR_T - K, 0]\,B(T,T+X) \quad (5)$$

The difference between (4) and (5) is clearly the term $B(T,T+X)$, which is the value at expiry (time T) of the annuity paying with frequency $1/\alpha$ for X years thereafter:

$$B(T,T+X) = \Sigma_{i\,=\,1,\frac{X}{\alpha}}\, Z(T,T + i\alpha)\,\alpha$$

(In the expression above $Z(t,T)$ is the price at time t of a discount bond maturing at time T. Even more similar to a CMS cap is a cash-settled European swaption, which is contractually designed to pay at time T)

$$\begin{aligned}\text{Payoff(EuroSwaption} - \text{CashSettled)} = \\ \text{Max}\,[\,SR_T - K, 0]\,A(T,T+X)\end{aligned} \qquad (6)$$

with

$$A\,(T,T+X) = \Sigma_{i\,=1,X/\alpha}\,\frac{1}{[1 + SR\,\alpha]^{i}} \qquad (7)$$

The important difference between (6) and (5) is that the future annuity B in (5) depends on the whole yield curve at time T. The "cash-settled annuity" A in expressions (6) and (7), on the other hand, depends purely on the appropriate swap rate SR_T at reset.

The payoff of the CMS cap is almost exactly linear[11] in the reset swap rate. The payoff from the cash-settled European swaption, on the other hand, displays significant convexity, since the swap rate enters not only as an argument of the Max [ ] operator but also, and non-linearly, in the term A. To the extent that the payoffs of both a cash-settled European swaption and the corresponding CMS caplet purely depend on the same swap rate, a static super- or sub-replicating portfolio of swaptions can be created (see Amblard and Lebuchoux, 2000), capable of reproducing the payoff of the caplet with arbitrary precision. See Figures 6 and 7.

The important point in the context of model risk is that (within the limit of the approximation in footnote 11) the price of the exotic product today can be expressed asymptotically exactly as a linear combination of prices of European cash-settled swaptions with increasing strikes. The construction with three strikes is shown in Figure 6. The market prices at the chosen strikes fully incorporate the impact of smiles on the CMS caplet. This price information is, however, available only if one assumes to know the implied volatility of European swaptions of arbitrary strikes. This is where step 2 (i.e., the transformation from a handful of truly transparent market benchmark prices/rates to a continuum of vanilla prices) enters the modeling process and introduces model risk: in order to obtain the close replication shown in Figure 6, the prices of payer swaptions 150 and 440 basis points out of the money are required; the corresponding implied volatilities are in practice available only by extrapolation of actually traded quantities.

If the model risk of a product to be replicated by a static portfolio replication is to be evaluated at a future point in time, the risk manager will first have to produce the future benchmark implied volatilities by applying the desired changes to their current values. At this point, however, the risk manager cannot make the assumption that the same extrapolation procedure valid today will apply in the future. By using one of the procedures suggested in step 2, he can nonetheless produce a reasonable distribution of future *contingent* plain-vanilla prices, and proceed to estimate the model risk accordingly.

---

[10] The notation $n \times m$ European swaption indicates an option expiring in n years' time to enter (pay or receive, as appropriate) an m-year swap

[11] The payoff is not exactly a linear function of the swap rate, because it occurs at time $T + \alpha$, and therefore depends on the forward rate resetting at time T and paying at time $T + \alpha$. While the correct treatment of this feature requires careful handling, the effect can be made quite small, and I shall neglect it in the discussion. Strictly speaking, the approach presented in the text would be exact for a CMS cap reset in arrears.

Figure 6: CMS cap and static hedges

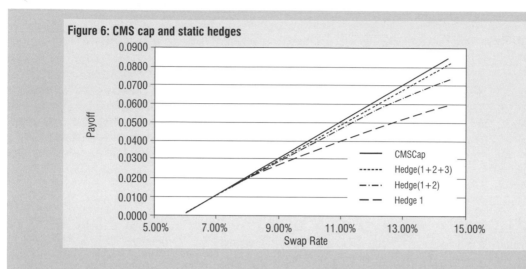

The payoff of a CMS caplet as a function of the swap rate at reset for a strike K of 6%. The caveat about the timing of the CMS caplet payment in footnote 11 applies. Starting from the bottom, the three concave lines represent the static replication of the caplet payoff based on a single cash-settled Eurpean swaption struck at 6% (Hedge1), two cash-settled swaptions, struck at 6% and 7.5% (Hedge(1+2)), and three cash-settled swaptions, struck at 6%, 7.5% and 10.4%. The portfolio so constructed is clearly sub-replicating, and therefore constitutes a (tight) lower bound for the price of the CMS caplet. By construction, this price includes all smile effects *today*. As for the CMS rate, it can be obtained by call/put parity after repeating the same calculation for a CMS floorlet. See Amblard and Lebuchoux (2000) for details.

Figure 7: Slippage of the various hedges

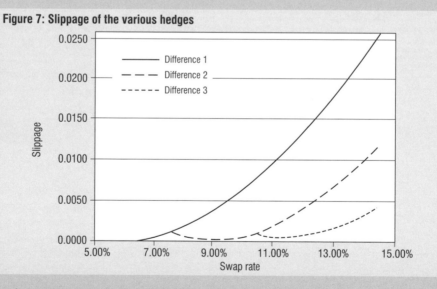

The differences between the true payoff of a CMS caplet (the same reservations about its payoff time expressed in footnote 11 and in the caption of Figure 6) and the static replication made up of the portfolio of cash-settled European swaptions described in the text and in the caption of Figure 6. The curve labeled Difference1 shows the difference between the payoff of the CMS caplet and Hedge1; Difference2 refers to the difference CMS Caplet – (Hedge1 + Hedge2); Difference3 to the difference CMS Caplet – (Hedge1 + Hedge2 + Hedge3). Despite the fact that, for a finite number of hedging cash-settled European swaptions the difference is unbounded as the swap rate goes to infinity, the associated prices of the swaptions themselves (which are progressively more and more out of the money) become smaller and smaller. The series of the prices converge very quickly.

prices, for a given model there is a well-defined procedure to effect this transformation. The risk manager, however, should not assume that the same methodology will be used in the future, and should explore the pricing impact of reasonable variations. As a concrete example, once the synthetic prices of FX or equity plain-vanilla options are available, one can derive the local volatility function, $\sigma(S_t, t)$ (the opaque model input), to be used in the DDKR approach. Despite the fact that, conceptually, there is a unique solution to the problem, the numerical methods presented by Derman, Kani and Zou (1996), Rebonato (1999) or Brigo and Mercurio (2000) all produce substantially different numerical outputs. Once again, in this respect the risk manager's views, however enlightened, about the "best" possible way to perform this transformation are not particularly relevant: what really matters is how the market will decide in the future that this operation should be carried out.

The synthetic prices of plain-vanilla products, however, need not be used as an intermediate step toward the estimation of the unobservable model inputs. Sometimes, in fact, they can be used directly as inputs to a model. This is obviously the case if the product to be valued is, for instance, a simple out-of-the-money call or put. But the synthetic plain-vanilla prices can also be used directly in an important and wide class of products that are far from being plain-vanilla. Before dealing with the transformation from the central to the right-most box at the top of Figure 4, I will deal with this situation by analyzing an interesting case study.

The example presented in the case study is important not just because of its intrinsic interest but because static replication techniques can have a rather wide range of applicability. Whenever this method can be profitably used it is particularly suited to the needs of a risk manager because it reduces the exploration of model scenarios to simple manipulations of plain-vanilla options, which, in turn, can be obtained via step 2 above. This topic is treated in more detail later.

In general, however, the risk manager will not be able to use directly a semi-continuum of plain-vanilla prices for pricing purposes, and he will have to obtain some intermediate opaque parameters or input functions to feed into a model. One such example is the local volatility surface to be used in the DDKR context, which can be obtained from the plain-vanilla prices using the well-known formula

$$\sigma^2_{K,T} = \frac{\dfrac{\partial C_{K,T}(0,S)}{\partial T} + K(r-d)\dfrac{\partial C_{K,T}(0,S)}{\partial K} + dC_{K,T}(0,S)}{\dfrac{\partial^2 C_{K,T}(0,S)}{\partial K^2} K^2} \tag{8}$$

Here, the user must perform accurate numerical differentiations of call prices (denoted by C) with respect to the strike, K, at maturity (T) in order to obtain the local volatility function; whatever numerical scheme is used, a very large number of "synthetic" plain-vanilla prices will be needed. Only after (8) has been evaluated at a very large number of points can the local volatility be fed into the pricing engine, and the actual evaluation of the desired non-plain-vanilla product begin.

Another area where the interpolated/extrapolated plain-vanilla prices are used to obtain the inputs for a complex model is the BGM approach for interest rates. I have shown elsewhere (Rebonato, 1999 and 2000) how either the caplet or the swaption prices can be exactly recovered using a BGM approach in an infinity of ways. Some of the possible calibrations of the instantaneous volatility functions that generate these prices can be financially more appealing than others, but, as emphasized above, it is the risk manager's task to explore the pricing impact of as wide a range of plausible choices as possible.

To give a few concrete examples, the instantaneous volatility functions, $\sigma_{inst}(t, T)$, could be assumed to be purely a function of time, $\sigma_{inst}(t)$; or to be a function of the individual forward rate, $\sigma_{inst}(T)$; one could impose that they should give rise to a time-homogeneous evolution of the term structure of volatilities, $\sigma_{inst}(T - t)$; or that they should be decomposable into the product (or the sum) of a time-homogenous component and a purely time-dependent or forward-rate-specific function: $\sigma_{inst}(t, T) = f(T) g(T - t)$ or $\sigma_{inst}(t, T) = h(t) g(T-t)$; they could be chosen so that the European swaptions underlying a given Bermudan swaption are all exactly priced (this task can also be accomplished in an infinity of ways, to each of which there corresponds a different forward-rate covariance matrix).

For each of these possible choices for the instantaneous volatility function there correspond different financial justifications, advantages and drawbacks – which are discussed at great length in Rebonato (2000) – and, needless to say, identical plain-vanilla prices, but different prices for exotic products. These topics have been treated at length elsewhere in the references provided, and will not be repeated here. In the context of model risk I will simply stress again that, unlike the trader, the risk manager must attempt to guess what the market's preferred approach will be in the future, not necessarily what the "truest" calibration should be. For the two (i.e., the best and the market-chosen) to be the same requires a very strong leap of faith, namely that the evolution toward more and more efficient and perfect markets is not only unstoppable but also progresses without local twists and turns. This assumption is highly questionable: it is my opinion that some of the derivatives markets have, in some respects, not fully recovered from the shock of the Russian crisis. On the one hand, the market events of summer 1998 have focussed the traders' attention on important ingredients (such as stochastic volatility) that had been neglected in some of the modeling approaches that were popular at the time. On the other hand, the faith in the constant and ever-ready availability of the market liquidity necessary to extract the model-implied fair value of some complex trades has been seriously shaken. This has brought about a mild but noticeable retrenchment from more sophisticated to simpler (and often less financially plausible) models. Continuous progress toward better and more sophisticated models should therefore not be taken for granted.

Step 4 – from opaque model inputs to prices of complex products

The last step in the process of obtaining a distribution of possible mark-to-model prices is feeding the opaque model inputs into the relevant models. This should be subjected to the same "stresses" as the inputs, and the same distinctions between "best" and "market-chosen" approaches applied.

The obvious – and very expensive – solution to this "model sampling" is to use a variety of modeling approaches. In some areas the task can be simplified by using a modeling framework general enough to encompass several sub-models as special cases. Once again, the BGM approach is useful and powerful in this respect, since there are suitable choices of the instantaneous volatility functions that can reproduce all the arbitrage-free models of the yield curve with deterministic volatilities (such as the Hull and White (1990), the BDT (1990), the Black Karasinski (1991), etc.). Therefore, the exploration of a relatively wide class of modeling approaches can be undertaken within the same framework. Similarly, Duffie, Pan and Singleton's (1999) affine jump-diffusion model incorporates as special cases a variety of models, such as pure diffusions, jump/diffusions, diffusive stochastic volatility models, and stochastic volatility models with discontinuous paths in the instantaneous variance.

Using these very general models in a flexible way has obvious advantages. However, I want to propose another approach that has sufficiently wide applicability, and that can circumvent in many important cases the need to use many different models (and to produce the accompanying transformation from the plain-vanilla prices to their opaque inputs). The approach is based on the idea of static replication, of which a particularly simple example was presented above for CMS caps. In that case the strategy was "strongly static," in that, once put in place, the replicating portfolio could be left unchanged out to *its own* expiry. So a moment's thought shows that this approach can be used only for European options, and that the payoff of the replicating portfolio must depend exclusively on the state variables that determine the payoff of the option to replicate. Quite clearly this severely restricts the domain of applicability.

Weak static replication, on the other hand, prescribes a portfolio of plain-vanilla options that will either have to be left unchanged until expiry, *or liquidated at a future point in time prior to their maturity*. The latter implies that their value will therefore depend on the implied volatilities that prevail at that time. Any possible realization of the latter will give rise to a different payoff upon liquidation.

Since the idea of (weak or strong) static replication is to match over a given region the boundary conditions of the complex instrument, different assumptions about the future implied volatility surface will give rise to different amounts of plain-vanilla instruments needed to match the payoff at the boundary. This, in turn, gives rise to a different price for the replicating portfolio of plain-vanilla options and hence to the price for the complex instrument.

The idea of static replication for pricing purposes is not new (see, for example, Derman, Kani, Ergener and Bardhan, 1995, Rebonato, 1999), and it has mainly been presented as a computational technique to arrive at results that could be derived in alternative (and more cumbersome) ways. In the context of the management of model risk, however, its potential is much wider and, I believe, it has been poorly exploited. The fundamental idea can be summarized as follows: if the quality and desirability of a model are assessed on the basis of its ability to reproduce desirable future prices for plain-vanilla options of different strikes (i.e., a desirable future smile surface), why not concentrate directly on these plain-vanilla prices, rather than proceeding via the intermediate model-building stage? This can be of use whenever the price of a non-plain-vanilla option can be expressed as a linear combination of calls and puts of different strikes and maturities.

It is well known how this can be done for known-boundary problems such as single or double continuous knock-out barriers, up-and-out options with rebates, and so forth. Rebonato (1999) shows how, in a risk management context, the future values of these products can be valued in the presence of arbitrary user-assigned smiles. But more exciting recent developments have shown that this approach can also be used for a much wider class of problems. American options – a free-boundary problem where the exercise strategy is not known *a priori* – are one such case (Jaeckel and Rebonato, 2000). Andersen and Andreasen (2000) and Andersen, Andreasen and Eliezer (2000) extend the approach to discretely monitored barriers, and combine their results to obtain a general solution for arbitrary knock-out regions (single, double, curved, partial, and discretely monitored barriers). Work is in progress to apply the same approach to Bermudan swaptions.

Appealing as it is, the approach requires careful analysis because it assumes that the user can freely assign a *future* implied volatility surface. Since this is an unconventional procedure, it is important to explore carefully to what extent, and in what contexts, this is a legitimate exercise.[12] I intend to show that the approach can have useful but different applications for risk managers and traders; I shall therefore refer collectively to "users" in the first part of the discussion, before the domain of applicability of the technique has been made clear.

To begin with I shall always assume that the possible future implied volatility surface being considered is admissible (see footnote 9). Note that, because of call/put parity, an admissible smile surface automatically ensures that the forward contract is correctly priced, and therefore the user specifying an admissible future implied volatility surface does not have to take into account the forward condition separately.

Let us now consider a two-period trading horizon and the smile surface today; in other terms, today's prices of calls and puts of all strikes maturing at times t_1 and t_2 are assumed to be available. From the call prices, $\{C\}$, and using (1), one can obtain the unconditional (risk-neutral)[13] probability densities $p(S_{t(0)} \rightarrow S_{t(i)})$, $i = 1,2$:

$$\frac{\partial^2 C(S = S_{t(0)}, K, T)}{\partial K^2} = p(S_{t(0)} \rightarrow S_{t(i)} = K) \qquad (9)$$

In the expression above, $p(S_{t(0)} \rightarrow S_{t(i)} = K)$ indicates the probability for the stock price to move from the value $S_{t(0)}$ today to value K at time $t(i)$. To the extent that prices of calls of all strikes and maturities are given by the market, today's unconditional probability density can therefore be assumed to be market-given: the user has no freedom to modify it, or to have "views" about it.

For future discussion, it is essential to make a distinction at this point between the "true" price functional, and the Black and Scholes pricing formula. The former depends on today's value of the stock price, the residual time to maturity, the strike of the option, an unknown set of parameters describing the "true" dynamics (diffusion coefficients, jump amplitudes, etc.) and, possibly, on the past history. The parameters describing the process of the underlying (volatility, jump frequency, jump amplitude, etc.) can, in turn, themselves be stochastic. However, they are all, obviously, strike-independent. The unknown "true" parameters and the full history at time t will be symbolically denoted by $\{\alpha_t\}$ and $\{F_t\}$ respectively.[14] The Black and Scholes formula, on the other hand, depends on today's value of the stock price, the residual time to maturity, the strike of the option, and a single strike-dependent parameter (the implied volatility). If, with obvious notation, the true functional is denoted by $C(S_t, T-t, K, \{\alpha_t\}, \{F_t\})$ and the Black and Scholes formula by $BS(S, T-t, K, \sigma_{impl}(t, T, K))$, then we would like to be able to write

$$C(S, T-t, K, \{\alpha_t\}, \{F_t\}) = BS(S, T-t, K, \sigma_{impl}(K)). \qquad (10)$$

As of today this expression is certainly well defined, since, from the knowledge of the

---

[12] The material from here to the end of this section has been adapted from the introductory section of Jaeckel and Rebonato (2000).

[13] All the probability density referred to in this section is risk-neutral. To lighten the notation, and for an easier flow of expression, the qualifier "risk-neutral" is often omitted.

[14] More technically, $\{F_t\}$ is the filtration generated by the evolution of the stock price and of whatever stochastic parameters describe its process.

evolution of the stock process and of its stochastic parameters (if any), we know what values to input in the true pricing functional. As a consequence, as of today, even if the user does not know the true functional C, she can still write

$$\frac{\partial^2 C(S_0, K, T, \{\alpha_0\}, \{F_0\})}{\partial K^2} =$$

$$\frac{\partial}{\partial K}\left[- N(h_2) + \frac{\partial BS}{\partial \sigma_{\text{impl}}} \frac{\partial \sigma_{\text{impl}}}{\partial K}\right] = \tag{11}$$

$$p(S_0 \rightarrow S_t = K)$$

where use has been made of the fact that $\frac{\partial BS}{\partial K} = -N(h_2)$, and h_2 is given by

$$h_2 = \frac{ln\ (S/K) + r\ t -\frac{1}{2}\ \sigma^2\ t}{\sigma\sqrt{t}}$$

It is important to stress again the fundamental difference between (11) and (9): if the trader assumes one knows how the function $\sigma_{\text{impl}}(0, T, K)$ changes with strike – i.e., if the trader assumes to have views about the "floating," "sticky" or otherwise nature of the smile, as expressed by the term $\partial\sigma_{\text{impl}}/\partial K$ – then the risk-neutral unconditional probability densities for all maturities can be obtained analytically *even if the true functional C is not known.*

What one would like to be able to do is to repeat the same reasoning forward in time, and obtain, by so doing, expressions for the *conditional* probability densities. In other words, it would be tempting to reason as follows: using Kolmogorov's equation, one might like to be able to write that these unconditional probability densities at times 1 and 2 are linked by

$$p(S_{t(0)} \rightarrow S^*_{t(2)}) = \int p(S_{t(0)} \rightarrow S'_{t(1)})\ p(S'_{t(1)} \rightarrow S^*_{t(2)} \mid S_{t(1)} = S')\ dS'_{t(1)} \tag{12}$$

where the quantity $p(S'_{t(1)} \rightarrow S^*_{t(2)} \mid S_{t(1)} = S')$ now denotes the *conditional* probability of the stock price reaching S^* at time $t(2)$, given that it had value S' at time $t(1)$. Notice, however, that the integral (12) can be used to obtain information about future *conditional* price densities if and only if a future state of the world is fully determined by the realization of the stock price. In general, however, this will not be the case. If, for instance, the "true" process for the stock price were driven by a stochastic volatility, (12) would require a double integration over future price and volatility values:

$$p(S_{t(0)} \rightarrow S^*_{t(2)}, \sigma_{t(0)} \rightarrow \sigma^*_{t(2)}) =$$

$$\int p(S_{t(0)} \rightarrow S'_{t(1)}, \sigma_{t(0)} \rightarrow \sigma'_{t(1)})p(S_{t(1)} \rightarrow S^*_{t(2)}, \sigma_{t(1)} \rightarrow \sigma^*_{t(2)} \mid S_{t(1)} = S', \sigma_{t(1)} = \sigma')S'_{t(1)}\ d\sigma'_{t(1)} \tag{12'}$$

where $p(\mathbf{S}_{t(0)} \rightarrow S^*_{t(2)}), \sigma_{t(0)} \rightarrow \sigma^*_{t(2)})$ is now the unconditional joint probability density that the stock price should have value S^* at time t_2 and the volatility should assume value σ^*, also at time t_2, given that they have values $S_{t(0)}$ and $\sigma_{t(0)}$ today, and $p(S_{t(1)} \rightarrow S^*_{t(2)}, \sigma_{t(1)} \rightarrow \sigma^*_{t(2)} \mid S_{t(1)} = S', \sigma_{t(1)} = \sigma')$ is the conditional probability of reaching state S^* and σ^* at time t_2, given that the stock price and the volatility had values S' and σ' at time t_1.

Since expressions such as (12′) quickly become more cumbersome if one wants to include explicitly all the stochastic variables that specify a future state, it is more convenient to speak simply of conditional and unconditional probability densities of reaching *states*. Also, if, instead of a continuum of states, one assumes that there exists only a discrete set of possible future states, one can restate more concisely (12′) in matrix form. The equivalent, discrete-price expression in terms of transition matrices is given by

$$\Pi \boldsymbol{p}^1 = \boldsymbol{p}^2$$

where

$$
\boldsymbol{p}^1 = \begin{pmatrix} p_1^1 \\ p_1^1 \\ \vdots \\ p_n^1 \end{pmatrix}, \quad
\boldsymbol{p}^2 = \begin{pmatrix} p_1^2 \\ p_2^2 \\ \vdots \\ p_n^2 \end{pmatrix} \text{ and } \Pi =
\begin{pmatrix}
\pi_{11} & \pi_{12} & & \pi_{1n} \\
\pi_{21} & \ddots & & \vdots \\
& & \ddots & \\
\pi_{n1} & \cdots & & \pi_{nn}
\end{pmatrix}
\tag{13}
$$

In (13) p_n^m means the probabilty of being in state m at time t_n, and π_{jk} is the conditional probability of going from state k at time t_1, to state j at time t_2. These conditional probabilities are not all independent. Since, from a given state, the probability of reaching some other state is unity, one must impose a probability normalization condition from each parent state. This provides n equations ($\Sigma_k \pi_{jk} = 1$). It is therefore easy to see that (13) together with the normalization condition provides $2n$ constraints, which do not uniquely specify the n^2 elements of the matrix Π. As a consequence, a number of transition matrices satisfy (13) – which is another way of saying that a variety of processes can account for today's option prices (as embodied by the vectors $\boldsymbol{p}^1$ and $\boldsymbol{p}^2$). Similarly, an infinity of conditional probability densities satisfy the Kolmogorov equation (12′), with the link between the probability density and the prices explicitly given by

$$
p(S'_{t(1)} \rightarrow S^*_{t(2)} \mid S_{t(1)} = S') = \frac{\partial^2 C\,(S = S',\, K = S^*,\, T = t(2) - t(1))}{\partial K^2}
\tag{14}
$$

As long as (12′) or (13) is satisfied, an infinity of future smile surfaces are therefore compatible with today's prices of plain-vanilla options. If the admissible future smile surface assumed by a trader (trader 1) belongs to this set, he can rest assured that no static, model-independent, strategy can arbitrage his prices. Another trader (trader 2), with superior and correct knowledge about the "truth" of a specific process, can, of course, arbitrage trader 1, but she can do that only by engaging in a dynamic, model-dependent strategy. Since we consider, in this section, the situation of users who have views about future smile surfaces but are "agnostic" about true models, the possibility of model-driven arbitrage is not our main concern.

It is easy to see, however, that a trader can believe that a single (admissible) future volatility surface will prevail at time t if and only if she believes that all the (possibly unknown) parameters driving the process for the stock price (volatility, jump amplitude ratio, jump frequency, etc.) fall in one of two classes:

i) either they are fully deterministic (i.e., constant or, at most, purely dependent on time);

ii) or their value at time t depends at most on the time-t realization of the stock price itself.

Since the most common processes are jump-diffusions,[15] let us analyze in this light the implications of i) and ii) above. If the process is a pure diffusion, then the volatility must have the form σ_0 or $\sigma(t)$, for case i) to apply, and $\sigma(S_t, t)$ for case ii). If the volatility is of the form σ_0 or $\sigma(t)$, then today's prices fully determine the future volatility surface (which, incidentally, can display no smiles). If the volatility is of the form $\sigma(S_t, t)$, we are back to the DDKR solution, which is unique. Once again, the future implied volatility surface is therefore uniquely determined by today's prices. If the user assigns a single future implied volatility surface different from the DDKR one, she is implicitly assuming that the process *cannot* be a diffusion without jumps: a stochastic volatility is not compatible with a unique future smile surface; a volatility of the form σ_0 or $\sigma(t)$ allows no smiles whatsoever; and a volatility of the form $\sigma(S_t, t)$ is compatible only with the DDKR implied smile surface.

If the user insists that a single future implied volatility surface will prevail, and that the process is no more complex than a jump diffusion, she must believe that, on top of a diffusion of type i) or ii), there must exist a jump component with parameters $\{j\}$ either constant $\{j_0\}$, or time dependent, $\{j(t)\}$, or at most dependent on time and on the realization of the stock price $\{j(S_t, t)\}$. These semi-agnostic views are logically consistent with assigning a single future implied volatility surface. Unfortunately, and for totally unrelated technical reasons, in the presence of jumps the replication method presented below becomes inapplicable.

These conclusions indicate that the method cannot be straightforwardly used by a trader, but can be of use to a risk manager, who is not interested in arbitrage-free option pricing but in the impact of different possible implied volatility scenarios on the future value of a portfolio of trades. The only constraint the risk manager would have to satisfy would be the admissibility of the implied volatility smile surface.

For this purpose the static replication method can provide an efficient and powerful tool for scenario and model stress analysis. Specifically, rather than stipulating a single future smile surface, the risk manager should provide a variety of possible future smile surfaces constrained to be admissible and to belong to the set of surfaces obtainable from the Kolmogorov equations (12). In the absence of a liquid market in forward-starting options (i.e., given the incompleteness of the volatility market), these joint conditions (admissibility and derivability from the Kolmogorov equations) are sufficient to ensure that no model-independent dynamic trading strategy can arbitrage any of the prices implied by the future volatility surface. In other terms, the financial universe under analysis can indeed be attained from today's prices. A separate note (Rebonato, 2000) shows how these Kolmogorov-compatible future implied volatility surfaces can be obtained in an efficient way.

---

[15] Merton (1990) and Neftci (2000) clearly highlight the high level of generality of mixed jump-diffusion processes.

Conclusion

I have tried to cover what I consider to be the most important conceptual aspects of model risk management. I have also attempted to indicate how my views can be put into practice in a variety of situations.

The conclusions I have drawn from the analysis presented might be, to some extent, controversial. In particular, I have argued that the "best" model for a trader need not be the "best" model for a risk manager. Therefore the common middle office's quest to mimic as closely as possible the modeling approach of the front-office traders might be misguided. In addition, the belief of those risk managers who maintain that if only they could avail themselves of the most sophisticated model in the market, model risk would be eliminated, is in my opinion both incorrect and dangerous. For the most sophisticated and financially "truest" model to be simultaneously of relevance to both the trader and the risk manager, the further Panglossian assumptions must be made that markets can only become progressively more perfect, liquid, rational, and efficient; that this progress is unstoppable; that it is rapid; and that it can suffer no detours. Recent market events have shown these assumptions to be dubious, to say the least. The market is fickle, and the path it follows often inscrutable.

From these considerations it would be equally wrong to derive a defeatist attitude and to conclude that the level of sophistication and market understanding of the risk manager can be lower than the trader's. What needs modeling for model risk management purposes is as complex, if not more, than the risk-neutral world of relevance to the trader; namely, the risk manager must be able to estimate how the fickle market might change its choice of favorite pricing measure in the future. This requires a solid conceptual understanding of asset pricing in incomplete markets, efficient implementation tools, and robust numerical techniques.

If this task is accomplished, a unified view of overall market risk as the combination of general market risk and model risk can be achieved. If this view is accepted, I have then shown that the concept of holding period should apply to model risk just as well as to general market risk.

Needless to say, much more work remains to be done in this area. For instance, I have barely touched upon the important question of how the distribution of differences between the mark-to-model and the market prices should be used to set limits and model provisions. Should the bank be more interested in the variance or in the tails of this distribution? The application of the vast literature about pricing in incomplete markets to model risk could also be profitably explored in much greater detail. From a different angle, rational bounds on the prices of options have received a lot of attention (see, for example, Neuberger and Hodges, 1998) and could be used in the context of pricing in incomplete markets to establish bounds that cannot be trespassed, even by the fickle market.

Despite these omissions and shortcomings, I would be delighted if the thoughts I have expressed here could constitute a useful starting point for further work in the area.

Summary

Riccardo Rebonato presents a new, quantitative approach to managing model risk. A careful definition of model risk shows that it is inextricably bound up with asset pricing in incomplete markets. Several practical examples have been chosen to illustrate the most important conceptual aspects of model risk management. He argues that the "best" model for a trader need not be the "best" model for a risk manager. Therefore the common middle office's quest to mimic as closely as possible the modeling approach of the front-office traders might be misguided.

Acknowledgement: It is a pleasure to acknowledge useful discussions with my colleagues, Dr Chris Hunter and Dr Mark Joshi. I have also benefitted from useful conversations with a former colleague, Dr Emanuele Amerio. As the standard disclaimer goes, all the remaining errors are mine. The opinions expressed in this article should not be attributed to my employer, the Royal Bank of Scotland Group, which, however, I wish to thank for providing a stimulating environment in which the ideas presented here can find practical application.

Suggested further reading

Amblard, G. and Lebuchoux, J. (2000) "Models for CMS caps" in "Euro Derivatives," published by *Risk*, September.

Andersen, L. and Andreasen, J. (2000) "Static barriers," *Risk*, September.

Andersen, L., Andreasen, J. and Eliezer, D. (2000) "Static replication of barrier options," Working Paper, GenRe Financial Products, http://www.ssrn.com

Bingham, N.H. and Kiesel, R. (1998) "Risk neutral valuation," *Springer Finance*, Springer Verlag, Berlin Heidelberg, New York.

Björk, T. (1998) *Arbitrage Theory in Continuous Finance*, Oxford University Press, Oxford.

Black, F., Derman, E. and Toy, W. (1990) "A one-factor model of interest rates and its application to Treasury bond options," *Financial Analysts Journal*, pp. 33–339.

Black, F. and Karasinski, P. (1991) "Bond and option pricing when short rates are lognormal," *Financial Analysts Journal*, July-August.

Brigo, D. and Mercurio, F. (2000) "A mixed up smile," *Risk*, September, pp. 123–126.

Dembo, R. (2000) "Mark to future" in *Visions of Risk*, Alexander, C. (ed.), Financial Times-Prentice Hall, London.

Derman, E., Kani, I., Ergener, D. and Bardhan, I. (1995) "Static option replication," Goldman Sachs, Quantitative Strategies Research Notes, Working Paper available at http://www.gs.com/gs/

Derman, E., Kani, I. and Zou, J. (1996) "The local volatility surface: unlocking the information in index option prices," *Financial Analysts Journal*, July/August, pp. 25–36.

Duffie, D. (1996) *Dynamic Asset Pricing Theory*, 2nd Edition, Princeton University Press, Princeton, New Jersey.

Duffie, D., Pan, J. and Singleton, K. (1999) "Transform analysis for affine jump-diffusions," Working Paper, Graduate School of Business, Stanford University.

Dupire, B. (1993) "Pricing and hedging with smiles," Working Paper, Paribas Capital Markets Swaps and Options Research Team.

Dupire, B. (1994) "Pricing with a smile," *Risk*, 7, pp. 32–39.

Hull, J. and White, A. (1990) "Pricing interest-rate derivative securities," *Rev. Fin. Stud.*, 3, p. 454.

Jackwerth, J.C. (1997) "Recovering risk aversion from option prices and realized returns," Working Paper, London Business School.

Jaeckel, P. and Rebonato, R. (2000) "Valuing American options in the presence of user-defined smiles and time-dependent volatility: scenario analysis, model stress and lower-bound pricing applications," submitted to *Journal of Risk*.

Jamshidian, F. (1997) "Libor and swap market models and measures," *Finance and Stochastics*, Vol. 4, September, pp. 293–330.

Marris, D. (1999) "Financial option pricing and skewed volatility," MPhil Statistical Science, Statistical Laboratory, University of Cambridge.

Merton, R. (1990) *Continuous Time Finance*, Blackwell, Oxford.

Mirfendereski, D. and Rebonato, R. (2000) "Closed-form solutions for option pricing in the presence of volatility smiles: a density-function approach," accepted in *Journal of Risk*.

Neftci, S. (2000) "An introduction to the mathematics of financial derivatives," 2nd Edition, Academic Press, New York.

Neuberger, A. and Hodges, S. (1998) "Rational bounds for the prices of exotic options," IFA Working Paper 281-1998.

Rebonato, R. (1999) *Volatility and Correlation*, John Wiley, Chichester, UK.

Rebonato, R. (2000) "Building admissible Kolmogorov-compatible future implied volatility surfaces," Working Paper, Royal Bank of Scotland QuaRC.

Rebonato, R. and Jaeckel, P. (2000) "Linking caplet and swaption volatilities in a BGM framework: approximate solutions," submitted to *Journal of Comp. Finance*.

Rubinstein, M. (1994) "Implied binomial trees," *Journal of Finance*, Vol. 49, No. 3, pp. 771–818.

Schoenbucher, P.J. (1998) "A market model for stochastic implied volatility," Working Paper, Department of Statistics, Bonn University, June.

CREDIT RISKS

2

Contributors

Michael Gordy is an economist in the Research and Statistics division of the Federal Reserve Board. His current research focuses on the design, calibration, computation, and validation of models of portfolio credit risk. He received his PhD in Economics from MIT in 1994 and a BA in Mathematics and Philosophy from Yale University in 1985.

Mark Davis is Professor of Mathematics at Imperial College London, involved in research and teaching in financial mathematics, with an accent on incomplete markets and modeling credit risk. From 1995–99 he was Head of Research and Product Development at Tokyo-Mitsubishi International. He holds a PhD in Electrical Engineering from the University of California, Berkeley.

Violet Lo is a quantitative analyst in the Market Risk Engineering Group at Deutsche Bank AG, London. Her current research focuses on market and credit risk, interest rate and credit derivatives. She previously worked in the Research and Product Development Group at Tokyo Mitsubishi International London. Before joining TMI, she lectured in the Mathematics Department at the University of Manchester Institute of Science and Technology. She received a PhD in Probability at Cambridge University in 1998.

Dilip Madan obtained PhD degrees in Economics (1971) and Mathematics (1975) from the University of Maryland and then taught econometrics and operations research at the University of Sydney. His research interests developed in the area of applying the theory of stochastic processes to the problems of risk management. In 1988 he joined the Robert H. Smith School of Business where he now specializes in mathematical finance.

John Hull is the Maple Financial Group Professor of Derivatives and Risk Management in the Joseph L. Rotman School of Management at the University of Toronto. He has written two popular books: *Options, Futures, and Other Derivatives* and *Introduction to Futures and Options Markets*.

Alan White is Professor of Finance in the Joseph L. Rotman School of Management at the University of Toronto. He has published many articles on derivatives and risk management in practitioner and academic journals.

Contents

Introduction

During the last few years there has been an enormous resurgence of interest in the pricing of credit risky securities and the measurement and management of credit risks. This has driven growth in new markets for credit derivatives and focused the attention of regulators on the need to re-assess credit risk capital requirements. The Basel 2 Accord that will be implemented in 2004 is likely to be a driving force behind the continual development of new methods for measuring, pricing and hedging credit risks.

The chapters in this part have been chosen to represent the current state of the art. It begins with a chapter by Michael Gordy of the US Federal Reserve, presenting a general framework for credit Value-at-Risk (VaR) models. CreditMetrics and CreditRisk$^+$ are encompassed within this framework and are discussed as special cases of Gordy's model. They use different mappings from risk factor realizations to conditional default or migration probabilities for the obligors; however the most significant difference concerns their distributional assumptions on the systematic risk factors. Using test portfolios that reflect the size and quality of loans normally experienced by real banks, simulations show that CreditRisk$^+$ measures are very sensitive to distributional parameter assumptions. The general effects of distributional assumptions on the VaR measure are analyzed using an asymptotic analysis (see pp. 122–140).

The next chapter presents two models for correlated defaults in bond portfolios. Mark Davis of Imperial College and Violet Lo of Deutsche Bank, London examine transactions in collateralized bond obligations, whose performance depends on the defaults of an underlying high-yield portfolio of bonds. The risk of a collateralized bond obligation will be reduced by diversification in the underlying portfolio, but it is not easy to assess how effective this will be. Davis and Lo introduce two classes of probabilistic models: default "injection" (a static model where default on one bond triggers defaults

on others) and default "burst" (a stochastic process model where default on one bond induces a high risk period with increased default probabilities for all bonds). Both models produce fat-tailed default distributions as correlation between defaults increases and the chapter explains how to quantify this increased correlation risk (see pp. 141–151).

Pricing the risks of default is the subject of the next chapter by Dilip Madan of the University of Maryland. It surveys the wide variety of models that have been proposed for pricing simple contingent claims: from the option theoretic models of Merton, Longstaff and Schwartz or Madan, Carr and Chang; to hazard rate models of default by Jarrow and Turnbull, Duffie and Singleton or Jarrow, Lando and Turnbull. Most of this work concerns the time or probability of default with little attention focused on recovery rates. However the chapter also draws on recent papers by Madan and Unal that attempt to assess recovery rates from market data (see pp. 152–170).

The final chapter in Part 2 is by John Hull and Alan White of the University of Toronto. It compares two approaches for estimating default probabilities: those that are based on historical data and those that are based on risk-neutral valuation methods. The default probabilities that are calculated from bond prices are much higher than those estimated from historical data; because the probabilities that are backed-out from bond prices are risk-neutral, whereas those calculated from historical data are real-world probabilities. The conclusion is that historically estimated default probabilities may be suitable for the computation of credit VaR by middle office risk management whereas risk-neutral default probabilities should be used in the front office for valuing default dependent derivatives (see pp. 171–180).

Carol Alexander,
Professor of Risk Management,
ISMA Centre, University of Reading, UK

What wags the tail? Identifying the key assumptions in models of portfolio credit risk

by Michael B. Gordy

Recent years have seen a dramatic increase in effort and resources devoted to modeling credit risk on a portfolio basis. In all of the major markets, there are banks and other financial institutions in the process of selecting and implementing credit Value-at-Risk (VaR) models. The best choice of model for an institution depends, in general, on the complexity of the institution's portfolio, on the sorts of data available in its information systems, and on the institution's portfolio management policies. For example, a simple actuarial model of loss might be appropriate for an institution with a hold-to-maturity portfolio of term loans to middle-market borrowers, whereas an investment bank with an actively traded portfolio is more likely to require a sophisticated mark-to-market approach.

Let us assume that a model has been chosen and implemented. Table 1 presents a simplified version of a report delivered to senior management. In this example, management has selected a one-year risk horizon, and defined Value-at-Risk as the 99.8th percentile of the loss distribution. Managers can draw on experience to decide whether the model's assessment of expected loss, here stated to be 1.4 percent of total portfolio exposure, is reasonable. For Value-at-Risk, however, experience provides little guidance, as VaR at the 99.8th percentile level represents a one-in-500-year event. Backtesting is similarly fruitless. More than with most financial models, therefore, it is important that senior management understand the sensitivity of reported VaR to the assumptions embedded in the chosen model and to uncertainty in parameter calibration.

Table 1: A simple credit VaR report

Portfolio size	$42,100m
Expected loss	$589.4m
VaR (99.8 %)	$2444.6m

This article offers a general approach to opening the black box of a portfolio credit risk model. We begin with a summary of two influential benchmarks in the development of credit VaR models, Credit Suisse Financial Products' CreditRisk[+]

This paper draws heavily on "A Comparative Anatomy of Credit Risk Models," published in the *Journal of Banking & Finance*, January 2000. The interested reader is referred to that study for greater detail on the models and on the calibration methods used here. The views expressed herein are my own and do not necessarily reflect those of the Board of Governors or its staff. Please address correspondence to the author at Division of Research and Statistics, Mail Stop 153, Federal Reserve Board, Washington, DC 20551, USA. Phone: (202) 452-3705. Fax: (202) 452-5295. E-mail: michael.gordy@frb.gov and the RiskMetrics Group's CreditMetrics. Although the two models appear to be quite different in their characterization of credit risk, we go on to show that the underlying probabilistic structures are in fact similar, and that the two models can be seen as special cases of a much broader class of risk-factor models. Placing the models within a unified and generalized framework not only helps to make clear the structural parallels between them but also serves to highlight their shared limitations.

We then develop comparative simulations, taking care to construct test deck portfolios with quality and loan size distributions similar to real bank portfolios, and to calibrate correlation parameters in CreditMetrics and CreditRisk$^+$ in an empirically plausible and mutually consistent manner. An especially striking result from the simulations is the sensitivity of CreditRisk$^+$ to a seemingly innocuous distributional parameter. Then we show how large-portfolio asymptotic analysis can be used to shed light on this result and, more generally, to understand the key role of embedded distributional assumptions in determining the reported VaR. We conclude with some implications for model validation.

Summary of the models

Here we give an introduction to CreditRisk$^+$ and CreditMetrics. For convenience in exposition, we describe the models as they would be applied to a portfolio of bonds. Our choice of notation is intended to facilitate comparison of the models, and may differ considerably from what is used in the original manuals.

CreditRisk$^+$

CreditRisk$^+$ is essentially a model of *default risk*. Each obligor has only two possible end-of-period states, default and non-default. In the event of default, the lender suffers a loss of fixed size; this is the lender's *exposure* to the obligor. The distributional assumptions and functional forms imposed by CreditRisk$^+$ allow the distribution of total portfolio losses to be calculated in a convenient analytic form.

Default correlations in CreditRisk$^+$ are assumed to be driven entirely by some finite set of "risk factors." These risk factors represent the various sources of systematic risk which influence the health of many individual firms. The identity of the factors is left abstract in CreditRisk$^+$, but in principle would embrace macroeconomic variables, changes in commodity prices, the emergence of major new technologies, etc. We represent these risk factors as a vector of K variables $X = (X_1, ..., X_K)$.

Aside from the systematic risk factors, all other sources of default risk are assumed to be idiosyncratic to the individual firms; that is, holding fixed any given outcome of X, defaults of individual obligors are independent events. We write $p_i(x)$ to denote the probability of default by obligor i conditional on obtaining the realization x of X. In CreditRisk$^+$, the conditional default probability function $p_i(x)$ depends on the initial rating grade γ_i of obligor i, the realization x of the risk factors, and the vector of "factor loadings" $(w_{i1},...,w_{iK})$ which measure the sensitivity of obligor i to each of the risk factors. The function is specified as

$$p_i(x) = \bar{p}_{\gamma(i)} \left(1 + \sum_{k=1}^{k} w_{ik}(x_k - 1) \right) \tag{1}$$

where $\bar{p}_\gamma$ is the unconditional default probability for a grade γ obligor.[1] The intuition behind this specification is that the risk factors X serve to "scale up" or "scale down" the unconditional $\bar{p}_\gamma$. A high value for x_k (over one) increases the probability of default for each obligor in proportion to the obligor's weight w_{ik} on that risk factor; a low value of x_k (under one) scales down all default probabilities.

Ex ante, we do not know what the realization of X will be, but (by assumption) do know the probability distribution over its possible outcomes. In CreditRisk$^+$, the factors $X_1, ..., X_K$ are independent gamma-distributed random variables with mean one and variance σ_k^2; $k = 1, ..., K$.[2] By construction, $E[\, p_i(X)\,] = \bar{p}_{\gamma(i)}$, i.e., the expected value of the conditional default probability across all possible values of X is simply the unconditional default probability. As long as the weights w_{ik} are positive numbers and sum to one or less, conditional probabilities will always be positive. It should be noted that it is possible for conditional probabilities to *exceed* one. This will tend to occur when $\bar{p}_\gamma$ or some of the σ_k are large. In practice, for reasonable calibrations of the model, this awkward possibility has no significant impact on the results for portfolios dominated by bankable credits (say, rated B or better on the S&P scale).

Loss in CreditRisk$^+$ is defined in book-value terms. In the event of default by obligor i, it is assumed that loss is a fixed and known fraction λ_i of bond face value A_i.[3] Otherwise, loss is zero. Value-at-Risk, VaR$_q$, is defined as the q-th percentile of the unconditional distribution of loss. Let $F(\cdot \mid x)$ denote the cumulative distribution of loss conditional on realization x of X. The assumed conditional independence of defaults, fixed loss given default, and functional form for $p_i(x)$ in equation (1) together imply that $F(\cdot \mid x)$ can be characterized in a tractable way. To get the unconditional distribution of loss, we simply integrate over the possible realizations of X:

$$\Pr(\text{Loss} \leq l) = F(l) = E[F(l \mid X)]. \tag{2}$$

The assumption that the X are mutually independent and gamma-distributed permits this integration to be done analytically, so we can avoid Monte Carlo simulation.[4] VaR$_q$ is the value of l such that $F(l) = q$.

---

[1] In the "plain-vanilla" version of CreditRisk$^+$, the w_{ik} sum exactly to one, so the expression for $p_i(x)$ reduces to $\bar{p}_{\gamma(i)}$ times the weighted sum of the x_k. The generalized version given here is equivalent to allowing for a "specific risk" sector as described in the CreditRisk$^+$ manual, §A12.3.

[2] This is a variant on the presentation in the CreditRisk$^+$ manual, in which X_k has mean μ_k and variance σ_k^2, and the conditional probabilities are given by $p_i(x) = \bar{p}_{\gamma(i)}(\sum w_{ik}(x_k/\mu_k))$. In our presentation, the constants $1/\mu_k$ are absorbed into the normalized x_k without any loss of generality.

[3] To facilitate the computation of the loss distribution, the loss exposure amounts $\lambda_i A_i$ are expressed as integer multiples of a "standardized loss unit" (e.g. $100,000). For reasonably small choices of this standardized unit, the round-off error induced by the discretization of loss exposures causes only a small loss of precision in the final results.

[4] The solution method for the unconditional $F(l)$ does not directly solve equation (2), but rather solves for the associated probability generating function. An additional assumption, known as the Poisson approximation, is imposed to make the pgf analytically tractable. Nonetheless, the intuition behind equation (2) is not misleading. See Gordy (2000a) or CSFP (1997) for details.

CreditMetrics

The CreditMetrics model for credit events is based loosely on Merton's model of bankruptcy, in which a borrower defaults when the value of its assets falls below the level needed to support its fixed liabilities. In the standard version of the Merton model, knowledge of the level of fixed liabilities and the current level and volatility of the value of the firm's assets (which can be inferred from the firm's equity price and volatility) are used to determine the firm's default probability. In the CreditMetrics version, the firm's default probability is taken directly from its credit rating. The firm's asset value and fixed liabilities are embedded implicitly in the model, but do not appear as quantities of direct interest.

Let R_i denote the return at the horizon on the firm's asset value. As in CreditRisk$^+$, it is assumed that the firm is affected by both systematic and idiosyncratic risk. We model R_i as a weighted sum of systematic risk factors X and idiosyncratic effects ε_i:

$$R_i = \sum_k X_k w_{ik} + \eta_i \varepsilon_i. \tag{3}$$

The vector of factor loadings $w_{i1},...,w_{iK}$ determines the relative sensitivity of obligor i to each of the risk factors, and the weight η_i determines the relative importance of idiosyncratic risk for the obligor. The risk factors X are assumed to be distributed multivariate normal with mean zero and covariance matrix Ω.[5] The ε_i are assumed to be iid $N(0,1)$.

When the realization of the asset value return falls under a threshold value, the obligor defaults. Calibration of the default thresholds, denoted by Z_i, requires that we know the unconditional probability of default for each grade. For each obligor, we find the value of Z_i so that $\Pr(R_i \leq Z_i) = \bar{p}_{\gamma(i)}$, where, as above, $\bar{p}_\gamma$ is the unconditional default probability for grade γ. By construction, R_i is distributed normal with mean zero and variance $w_i' \Omega w_i + \eta_i^2$, so we have

$$\bar{p}_{\gamma(i)} = \Phi \left(Z_i \sqrt{w_i' \Omega w_i + \eta_i^2} \right)$$

where Φ is the standard normal cumulative distribution function (cdf).[6] The solution for Z_i is therefore

$$Z_i = \sqrt{w_i' \Omega w_i + \eta_i^2} . \Phi^{-1} (\bar{p}_{\gamma(i)}).$$

Observe that Z_i is directly proportional to the standard deviation of R_i. If that latter is doubled, the former is doubled to compensate, and nothing changes. Thus, the variance of R_i is superfluous information and can be normalized out. Without loss of generality, we re-scale the factor loadings for obligor i so that $w_i' \Omega w_i + \eta_i^2 = 1$. We then have $Z_i = Z_\gamma = \Phi^{-1}(\bar{p}_\gamma)$ for all obligors i in grade γ. For essentially the same

---

[5] In the CreditMetrics Technical Document, it is recommended that the X be taken to be country/industry stock market indexes. The ready availability of historical data on stock indexes simplifies calibration of Ω. More importantly, basic information on a company's geographic and business line exposure can be applied to setting the weights w_i. The mathematical framework of the model, however, imposes no specific identity on the X.

[6] We use matrix notation w_i to refer to the column vector of factor loadings for i, and the notation w_i' to refer to its transpose.

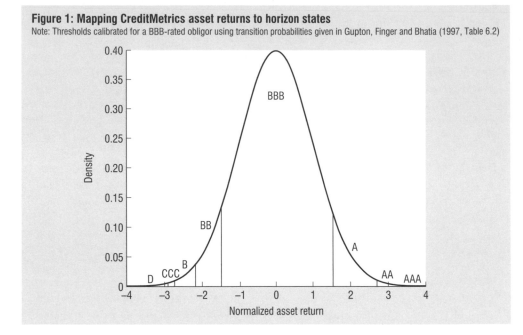

Figure 1: Mapping CreditMetrics asset returns to horizon states
Note: Thresholds calibrated for a BBB-rated obligor using transition probabilities given in Gupton, Finger and Bhatia (1997, Table 6.2)

reason, the variances of the risk factors X can be absorbed into the factor loadings. Without loss of generality, we impose ones on the diagonal of matrix Ω, which can then be interpreted as a matrix of factor correlations.[7]

This framework generalizes naturally to accommodate migration across non-default states as well. Let there be G "live" rating grades, and denote default as grade $G + 1$. Instead of having a single threshold for each initial grade, we now have a vector of thresholds $Z_{\gamma,1}, ..., Z_{\gamma,G}$. If $R_i \leq Z_{\gamma,G}$ then obligor i defaults. If $Z_{\gamma,G} < R_i \leq Z_{\gamma,G-1}$ then obligor i migrates to grade G at the horizon, and so on. If $Z_{\gamma,1} < R_i$, then obligor i migrates to grade 1 at the horizon. The $Z_{\gamma,g}$ thresholds are calibrated so that the unconditional probability of migrating from grade γ to grade g matches the value from an empirical transition matrix.[8] Figure 1 shows how the possible realizations of R_i are divided into bins for a BBB-rated obligor. The vertical lines mark the $Z_{BBB,g}$ thresholds for each final state. The areas under the curve within each bin correspond to the unconditional transition probabilities.

The ability to recognize the risk of rating migration makes CreditMetrics well suited to mark-to-market valuation. When an obligor ends in a non-default state at the horizon, CreditMetrics uses forward credit spreads for the final grade to discount the bond's remaining contractual cash flows.[9] When an obligor ends in the default state, recovery value is drawn as dollar face value times a beta-distributed

---

[7] Also for the same reason, we could have allowed for non-zero means of the X factors and the ε, but these means would have washed out of the final analysis.
[8] Let $\bar{p}_{\gamma,g}$ denote the empirical transition probabilities. Then the Z thresholds are chosen so that $\Phi(Z_{\gamma,g-1}) - \Phi(Z_{\gamma,g}) = \bar{p}_{\gamma,g}$.
[9] While this discussion assumes a portfolio of bonds, CreditMetrics can accommodate more complex asset types such as loan commitments. See the CreditMetrics Technical Document, Chapter 4, and Finger (1998).

fractional recovery.[10] Mean and variance of a bond's fractional recovery can be set to reflect seniority and collateral. An important assumption, however, is that fractional recoveries are independent of the systematic risk factors.

The loss distribution is estimated by Monte Carlo simulation. To obtain a single trial for the portfolio, we first draw a single vector x as a multivariate $N(0,\Omega)$ and a set of iid $N(0,1)$ idiosyncratic ε. For each obligor, we form the return R_i, which is compared against the vector of threshold values $Z_{\gamma(i),1}, ..., Z_{\gamma(i),G}$ to determine the obligor's state at the horizon, which in turn determines the value of the bond at the horizon. These final values are summed to obtain the portfolio value. To estimate a distribution of portfolio outcomes, we repeat this process many times. Loss in CreditMetrics is defined as the difference between the expected portfolio value at the horizon and its realized value. The simulated portfolio losses are sorted to form a cumulative distribution for loss. For example, if the portfolio is simulated 100,000 times, then the estimated 99.5th percentile of the loss distribution is given by the 99,500th element of the sorted loss outcomes.

A unified approach to the models

At first glance, it appears that CreditMetrics and CreditRisk$^+$ embody fundamentally different views of portfolio credit risk. In CreditMetrics, correlation in firms' asset returns gives rise to clustering in defaults. In CreditRisk$^+$, default probabilities increase or decrease in response to background systematic factors. To the extent that two obligors are sensitive to the same set of background factors, their default probabilities will move together. These co-movements in probability give rise to clustering in defaults. This section shows that the difference in these views is one of mathematical language and not one of substance. We present the two models as special cases of a more general class of portfolio credit risk models. Placing the models within a unified and generalized framework not only helps to make clear the structural parallels between them but also serves to highlight their shared limitations.

A complete specification of a risk-factor model of portfolio credit risk has four components. The first is a set S of possible states at the horizon. In CreditRisk$^+$, S has only two elements, "survive" and "default." In CreditMetrics, S depends on the chosen rating scale. If we adopt, say, the S&P scale, then S = {AAA, AA,..., CCC, Default}.[11] The second component is a set of systematic risk factors X with joint distribution function $H(x)$. In CreditRisk$^+$, the X are assumed to have independent gamma distributions. In CreditMetrics, the X are multivariate normal.

The third component is a mapping $f_i(s \mid x)$ for obligor i from realizations of X to a conditional probability distribution over the states $s \in$ S. In CreditRisk$^+$, this mapping is straightforward. For the default state we have $f_i(\text{Default} \mid x) = p_i(x)$, and for the non-default state we have $f_i(\text{Survive} \mid x) = 1 - p_i(x)$, where $p_i(x)$ is given by equation (1). The mapping for CreditMetrics may seem less obvious, but it takes on a simple form.[12] The probability given $X = x$ that obligor i will migrate to grade g is

---

[10] CreditMetrics also tracks coupons received in the intra-horizon period, and assumes these coupons are reinvested at the Treasury rate. In the event of default, it is assumed that all coupons due *prior* to the horizon date are received in full.

[11] The set S need not be discrete. In KMV's model, S contains Default and a continuum of possible EDF values at the horizon.

given by

$$
\begin{aligned}
f_i(g \mid x) &\equiv \Pr(s_i = g \mid X = x) = \Pr(Z_{\gamma,g} < R_i \le Z_{\gamma,g-1} \mid X = x) \\
&= \Pr(R_i \le Z_{\gamma,g-1} \mid X = x) - \Pr(R_i \le Z_{\gamma,g} \mid X = x) \\
&= \Pr(Xw_i + \eta_i \varepsilon_i \le Z_{\gamma,g-1} \mid X = x) - \Pr(Xw_i + \eta_i \varepsilon_i \le Z_{\gamma,g} \mid X = x) \\
&= \Pr(\varepsilon_i \le (Z_{\gamma,g-1} - Xw_i)/\eta_i \mid X = x) - \Pr(\varepsilon_i \le (Z_{\gamma,g} - Xw_i)/\eta_i \mid X = x) \\
&= \Phi((Z_{\gamma,g-1} - xw_i)/\eta_i) - \Phi((Z_{\gamma,g} - xw_i)/\eta_i).
\end{aligned}
\tag{4}
$$

Risk-factor models always assume that the outcomes of any two obligors are independent conditional on X. Thus, for any realization x of X, any two obligors i and j, and any two final states s_i and s_j, the joint conditional probability that i will land in state s_i and j will land in state s_j is simply the product of the two conditional probabilities $f_i(s_i \mid x)$ and $f_j(s_j \mid x)$. Conditional independence is indeed a powerful assumption. It implies that the distribution $H(x)$ and the conditional probability functions $f_i(s \mid x)$ together give us a complete description of the probabilistic structure of obligor defaults and migrations. This parsimony is what makes it possible to calibrate the models with our limited data, and also greatly simplifies computation. However, in practice it often causes us to ignore concentrations of risk within a portfolio. If, for example, we assign factors to represent geographic risk at the country level, we are assuming that regional risk is immaterial. A portfolio of loans to New England firms would have VaR equal to that of an otherwise comparable portfolio of firms from across the United States.

The final component is a pricing method for determining loss in each final obligor state. Let $L_{i,s}$ be the loss incurred on obligor i in final state s. To allow for the case in which loss is stochastic, we define $\Lambda_{i,s}(\cdot \mid x)$ as the cumulative distribution function for $L_{i,s}$. Conditional on $X = x$, we assume that the $L_{i,s}$ are drawn independently across obligors. Under a book-value definition of loss, as in CreditRisk$^+$, $L_{i,\text{Survive}}$ is identically zero. CreditRisk$^+$ assumes fixed fractional recovery, so $L_{i,\text{Default}} = \lambda_i A_i$. (Thus, in CreditRisk$^+$, the $\Lambda_{i,s}$ distributions are degenerate.) In CreditMetrics, credit spreads are taken to be fixed, so $L_{i,g}$ is non-stochastic for non-default grades g. In the case of default, fractional loss λ_i is drawn as an independent beta random variable, so the distribution of $\lambda_{i,\text{Default}}$ is a simple transformation of the beta distribution.

Viewing risk-factor models in this abstract and generalized framework can often provide insight into what makes them tick. For present purposes, the most immediate insight is that the models do not differ fundamentally in structure or in their characterization of credit risk. From equation (4), we see how the mathematics of correlated asset returns can easily be re-cast into the mathematics of co-moving migration probabilities.[13] Differences between the models in solution techniques and suggested methods for parameter calibration may be of practical relevance to users but are not in any mathematical way intrinsic to the models. Breaking the models into components also encourages hybridization. For example, in the section below, we require a book-value version of CreditMetrics. As the above analysis makes

[12] In independent work, Koyluoglu and Hickman (1998) derive the conditional default probability function for a book-value version of CreditMetrics, and note its utility in mapping CreditMetrics to the CreditRisk$^+$ framework.

[13] One can also map in the other direction. That is, one can describe defaults in CreditRisk+ in terms of an unobserved random variable crossing a threshold value. See Gordy (2000a, §3.2).

clear, all we need to do is reduce the set S to default and non-default, and adopt the book-value pricing method.

Perhaps more importantly, this exercise in comparative anatomy of the models gives due prominence to the distributions imposed on the systematic risk factors. Because it is assumed that all other sources of risk are idiosyncratic, the systematic factors are the main drivers of risk at the portfolio level. Our choice of distribution to impose on the systematic factors is, in practice, made for convenience in modeling and not from empirically-derived beliefs. In the case of CreditMetrics, one could substitute any member of the symmetric stable class of distributions (of which the normal distribution is only a special case) without requiring significant change to the methods of model calibration and simulation. Even if parameters were recalibrated to yield the same mean and variance of portfolio loss, the overall shape of the loss distribution would differ, and therefore the tail percentile values would change as well. The choice of the gamma distribution in CreditRisk^{+} is entirely motivated by analytical tractability. On page 133 we show how small deviations from the gamma specification can lead to significant differences in VaR.

Finally, the generalized framework points to limitations of the present generation of models. Observe that the generalized pricing method allows the distribution of bond value at the horizon to depend on the realization of X, as well as on the obligor's outcome. Empirically, we tend to observe lower recoveries and higher credit spreads during a recession than during an economic expansion. Conditioning the distribution of the horizon price on X would allow us to capture systematic risk in recoveries and spreads without requiring fundamental changes to our Monte Carlo simulation methods.

Comparative simulations

For any particular portfolio of interest, estimates of credit VaR may vary significantly across models. To gain insight into what drives these differences, we perform comparative simulations between CreditRisk^{+} and CreditMetrics on a range of "test deck" portfolios. The simulations also help to identify the parameters or portfolio characteristics to which each model is most sensitive. Emphasis is placed on relevance and robustness. By relevance, we mean that the simulated portfolios and calibrated parameters ought to resemble their real-world counterparts closely enough for conclusions to be transferable. By robustness we mean that the conclusions ought to be qualitatively valid over an empirically relevant range of portfolios.

To allow more direct comparison with CreditRisk^{+}, we work with a book-value version of CreditMetrics. Under book valuation, the only relevant horizon states are default and non-default. Following the same logic as the derivation of equation (4), we can show that the conditional probability of default is

$$p_i(x) = \Phi((Z_{\gamma(i)} - xw_i)/\eta_i) \tag{5}$$

where $Z_\gamma = \Phi^{-1}(\bar{p}_\gamma)$.[14] In the event of default, we assume that loss is a fixed fraction λ of the face value. In the discussion below, the restricted CreditMetrics is designated

---

[14] With only two states, we can simplify notation by writing the conditional probability of default as $p_i(x)$ (as in CreditRisk^{+}) as a shorthand for $f_i(\text{Default} | x)$.

"CM2S" ("CreditMetrics two-state") whenever distinction from the full Credit-Metrics model needs emphasis.

This section presents our main simulations. First, we construct a set of "test deck" portfolios. All assets are assumed to be ordinary term loans. The size distribution of loans and their distribution across S&P rating grades are calibrated using data from two large samples of mid-sized and large corporate loans. Second, default probabilities and factor loadings in each model are calibrated using historical default data from the S&P ratings universe. We calibrate each model to a one-year risk horizon. We then go on to present simulation results.

Portfolio construction

Construction of a test deck loan portfolio requires choices along three dimensions. The first is *credit quality*, i.e., the portion of total dollar outstandings in each rating grade. The second is *obligor count*, i.e., the total number of obligors in the portfolio. The third is *concentration*, i.e., the distribution of dollar outstandings within a rating grade across the obligors within that grade. Note that the total portfolio dollar outstandings is immaterial because losses are calculated as a percentage of total outstandings.

In our simulations, the range of plausible credit quality is represented by four credit quality distributions, which are labeled "High," "Average," "Low," and "Very Low." The first three distributions are taken from internal Federal Reserve Board surveys of large banking organizations. The "Average" distribution is the average distribution across the surveyed banks of total outstandings in each S&P grade. The "High" and "Low" distributions are drawn from the higher and lower quality distributions found among the banks in the sample. The "Very Low" distribution is not found in the Federal Reserve sample but is intended to represent a very weak large bank loan portfolio during a recession. Speculative grade (BB and below) loans account for half of outstandings in the "Average" portfolio, and 25 percent, 78 percent and 83 percent in the "High," "Low," and "Very Low" quality portfolios respectively.

Realistic calibration of obligor count is likely to depend not only on the size of the hypothetical bank but also on the bank's business focus. A very large bank with a strong middle-market business might have tens of thousands of rated obligors in its commercial portfolio. A bank of the same size specializing in the large corporate market might have only a few thousand. For the "base case" calibration, we set $N = 5000$. To establish robustness of the conclusions to the choice of N, we model portfolios of 1,000 and 10,000 obligors as well. In all simulations, we assume each obligor is associated with only one loan in the portfolio.

Portfolio concentration is calibrated to match properties of the size distribution of loans in the Society of Actuaries (1996) (hereafter cited as "SoA") sample of mid-sized and large private placement loans (see also Carey, 1998). We divide the total number of obligors N across the rating grades so that the ratio of mean loan sizes across any two grades matches the same ratio from the SoA data. For each rating grade, we divide total exposure within the grade across its obligors so that, up to a scaling factor, the distribution of loan sizes matches the SoA distribution.[15] This method ensures that the shape of the distribution of loan sizes within a grade will not be sensitive to the distribution of total exposure across grades.

[15] For a more precise description of the method used to calibrate loan size distributions to the SoA data, see Gordy (2000a, §4.1).

In all simulations below, it is assumed that loss given default is a fixed proportion $\lambda = 0.3$ of book value, which is consistent with the average historical loss given default experience for senior unsecured bank loans.[16] Percentile values on the simulated loss distributions are directly proportional to λ. Holding fixed all other model parameters and the permitted probability of bank insolvency, VaR given, say, $\lambda = 0.45$ would simply be 1.5 times VaR given $\lambda = 0.3$.

Default probabilities and correlations

In any model of portfolio credit risk, the structure of default rate correlations is an important determinant of the distribution of losses. Special attention must therefore be given to mutually consistent calibration of parameters which determine default correlations. In the exercises below, we calibrate CreditMetrics and CreditRisk[+] to yield the same unconditional expected default rate for each rating grade and the same default correlation between any two obligors within a single rating grade.[17]

For simplicity, we assume a single systematic risk factor X. Within each rating grade, obligors are statistically identical except in loan size. That is, every obligor of grade γ has unconditional default probability $\bar{p}_\gamma$ and has the same weight w_γ on the systematic risk factor. (The value of w_γ will, of course, depend on the choice of model.) The $\bar{p}$ values are set to the long-term average annual default probabilities given in Table 6.9 of the CreditMetrics Technical Document, and are shown below in the first column of Table 2. Within-grade default correlations are estimated using data in Brand and Bahar (1998, Table 12) on historical default experience in each S&P grade.[18] Estimated values are reported in the second column of Table 2.

Table 2: Default probabilities, correlations and factor loadings*

	Historical experience			Factor loadings		
	$\bar{p}$	ρ	CM2S	CR+	CR+	CR+
σ				1.0	1.5	4.0
AAA	0.0001	0.0002	0.272	1.400	0.933	0.350
AA	0.0002	0.0004	0.285	1.400	0.933	0.350
A	0.0006	0.0009	0.279	1.200	0.800	0.300
BBB	0.0018	0.0003	0.121	0.400	0.267	0.100
BB	0.0106	0.0130	0.354	1.100	0.733	0.275
B	0.0494	0.0157	0.255	0.550	0.367	0.138
CCC	0.1914	0.0379	0.277	0.400	0.267	0.100

* Unconditional annual default probabilities $\bar{p}$ taken from the CreditMetrics Technical Document, Table 6.9. Default correlations and factor loadings from Gordy (2000a, Table 2)

The mapping from default correlations ρ_γ to the factor loadings w_γ is model-dependent. To calibrate CreditMetrics, we use

---

[16] The CreditMetrics Technical Document, §7.1.2, reports on available empirical evidence.
[17] Koyluoglu and Hickman (1998) also use expected default rate and within-grade default correlation to harmonize calibration of the two models.
[18] The estimation method is described in Gordy (2000a, Appendix B). For grades AAA and AA, there were no observed defaults in the sample, and only five defaults were observed for A-rated obligors. As the data are insufficient, we apply judgement in calibration of the $\bar{p}_\gamma$ and ρ_γ for these grades.

$$\rho_\gamma = \frac{\Phi(Z_\gamma, Z_\gamma, w_\gamma^2) - \bar{p}_\gamma^2}{\bar{p}_\gamma(1 - \bar{p}_\gamma)} \tag{6}$$

where $\Phi(z_1, z_2, \xi)$ is the bivariate cumulative distribution function for two standard normal random variables with correlation ξ.[19] Given values for the thresholds Z_γ (which are functions of the $\bar{p}_\gamma$) and default correlations ρ_γ, non-negative w_γ are uniquely determined by the nonlinear equation (6). The solutions are shown in the third column of Table 2.

Under the generalized form of CreditRisk[+] with a single systematic factor and homogeneous buckets, the conditional probability of default reduces to

$$p_i(x) = \bar{p}_{\gamma(i)}(1 - w_\gamma + w_\gamma x). \tag{7}$$

Default correlation within grade γ is given by

$$\rho_\gamma = \frac{\bar{p}_\gamma}{1 - \bar{p}_\gamma}(w_\gamma \sigma)^2. \tag{8}$$

If we take the $\bar{p}_\gamma$ and ρ_γ as known for each of the G grades, then we have G equations of the form of equation (8). However, we have $G + 1$ unknowns, i.e., $w_1, ..., w_G$ and σ. For any given σ, the weights w_γ are uniquely determined, but there is no obvious additional information to bring to the choice of σ. As a practical matter, it is inevitably a matter of judgement. To explore the sensitivity of VaR to the choice, results are presented for three values of σ (1.0, 1.5, and 4.0). See the last three columns of Table 2 for the values of w_γ corresponding to each of these σ (with the products $w_\gamma \sigma$ held constant).[20]

To users of CreditRisk[+], our "top-down" approach to calibration should seem entirely natural. Users of CreditMetrics, however, may find it somewhat alien. The design of CreditMetrics facilitates a detailed specification of risk factors (e.g., to represent industry- and country-specific risks), and thereby encourages a "bottom-up" style of calibration. From a mathematical point of view, top-down calibration of CreditMetrics is equally valid, and is convenient for purposes of comparison with CreditRisk[+]. As an empirical matter, a top-down approach ought to work as well as a bottom-up approach on a broadly diversified bond portfolio, because the top-down within-grade default correlation should roughly equal the average of the bottom-up default correlations among obligors within that grade. The bottom-up approach, however, is better suited to portfolios with industry or geographic concentrations.

A limitation of our method of calibration is that it makes no use of historical default correlations between obligors of different grades. Cross-grade default correlations are determined as artifacts of the models' functional forms for $p_\gamma(x)$, the assumption of a single systematic risk factor, and the chosen factor loadings. In general, our calibrations for CreditMetrics and CreditRisk[+] yield quite similar cross-grade default correlations, but there are discrepancies for some cells. For example,

[19] Derivation of equation (6) follows from Proposition 1 in Gordy (2000a).
[20] When $\sigma = 1$ is used in our calibration of CreditRisk[+], a problem arises in that some of the factor loadings exceed 1. Such values imply that conditional default probabilities can be negative. In practice, so long as such obligors are relatively few and their negative weights relatively small in magnitude, the portfolio loss distribution can still be well-behaved. For the weights in the $\sigma = 1$ column, we have confirmed numerically that our simulations always produce valid loss distributions.

the default correlation between a BB issuer and a CCC issuer is 0.0204 in CreditMetrics and 0.0222 in CreditRisk[+]. Thus, while our method equalizes variance of loss across the two models given homogeneous (i.e., single-grade) portfolios, there will be slight differences given mixed-grade portfolios.

Main simulation results

Results for the main set of simulations are displayed in Table 3.[21] Each quadrant of the table shows summary statistics and selected percentile values for CreditMetrics and CreditRisk[+] portfolio loss distributions for a portfolio of a given credit quality distribution. The summary statistics are the mean, standard deviation, index of skewness and index of kurtosis. The latter two are defined for a random variable y by

$$\text{Skewness}(y) = \frac{E[(y - E[y])^3]}{V[y]^{3/2}}, \quad \text{Kurtosis}(y) = \frac{E[(y - E[y])^4]}{V[y]^2}.$$

Skewness is a measure of the asymmetry of a distribution, and kurtosis is a measure of the relative thickness of the tails of the distribution. High kurtosis indicates a relatively high probability of very large portfolio credit losses. These summary statistics are calculated analytically for the CreditRisk[+] model using the results of Gordy (1999), and are approximated for CreditMetrics from the Monte Carlo loss distribution.

The percentile values presented in the table are the loss levels associated with the 50 percent (median), 75 percent, 95 percent, 99 percent, 99.5 percent and 99.97 percent points on the cumulative distribution of portfolio losses. In many discussions of credit risk modeling, the 99th and sometimes the 95th percentiles of the distribution are taken as points of special interest. The 99.5th and 99.97th percentiles may appear to be extreme tail values, but are in fact of greater practical interest than the 99th percentile. To merit an AA rating, an institution must have a probability of insolvency over a one-year horizon of roughly three basis points (0.03 percent).[22] Such an institution therefore ought to hold capital (or reserves) against credit loss equal to the 99.97th percentile value. Capitalization sufficient to absorb up to the 99.5th percentile value of losses would be consistent with only a BBB− rating.

Table 3, for the average quality portfolio, illustrates the qualitative characteristics of the main results. The expected loss under either model is roughly 48 basis points of the portfolio book value. The standard deviation of loss is roughly 32 basis points. When the CreditRisk[+] parameter σ is set to 1, the two models predict roughly similar loss distributions overall. The 99.5th and 99.97th percentile values are roughly 1.8 percent and 2.7 percent of portfolio book value in each case. As σ increases, however, the CreditRisk[+] distribution becomes increasingly kurtotic. The standard deviation of loss remains the same, but tail percentile values increase substantially. The 99.5th and 99.97th CreditRisk[+] percentile values given $\sigma = 4.0$ are respectively 40 percent and 90 percent larger than the corresponding CreditMetrics values.

---

[21] In these simulations, there are $N = 5000$ loans in the portfolio, grade-specific loan size distributions are taken from the SoA sample, average severity of loss is held constant at 30 percent, and the weights w_γ and CreditRisk[+] parameter σ are taken from Table 2. CreditMetrics distributions are simulated using 200,000 portfolio trials.

[22] This is a rule of thumb often used by practitioners. Following the CreditMetrics Technical Document, we have taken a slightly lower value (0.02 percent) as the AA default probability.

Table 3: CreditMetrics vs CreditRisk[+]: main simulations

σ	CM2S	High quality portfolio			CM2S	Average quality portfolio		
		CR+				CR+		
		1.00	1.50	4.00		1.00	1.50	4.00
Mean	0.194	0.194	0.194	0.194	0.481	0.480	0.480	0.480
Std dev	0.152	0.156	0.156	0.156	0.319	0.325	0.325	0.325
Skewness	1.959	1.874	2.537	5.848	1.696	1.854	2.633	6.527
Kurtosis	9.743	8.432	13.531	65.004	8.137	8.374	14.220	75.694
0.5000	0.156	0.150	0.148	0.160	0.409	0.391	0.384	0.414
0.7500	0.257	0.257	0.240	0.222	0.624	0.612	0.567	0.520
0.9500	0.486	0.501	0.497	0.398	1.089	1.120	1.116	0.869
0.9900	0.733	0.745	0.794	0.858	1.578	1.628	1.749	1.916
0.9950	0.847	0.850	0.928	1.121	1.795	1.847	2.033	2.488
0.9997	1.342	1.277	1.490	2.345	2.714	2.736	3.225	5.149

σ	CM2S	Low quality portfolio			CM2S	Very low quality portfolio		
		CR+				CR+		
		1.00	1.50	4.00		1.00	1.50	4.00
Mean	0.927	0.927	0.927	0.927	1.107	1.106	1.106	1.106
Std dev	0.557	0.566	0.566	0.566	0.635	0.644	0.644	0.644
Skewness	1.486	1.883	2.734	6.990	1.393	1.885	2.747	7.060
Kurtosis	6.771	8.511	14.873	82.988	6.299	8.523	14.961	84.097
0.5000	0.809	0.769	0.753	0.815	0.977	0.926	0.906	0.979
0.7500	1.194	1.154	1.063	0.967	1.418	1.364	1.259	1.146
0.9500	1.989	2.045	2.041	1.585	2.316	2.379	2.376	1.854
0.9900	2.782	2.936	3.161	3.481	3.187	3.395	3.654	4.024
0.9950	3.124	3.320	3.664	4.504	3.562	3.832	4.227	5.192
0.9997	4.558	4.877	5.770	9.251	5.105	5.607	6.631	10.618

High, low, and very low quality portfolios produce different expected losses (19, 93, and 111 basis points, respectively) but similar overall conclusions regarding our comparison of the two models. CreditRisk[+] with $\sigma = 1.0$ produces distributions roughly similar to those of CreditMetrics, although as credit quality deteriorates the extreme percentile values in CreditRisk[+] increase more quickly than in CreditMetrics. As σ increases, so do the extreme loss percentiles.

Overall, capital requirements implied by these simulations may seem relatively low. Even with a low quality portfolio, a bank would need to hold only 4.5 percent–6 percent capital against credit risk in order to maintain an AA rating standard. It should be noted, however, that these simulations assume a broadly diversified portfolio. In real bank portfolios, there may sometimes be pockets of higher default correlation, due perhaps to imperfect geographic or industry diversification. Furthermore, it should be emphasized that these simulations incorporate only default risk. For high-rated long-maturity instruments, migration risk may be much more significant than default risk. Additional capital also must be held for other forms of risk, including market risk, operational risk, and recovery uncertainty.

To conclude this section, we explore the sensitivity of Value-at-Risk to the number of obligors in the portfolio and the distribution of loan size across obligors. As we would expect, increasing the number of obligors reduces VaR, but the benefit of adding obligors diminishes as the portfolio becomes larger. As shown in Table 4, increasing the number of obligors from 1,000 to 5,000 reduces VaR at the 99.5th and 99.97th percentiles by 12 percent–14 percent, while increasing portfolio size from 5,000 to 10,000 obligors reduces VaR by only 1.7 percent–2.5 percent. The overall qualitative nature of the results, and in particular the comparison between the two models, remains unchanged.

Table 4: Effect of obligor count on portfolio loss distributions*

| | $N = 1000$ | | $N = 5000$ | | $N = 10,000$ | |
	CM2S	CR+	CM2S	CR+	CM2S	CR+
Mean	0.480	0.480	0.481	0.480	0.480	0.480
Std dev	0.387	0.398	0.319	0.325	0.306	0.312
Skewness	1.672	2.245	1.696	2.633	1.734	2.788
Kurtosis	7.442	11.434	8.137	14.220	8.390	15.202
0.5000	0.383	0.370	0.409	0.384	0.410	0.380
0.7500	0.653	0.619	0.624	0.567	0.615	0.552
0.9500	1.235	1.251	1.089	1.116	1.064	1.097
0.9900	1.803	1.957	1.578	1.749	1.531	1.719
0.9950	2.044	2.278	1.795	2.033	1.750	1.999
0.9997	3.093	3.626	2.714	3.225	2.653	3.169

* Average quality portfolio with SoA loan size distributions. All CreditRisk+ simulations use $\sigma = 1.5$
Source: Gordy (2000a, Table 4)

The loan size distributions derived from the SoA data are likely to be somewhat skew in comparison with real bank portfolios. For $N = 5000$, the largest loans are more than 0.65 percent of the portfolio, which is not much below supervisory concentration limits. To examine the effect of loan size distribution, we construct portfolios in which all loans within a single rating grade have the same size. Compared with the SoA-calibrated portfolios, we find that tail percentiles are reduced by less than 3 percent. If one considers the magnitude of difference between the two loan-size distributions, the difference in model outputs seems minor. These results suggest that, with real bank portfolios, neither model is especially sensitive to the distribution of loan sizes.

Large-portfolio asymptotic properties of VaR models

The simulations of the previous section demonstrate that Value-at-Risk can be sensitive to calibration of a seemingly innocuous distributional parameter. When we vary the CreditRisk+ parameter σ while holding the $w_\gamma\sigma$ constant for each grade, the mean and standard deviation of loss remain unchanged, but the tail percentile values change markedly. In this section, we use large-portfolio asymptotic analysis to shed light on this sensitivity and, more generally, on the extent to which VaR is driven by the distributional assumptions embedded in the model.

Consider a simple book-value model of default risk with a single systematic risk factor and purely idiosyncratic recovery risk. We apply the model to a homogeneous portfolio of n obligors. Each obligor has the same unconditional default probability $\bar{p}$, the same conditional probability of default $p(x)$ (which we assume is strictly increasing in x), the same expected fractional loss given default $\bar{\lambda}$, and the same exposure size. We analyze the behavior of VaR as n grows toward infinity.

Let L_n denote book-value losses as a fraction of total portfolio book value. Using arguments based on the Law of Large Numbers, it can be shown that

$$\lim_{n \to \infty} \mathrm{VaR}_q(L_n) = \mathrm{E}[L_n \mid x_q] = \bar{\lambda} p(x_q), \tag{9}$$

where x_q is the qth percentile of the distribution of X. The intuition for the result is basic to portfolio management: as the size of a portfolio grows, idiosyncratic risks are diversified away. In the limit, one is left only with systematic risk. Therefore, VaR at the q-th percentile is, in the limit, determined by the conditional default probability associated with the q-th percentile of the distribution of the systematic factor.

This result can be generalized to allow for mark-to-market definitions of loss, for systematic risk in recoveries, and for portfolios which are heterogeneous in credit rating, factor loading, expected fractional loss given default, and (with very minor restrictions) exposure sizes – see Gordy (2000b) for details. The essential intuition remains the same.

The value of equation (9) is that it permits us to study the effect of key distributional assumptions and parameters on VaR in a convenient, controlled setting. The conclusions we draw from asymptotic analyses will be qualitatively valid for reasonably large portfolios. In the upper panel of Figure 2, we provide comparisons similar to those of Table 3. We plot the tail of the distribution of loss (as a percentage of total book value) for a homogeneous portfolio of infinitely many equal-sized loans to B+ rated obligors ($\bar{p} = 0.023$). We assume default correlation of 2 percent and expected loss given default of $\bar{\lambda} = 30$ percent of face value. Recall that rating grade and default correlation are sufficient to identify only the product $w\sigma$ in CreditRisk$^+$, and not the two parameters w and σ individually, so we present results for three different values of σ. We find that asymptotic VaR for CM2S falls in between VaR values from CreditRisk$^+$ with $\sigma = 1.0$ and $\sigma = 1.5$.[23] CreditRisk$^+$ with $\sigma = 4.0$ yields much higher tail percentiles. Comparing $\sigma = 4.0$ to $\sigma = 1.0$, VaR at the 99.5th percentile is more than 40 percent larger, and VaR at the 99.97th percentile is over twice as large.

Why does the choice of σ make such a big difference? At first glance, it would seem it ought to make no difference at all, because the default correlations depend only on the products $w_i \sigma$, which we hold constant. However, the shape (and not merely the scale) of the gamma distribution for the systematic factor X is sensitive to the choice of σ. This sensitivity is demonstrated in Figure 3, which plots gamma distributions with mean one and four different values of σ. Unlike the normal distribution, which has kurtosis equal to 3 regardless of its variance, the kurtosis of a gamma-distributed variable depends on its parameters.[24] A gamma random variable with

---

[23] Over this range of the tail, the CM2S loss distribution fits most closely to CreditRisk$^+$ with $\sigma \approx 1.2$, but the two tails differ slightly in shape.

[24] The invariance of the shape of the normal distribution to its location and scale parameters is what allows us to normalize variances to one in CreditMetrics without any loss in generality. Calibration is simplified, but at the expense of imposing very strong restrictions on the shape of the distribution

Figure 2: Asymptotic loss distributions for alternative models

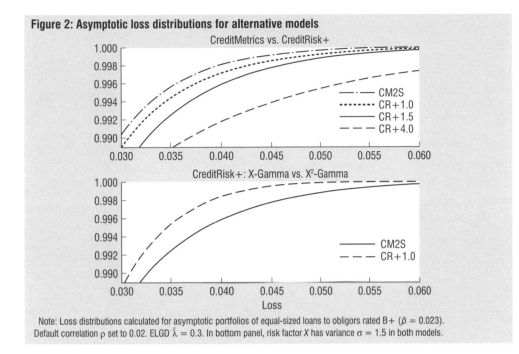

Note: Loss distributions calculated for asymptotic portfolios of equal-sized loans to obligors rated B+ ($\bar{p}$ = 0.023). Default correlation ρ set to 0.02. ELGD $\bar{\lambda}$ = 0.3. In bottom panel, risk factor X has variance σ = 1.5 in both models.

mean one and variance σ^2 has kurtosis $3(1 + 2\sigma^2)$. Using the Law of Large Numbers, one can easily show for any j that

$$\lim_{n \to \infty} \mathrm{E}\left[(L_n - \mathrm{E}[L_n])^j\right] \begin{aligned} &= \mathrm{E}[(\bar{\lambda}\, p(X) - \bar{\lambda}\bar{p})^j] \\ &= \bar{\lambda}^j \mathrm{E}[(\bar{p}(1 + w(X - 1)) - \bar{p})^j] = (\bar{\lambda}\bar{p}w)^j \mathrm{E}[(X - 1)^j]. \end{aligned} \tag{10}$$

Figure 3: Density of Credit risk$^+$ systematic factor for various σ

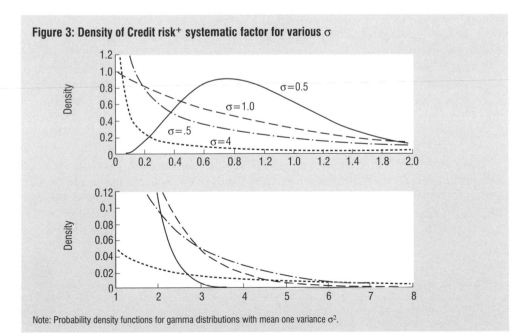

Note: Probability density functions for gamma distributions with mean one variance σ^2.

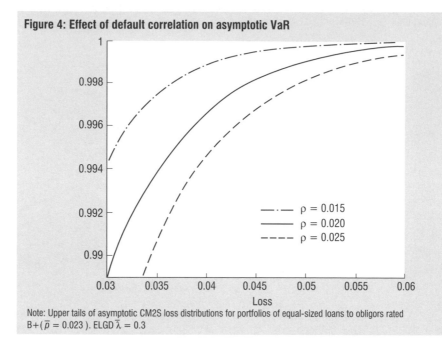

Figure 4: Effect of default correlation on asymptotic VaR

Note: Upper tails of asymptotic CM2S loss distributions for portfolios of equal-sized loans to obligors rated B+($\bar{p}$ = 0.023). ELGD $\bar{\lambda}$ = 0.3

From this result, one finds that the asymptotic kurtosis of L_n is equal to the kurtosis of X.[25] Therefore, by increasing σ and holding $w\sigma$ constant, we increase the asymptotic kurtosis of portfolio loss while leaving the asymptotic variance of portfolio loss unchanged. For percentiles q in the upper tail, higher kurtosis implies higher VaR$_q$.

As noted previously, the choice of distribution for X is motivated mainly by convenience and not by empirical observation. Asymptotic analysis is especially useful for exploring the consequences of alternative distributional assumptions, because equation (9) remains tractable as long as the cumulative distribution function for X is tractable. For example, in CreditRisk$^+$ we could assume that X^2 (rather than X) is gamma-distributed, while maintaining the assumption that X has mean one and variance σ^2. As an empirical matter, it would be difficult to distinguish this distribution from the ordinary gamma in standard CreditRisk$^+$ given only a short time series.[26] However, as shown in the bottom panel of Figure 2, the alternative distribution implies a much less fat-tailed asymptotic loss distribution. For σ = 1.5, VaR is reduced by 10 percent at the 99.5th percentile and by 24 percent at the 99.97th percentile.

Asymptotic approximation also simplifies sensitivity analysis. Practitioners may be especially concerned with the sensitivity of VaR to default correlations, which are difficult to estimate with precision given available data. For a homogeneous portfolio of B+ rated issuers, Figure 4 compares the upper tails of asymptotic CM2S loss distributions for three values of default correlation ρ. Compared with the base

[25] This result depends only on the linear form for $p(x)$. Under minor restrictions on the distribution of exposure sizes, it holds as well for portfolios which are heterogeneous in exposure size, $\bar{p}$, w and $\bar{\lambda}$.
[26] Gordy (2000a) shows how to calibrate an "exponentiated gamma" distribution to a mean and variance (Appendix D) and compares the two distributions graphically (Figure 2).

case of $\rho = 0.02$, reducing ρ to 0.015 reduces VaR by 14 percent and 17 percent at the 99.5th and 99.97th percentiles respectively. Increasing ρ to 0.025 increases VaR at these percentiles by 13 percent and 16 percent.

Conclusion

This article demonstrates that there is no unbridgeable difference in the views of portfolio credit risk embodied in CreditMetrics and CreditRisk[+]. The Merton framework of CreditMetrics can be mapped into the conditional probability framework of CreditRisk[+] without any difficulty. Indeed, both models can be viewed as special cases of a more general class of credit risk models. At a mathematical level, they differ most significantly in distributional assumptions on the systematic risk factors and in functional mappings from realizations of the risk factors to conditional default/migration probabilities for the obligors.

Simulations are constructed for a wide range of plausible loan portfolios and correlation parameters. The two models perform comparably on commercial loan portfolios of varying quality when the CreditRisk[+] volatility parameter σ is given a low value. However, higher values of σ raise VaR markedly, even though the mean and variance of the portfolio loss distribution are held constant.

Asymptotic methods are used to explore the sensitivity of VaR to distributional assumptions and parameters. We show that, for large portfolios, portfolio credit risk is simply a transformation of systematic risk. By tweaking the shape of the tail of the distribution of the systematic risk factors in the right way, one can increase or reduce VaR without altering those model outputs that one might have a reasonable hope of validating empirically. This sensitivity to unverifiable model assumptions ought to be of primary concern to practitioners. We conclude that the models are more likely to provide reliable measures for comparing the relative levels of risk in two portfolios than to establish authoritatively absolute levels of VaR for any given portfolio.

Summary

Michael B. Gordy shows how users of the current generation of credit Value-at-Risk models can open a model's "black box" and reveal its essential embedded assumptions. He shows how two influential models, CreditMetrics and CreditRisk[+], arise as special cases within a unified and generalized model framework. Placing the models within a common framework not only helps to make clear the structural parallels between them but also serves to highlight their shared limitations and helps us to design and calibrate comparative simulations on a level playing field. Using comparative simulations and large-portfolio asymptotic analysis, the article explores the sensitivity of reported VaR to distributional assumptions and to uncertainty in parameter calibration. It shows that credit VaR depends strongly on unverifiable assumptions on the properties of systematic risk.

Suggested further reading

Brand, L. and Bahar, R. (1998) "Ratings performance 1997: stability & transition," *Standard & Poor's Special Report*, August.

Carey, M. (1998) "Credit risk in private debt portfolios," *Journal of Finance*, 10:10, June, pp. 56–61.

Credit Suisse Financial Products (1997) *CreditRisk[+]: A Credit Risk Management Framework*, London: Credit Suisse Financial Products.

Finger, C.C. (1998) "Credit derivatives in CreditMetrics," *CreditMetrics Monitor*, August, pp. 13–27.

Gordy, M.B.(1999) "Calculation of higher moments in CreditRisk[+] with applications." Working paper.

Gordy, M.B. (2000a) "A comparative anatomy of credit risk models," *Journal of Banking and Finance*, 24:1, pp. 119–149.

Gordy, M.B. (2000b) "A risk-factor model foundation for ratings-based bank capital rules." Working paper.

Gupton, G.M., Finger, C.C. and Bhatia, M. (1997) *CreditMetrics – Technical Document*, New York: J.P. Morgan & Co. Incorporated, April.

Koyluoglu, H.U. and Hickman, A. (1998) "Reconcilable differences," *Risk*, 11:10, pp. 56–62.

Society of Actuaries (1996) *1986–92 Credit Risk Loss Experience Study: Private Placement Bonds* (Schaumberg, IL: Society of Actuaries).

Modeling default correlation in bond portfolios

by Mark Davis and Violet Lo

Figure 1 shows the structure of a typical collateralized bond obligation (CBO) transaction. The central box labeled SPV denotes a "special purpose vehicle," i.e., a company which is set up for this one transaction and dissolved when the transaction terminates. On the closing date of the transaction the SPV accepts principal payments from investors and purchases a portfolio of perhaps 60 high-yield bonds. All subsequent payments made to investors are derived from income received from the bond portfolio.

The investors are in two categories: noteholders (contributing perhaps 85 percent of the total principal) and equity investors. The former receive a specified coupon (= interest rate) on their investment and are repaid their principal at maturity; they are first in priority of payment. Their coupon is considerably less than the average coupon of the bond portfolio. The equity investors are paid residual receipts, with no guaranteed coupon or guarantee of principal repayment. If the SPV actually receives all coupon and principal payments due from the bond portfolio, then the noteholders will receive everything due to them and the equity investors will receive a very high return – perhaps in excess of 20 percent. If any of the collateral bonds defaults, then the equity investors will suffer a loss of return, but the noteholders are protected – up to a point – by the priority rule. (This is what justifies paying a lower coupon to them.) The equity investors are in effect making a leveraged investment in the high-yield portfolio.

Clearly, the performance of a CBO depends entirely on the default performance of the underlying high-yield portfolio. The rating agencies (S&P, Moody's et al.) give credit ratings to companies or individual debt issues, and publish comprehensive statistics of default performance in the various rating categories. Reassuringly, it is indeed true that the historically experienced default rates are a monotone function of the rating category. The yield on lower-rated bonds is higher, to compensate investors for increased default risk. The idea of a CBO is to concentrate this risk, shifting the equity investors to the high-risk end of the risk/return curve. At the

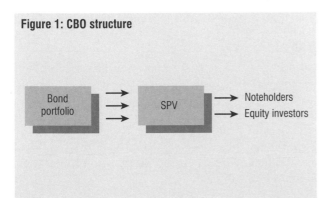

Figure 1: CBO structure

Bond portfolio → SPV → Noteholders / Equity investors

same time, the overall risk is reduced by diversification, in that the SPV invests in a medium-size portfolio of bonds rather than in just one high-yield issue.

The most difficult question to answer in analyzing CBOs is: how effective is this diversification? Obviously, this depends on "correlation." If the 60 bonds default independently, it is an easy matter to predict the default performance of the portfolio from the rating agencies' default statistics. However, there is clearly the potential for "concentration risk" – default of a whole subset of the bond portfolio might be triggered by some common event which affects all the issuers in that subset. The rating agencies deal with this question in various ways. We will describe one of them, Moody's Binomial Expansion Technique, below. This provides in many cases an effective, or at least systematic, solution to the problem. However it does not model the actual default events in the portfolio, since a smaller, "equivalent" portfolio is considered. It is also a static model in that it only concerns the amount of default in a fixed time interval, with no consideration of the times at which defaults take place.

To overcome these drawbacks we introduce two classes of probabilistic models. The first is a static model involving "default infection" – default of one bond may trigger default of other related bonds. The other model takes a somewhat similar approach, but in a continuous time stochastic process context. Here, as soon as one bond defaults we enter a "high risk" period, lasting a random length of time, in which default intensities for the other bonds are increased. The tendency therefore is for occasional periods of high credit spreads and "bursts" of default – a much more realistic model than one assuming constant credit spreads.

As will be seen, the common feature of these models is heavy-tailed default distributions. As correlation (or "infection") increases, more weight is pushed out with the tails of the distribution, increasing the risk to the supposedly secure noteholders. The main purpose of the analysis is to quantify this extra risk.

The most obvious feature of this whole area is lack of data. Default events are infrequent and data collected over many years can hardly be supposed to be a sample from a stationary process. Thus reliable statistical estimates of distributional parameters are practically impossible to obtain, particularly the key correlation estimates. In these circumstances there is no point in introducing complicated models with lots of additional parameters. Our philosophy is to introduce the simplest models with the smallest number of extra parameters (never more than one or two) that will capture "concentration risk" in a credible way. Even if statistical estimates are hard to come by, plausible ranges of the parameters can be arrived at on intuitive grounds. Analysis using plausible values gives bounds on asset values and is certainly better than ignoring concentration risk altogether.

Moody's diversity scores and BET

Consider a collateral portfolio consisting of, say, $n = 60$ bonds. Assume for simplicity that the bond issuers all have the same credit rating and that the notional amounts of the bonds are equal. Moody's and other rating agencies have assembled statistics of defaults in the various rating classes over the past 20 years from which we can infer a distribution function for the default time. We can thus estimate the default probability p for any of the bonds in the portfolio over a given period, say ten years. If we assume that all the bonds are independent, then the distribution function for the number K defaulting is the binomial distribution

$$P[K = k] = C_k^n \, p^k \, (1-p)^{n-k}, \qquad\qquad (1.1)$$

where C_k^n is the binomial coefficient, $C_k^n = n!/(k!(n-k)!)$. The expected number of defaults and the variance are np, $np(1-p)$ respectively.

Moody's Binomial Expansion Technique (BET) – see Moody's Investment Services (1997) – is based on the idea that issuers in the same industry sector are related, while issuers in different industry sectors can be treated as independent.[1] Moody's defines 32 industry sectors and the diversity score table shown in Table 1.

Table 1: Moody's diversity scores

Number of firms in the same industry	Diversity score
1	1.0
2	1.5
3	2.0
4	2.3
5	2.6
6	3.0
7	3.2
8	3.5
9	3.7
10	4.0
10 or more	Evaluated case by case

For example, suppose our portfolio of 60 bonds is distributed as in Table 2.

Table 2: Portfolio distribution

No of issuers in sector	1	2	3	4	5
No of incidences	2	7	6	4	2
Diversity	2	10.5	18	9.2	5.2

Thus there are two cases in which issuers are the only representatives of their industry sector, seven cases in which pairs of issuers are in the same sector, etc. The diversities, taken from Table 1, are given in the third row; the total diversity score is 45.

In Moody's Binomial Expansion Technique we consider the original portfolio of 60 bonds to be equivalent to a portfolio of 45 *independent* bonds with the same default probability but with notional value 60/45 times the original notional. Thus the expected loss, expressed in dollar terms, is the same ($= 60p$). The distribution of the number defaulting in the equivalent portfolio is

$$P[k \text{ defaults}] = C_k^d \, p^k \, (1-p)^{d-k}$$

where d is the diversity score. The main purpose of the BET is to evaluate the losses suffered by the noteholders. Because of the payment priority rule, the noteholders experience no losses up to some level of default, and progressively increasing losses after that. To give a simple evaluation, we calculate the expected loss for an option-

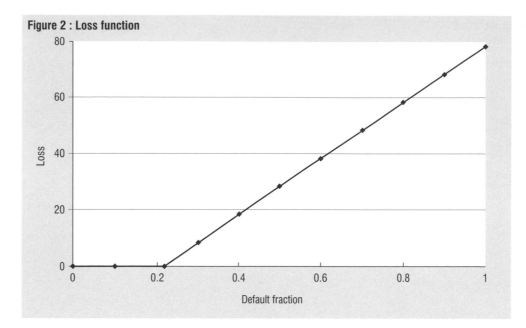

Figure 2 : Loss function

like loss function $L(x) = 100 \max(x - K,0)$ as shown in Figure 2,[2] where x denotes the fraction of the portfolio notional that defaults.

For the original portfolio with diversity score 60 and individual default probability 0.1, the expected number of defaults is $m = 6$ and the standard deviation is $r = 2.32$. To close approximation therefore, $m + 3\sigma = 13$ and we take the threshold level K as $13/60 = 0.217$. We now plot, in Figure 3, the expected loss and the loss probability[3] as a function of diversity score.

As we can see, both expected loss and loss probability increase as the diversity is reduced, even though the *expected* proportion of default is constant. For our specimen portfolio with diversity 45, the loss probability is 1.2 percent, more than double the loss probability for diversity 60 (0.57 percent).

Infectious defaults

This idea was introduced in Davis and Lo (1999). Rather than replacing the original portfolio by a smaller "equivalent" portfolio we wanted to give a probabilistic model for interaction effects in the original portfolio. To describe this, let n be the portfolio size and Z_i be random variables such that $Z_i = 1$ if bond i defaults and $Z_i = 0$ otherwise. The number defaulting is thus $N = Z_1 + Z_2 + \dots + Z_n$. The value of Z_i is determined as follows. For $i = 1, \dots, n$ and $j = 1, \dots, n$ with $j \neq i$ let X_i, Y_{ij} be independent Bernoulli random variables with $P[X_i = 1] = p$, $P[Y_{ij} = 1] = q$. The constant q is the infection parameter. Then

$$Z_i = X_i + (1 - X_i)\left(\left(1 - \prod_{j \neq 1} (1 - X_j\,Y_{ji})\right)\right). \tag{2.1}$$

The idea here is that bond i may default "directly" ($X_i = 1$) or may be "infected" by default of bond j. Indeed, the second term in (2.1) is equal to 1 when $X_i = 0$ and for

---

[2] The scaling factor 100 is for graphical convenience. The units are arbitrary.
[3] i.e., the probability that losses exceed 0.217.

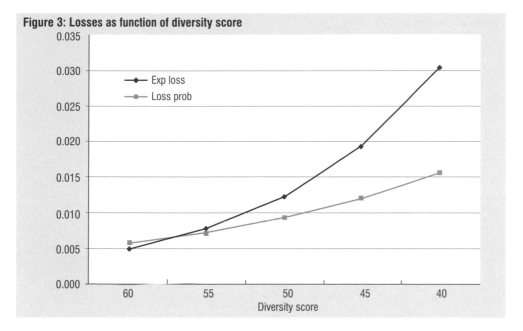

Figure 3: Losses as function of diversity score

some j both X_j and Y_{ji} are equal to 1. It is shown in Davis and Lo (1999) that the distribution of N is

$$P[N = k] = c_k^n \, \alpha_{nk}^{pq} \qquad (2.2)$$

where

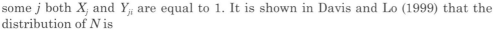

$$\alpha_{nk}^{pq} = p^k \, (1-p)^{n-k}(1-q)^{k(n-k)} + \sum_{i=1}^{k-1} c_i^k \, p^i \, (1-p)^{n-i}(1-(1-q)^i)^{k-1} \, (1-q)^{i(n-k)}.$$

The expected value is

$$EN = n \, (1 - (1-p)(1-pq)^{n-1}). \qquad (2.3)$$

When $q = 0$, (2.2) and (2.3) reduce to the binomial distribution with parameter p. When q > 0, EN is increased because we have provided more ways in which each bond can default. However, we want to consider, as in the diversity score analysis, a situation in which the probability of default for each individual bond is fixed at p. To achieve this, we need to *rescale p*, i.e., find the number $\hat{p}(q)$ such that $(1 - \hat{p}(q))$ $(1 - \hat{p}(q)q)^{n-1} = 1 - p$. We have $\hat{p}(0) = p$ and $\hat{p}(q) < p$ for q > 0. Then $EN = np$ when the infection model parameters are $\hat{p}(q)$, q, but the *variance* is increased, as we shall see below.

The next step is to bring in the industry sector distribution. As in the diversity score analysis, we assume that bonds in m different industry sectors default independently. Within each industry sector i we assume that an infection model holds with parameters $(p_i = \hat{p}(q_i), q_i)$. The parameters required are p, the marginal default probability, and q_i, the infection parameter for sector i. Generally it is reasonable to take $q_i = q$ for some fixed q, reducing the model parameters to two (p, q).

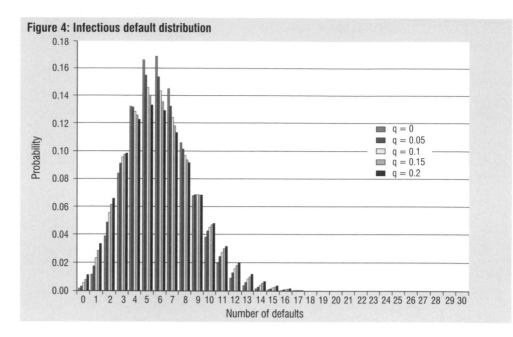

Figure 4: Infectious default distribution

The probability of k_i defaults in sector i, $i = 1, \ldots, m$ is

$$\prod_{i=1}^{m} F(k_i, n_i, p_i, q_i)$$

where n_i is the number of bonds in sector i and $F(k, n, p, q)$ is the distribution function (2.2). The probability that the total number of defaults is k is therefore

$$\sum_{\alpha \in A_k^m} \prod_{i=1}^{m} = F(k_i, n_i, p_i, q_i) \tag{2.4}$$

where m is the number of industry sectors and A_k^m is the set of arrangements $a = \{k_1, \ldots, k_m\}$ of k defaults in the m industry sectors.

Calculating (2.4) is not completely straightforward, even for moderate n, since the number of elements in A_k^m can be extremely large. Effective computational methods based on an idea we call "superboxes" have been developed and are described in Davis and Lo (1999). Figure 4 shows the default distributions for values of the infection parameter q ranging from 0 to 0.4, for the 60-bond portfolio with industry distribution as in Table 2. The individual default probability is $p = 0.1$, so all distributions have mean 6. The case $q = 0$ is the binomial (60, p) distribution. As can be seen, the infection process increases the variance, pushing more weight out into the tails of the distribution. Figure 5 shows the expected loss probability using the same parameters as above (i.e., the threshold K is 13/60 corresponding to default of 13 bonds). Comparing Figures 3 and 5 we see that infection has a very similar qualitative effect to reduction in diversity. In terms of expected loss, a diversity score of 45 corresponds to an infection parameter $q = 0.08$ for this portfolio.

Figure 5: Infectious default loss

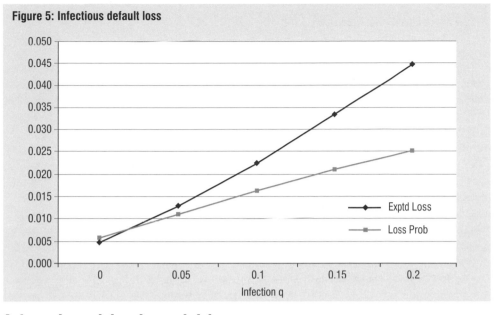

A dynamic model: enhanced risk

The infectious defaults model gives a convenient family of distributions for analyzing defaults in a given time interval. However, this is not the whole story. If we wish to simulate the performance of a CBO structure, for example, the question of *when* defaults occur is as important as *how many* occur. To model this we need a stochastic process model that produces sequences of random default times according to some prescribed mechanism.

Let us start with the simplest case, in which there are n independent bonds, each having a default time that is exponentially distributed with parameter λ. The probability of default for any one bond in a time interval T is then $p = 1 - e^{-\lambda T}$ and the distribution of the number defaulting is binomial (n, p). This is the case analyzed in the previous sections with diversity equal to n or infection parameter $q = 0$. Let N_t denote the number of defaults in the interval $[0, t]$. It is easy to see that the process

$$M_t = N_t - \int_0^t \lambda (n - N_s)\, ds \tag{3.1}$$

is a martingale: we have

$$P[\text{default in } [t, t + dt] \mid N_t] = E\,[dN_t \mid N_t] = \lambda\,(n - N_t)\,dt \tag{3.2}$$

i.e., the default or "hazard" rate is proportional to the number of bonds still "alive." Denoting $m(t) = EN_t$ we see by taking expectations in (3.1) that

$$m(t) = n\lambda t - \int_0^t \lambda m(s)\, ds$$

which is easily solved to give

$$m(t) = n(1 - e^{-\lambda t}),$$

in agreement with the binomial distribution.

The martingale method gives us a convenient simulation methodology: rather than simulating default times for each of the n bonds we can just generate successive jump times of N_t. Denoting these T_1, T_2, ... we know from (3.1) or (3.2) that $T_{i+1} - T_i$ is exponentially distributed with parameter $\lambda(n - i)$. Usually there will only be a few T_is in the interval $[0,T]$ of interest. This kind of approach has been emphasized by Duffie and Singleton (1998).

To introduce some interaction effects into this model we would like to capture the idea that incidence of a default puts everybody else "at risk," at least for a while. This accords with evidence (from, say, the Russian default of 1998) that when a default takes place, credit spreads for other issuers are increased, settling back to "normal" levels after some time. In mathematical terms the assumptions are as follows. Initially each bond has hazard rate λ, so the total hazard rate is $n\lambda$. When a default happens, the hazard rate for *all remaining bonds* is increased by a factor $a > 1$, so the total hazard rate is $a(n - 1)\lambda$. The multiplying factor continues to be a for an exponentially distributed time with parameter μ, after which it reverts to 1 until the next default happens. Thus "normal" periods alternate with "enhanced risk" periods triggered by an actual default.

The process just described is a piecewise-deterministic Markov process (PDP) in the terminology of Davis (1993). The state space is the $2(n + 1)$-point set $E = \{(i, j): i = 0,1; j = 0,1, ... ,n\}$ and x_t is the value of the process at time t. Index $i = 0,1$ corresponds to normal and enhanced risk respectively, while j is the number of bonds still alive. Thus the starting point is $(0, n)$. The generator A for this process, acting on a test function $f: E \to R$, is

$$
\begin{aligned}
Af(0, j) &= j\lambda(f(1, j - 1) - f(0, j)), j > 0 \\
Af(0, 0) &= 0 \\
Af(1, j) &= aj\lambda f(1, j - 1) + \mu f(0, j) - (aj\lambda + \mu)f(1, j), j > 0 \\
Af(1, 0) &= \mu(f(0, 0) - f(1, 0)).
\end{aligned}
$$

In state $(0, j)$ the hazard rate is $j\lambda$ and the process moves to $(1, j - 1)$ (one extra default, enhanced hazard). In state $(1, j)$ the hazard rate is $h = aj\lambda + \mu$ and the process moves either to $(1, j - 1)$, with probability $aj\lambda/h$, corresponding to another default, or to $(0, j)$, with probability μ/h, corresponding to the end of an enhanced risk period.

We can compute the distribution of the number of defaults in a fixed time $[0,T]$ by solving the backward equation

$$\frac{\partial}{\partial t} v(t, x) + Av(t, x) = 0, (t, x) \in [0, T] \times E \tag{3.3}$$

$$v(T, x) = l(x), x \in E. \tag{3.4}$$

As shown in Davis (1993), the solution $v(t,x)$ is in probabilistic terms

$$v(t, x) = E_{t,x} l(x_T).$$

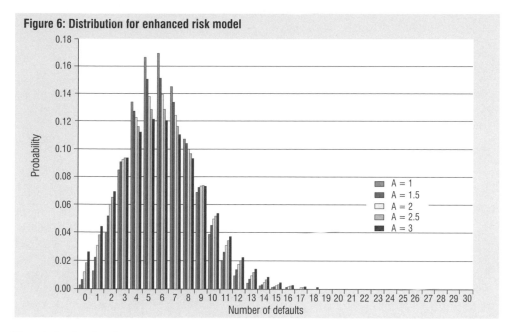

Figure 6: Distribution for enhanced risk model

If we take $l = l_k$ where

$$l_k(0, n - k) = l_k(1, n - k) = 1$$
$$l_k(i, j) = 0, j \neq n - k$$

and denote by v_k the corresponding solution of (3.3), (3.4) then clearly $v_k(0, (0, n))$ is the probability of just k defaults in $[0, T]$ starting with a portfolio of size n. Since E is a finite set, (3.3), (3.4) is just a linear ordinary differential equation of dimension $2(n + 1)$. It can be solved by computing the matrix exponential or by direct application of Runga-Kutta integration.

As in the infection model, the expected number of defaults increases as we increase the "enhancement factor" a. To get the correct comparison we must rescale λ so that the individual default probabilities are equal to some prescribed value. Here we take, as before, a portfolio of 60 bonds and a T = ten-year time horizon. If $a = 1$, the individual default probability is $p = 1 - e^{-\lambda T}$. For comparison with previous results we take $p = 0.1$ which implies $\lambda = 0.0105$. The distribution is then binomial (n, p) as noted earlier. For $a > 1$ we choose $\lambda = \lambda_a$ such that the mean is equal to np and calculate the distribution as described above. As regards μ, we somewhat arbitrarily take $\mu = 0.5$ corresponding to an average two-year period before "normal" conditions resume. Figure 6 shows the distribution functions for a ranging from 1 to 3. As we can see, the results are qualitatively very similar to the infection model, with weight being pushed out into the tail as a increases. The expected losses and loss probabilities, analogous to those computed earlier, are shown in Figure 7.

In terms of expected loss, $a = 2$ is roughly equivalent to $q = 0.1$ in the infection model.

Of course, other similar models are easily envisaged. For example, we could apply the enhanced risk model within industry sectors, assuming that the industry sectors are independent. It depends on the application; the model we have given concentrates on the systematic risk affecting all issuers.

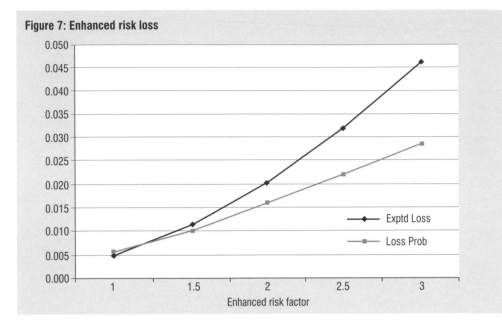

Figure 7: Enhanced risk loss

Parameter estimation and applications

Estimation is plagued by lack of data. However, both the infection and enhanced risk models (leaving aside μ, the value of which does not seem critical) have only two parameters and hence are fully determined once two statistics of the distribution – for example, the mean and variance – are given. Our suggestion is to use Moody's default statistics to estimate the variance of the number of defaults over the desired time horizon. This information, together with Moody's own empirical distributions, then fixes the model parameters.

For a CBO structure, there are two questions of interest that can be addressed using our models: the credit rating of the notes (or senior tranches for a multi-tranche CBO) and the expected returns and return volatility of the equity tranche. For the former, infectious defaults provides an alternative to the diversity score analysis that is in some ways attractive. For the latter, a dynamic model is essential, and the enhanced risk model combines realistic patterns of default with ease of simulation.

Conclusion

Any analysis of financial products involving portfolios of bonds or other debt must address the issue of concentration risk. As indicated in this chapter this is in many cases both the crucial risk factor and the hardest to quantify. Concentration risk may arise from general economic factors affecting wide categories of issuers or from interaction effects between issuers active in, or exposed to, the same industry sectors.

Moody's Diversity Score and Binomial Expansion Technique (BET) deal with the latter interactions in a convincing way. They have however some shortcomings: they cannot predict actual numbers of defaults since the analysis concerns a hypothetical "equivalent portfolio", and as a static model they cannot be used to predict default timing. To handle these two problems we introduced the infectious defaults and enhanced risk models respectively. These are probabilistic models based on a simple description of the interaction effects, specified by an absolute minimum of extra parameters. They are easily calibrated against diversity scores, and direct parameter estimation may be possible by looking at the variability of default, as well as averages, in the various rating categories. Finally, these models offer flexibility in that they are easily extended to cover a repertoire of different kinds of interaction that the analyst may wish to include.

Summary

The performance of a CBO structure is critically dependent on the correlation of defaults in a medium-sized portfolio of bonds. Two classes of purely probabilistic models to handle these interaction effects are introduced. In the first, it is supposed that default of an issuer in a particular industry sector may trigger defaults of other issuers in the same sector by an "infection" mechanism. As infection increases default distribution has increased variance and heavier tails, quantifying the concentration risk. The second model is a continuous-time stochastic process called an enhanced-risk model, that exhibits very similar features. In this case the incremental default probability is increased for all other issuers for a certain random period following occurrence of a default. **Mark Davis** and **Violet Lo** conclude with some comments on parameter estimation and applications of these models in CBO analysis.

Suggested further reading

Davis, M. and Lo, V. (1999) "Infectious defaults," *CreditMetrics Monitor*, RiskMetrics Group.

Davis, M.H.A. (1993) *Markov Models and Optimization*, Chapman and Hall, London.

Duffie, D. and Singleton, K. (1998) *Simulating Correlated Defaults*, working paper, Graduate School of Business, Stanford University.

Moody's Investment Services (1997) *The Binomial Expansion Technique*.

Pricing the risks of default

by Dilip B. Madan

Default may generally be defined as the failure of a counterparty to deliver in full the agreed-upon quid pro quo as per contract. Examples cover a range of activities such as the failure of timely loan repayments, airline bankruptcies and their related inability to honor their ticket sales, or babysitters not showing up. Primarily the stronger party collects quid pro quo first and the weaker waits, so we buy the airline ticket or deliver labor on jobs and then wait for the ride or wages as the case may be. Sometimes this may be reversed, as when banks provide individuals with housing loans and then wait for their repayments over 30 years. The timing of the default is in many cases after the delivery of the quid pro quo, but it can be before, as when the babysitter doesn't show. The cost of the default, on the counterparty, goes beyond the loss of the quid pro quo and includes an assessment of the inconvenience of the absence of delivery that was being relied upon – otherwise the babysitter not showing up is no default as then he is not paid for services he did not render.

Associated with each default is the *default time* that we take to be the time at which it is announced that the quid pro quo will not be paid in full. But as there is in general some partial payment, we also have to assess the risk of the default magnitude. This magnitude can be difficult to assess as it amounts to ascertaining what it may cost the counterparty to restore the status quo of the contract in either dollar or utility terms. For example, one may get babysitting services at short notice for a relatively high rate and the cost of the default is this higher value and not the value of the original fee. In other situations it is impossible to restore the status quo, as for example when you promise to deliver an original painting by Renoir and find it destroyed in transport, or an e-commerce site delivers a three-year-old their Christmas present two weeks late. We then have to resort to mechanisms for compensating monetarily for a wide array of intangible welfare losses.

Our focus here will be restricted to financial contracts where all deliveries and payments are sums of money, albeit at different times and under different contingencies. The *default magnitude* is then the shortfall in the payment delivered relative to the promised contractual payments. Financial claims can be quite complicated even though they deal only with money transfers as they may involve multiple transfers among many parties under a variety of contingencies. One only has to consider the myriad life insurance and retirement plans to appreciate the level of the underlying complexity. To this we may add convertible bonds that are callable and putable as well as swaps and options to swap, or swaptions.

The success of modern finance in dealing with this maze of securities and associated eventualities lies in the reduction of these complicated claim structures to a portfolio of simpler claims. The simpler claims may be described as unit face state contingent bonds that pay off a dollar when a particular eventuality is realized. We will concentrate our efforts on assessing these simpler securities, commenting on how they are employed in practice to manage the structure of the more complex claims of interest. The events of interest to us here are the default time and its magnitude.

Much of the literature and the models we will survey are concerned with pricing these simpler securities. After a general discussion of the properties of these securities, we will consider the various models that have been proposed to price them. We will then look at option-theoretic models that have as their cornerstone the property of defining the precise default event, what are now called hazard rate models that focus their attention directly on event probabilities and their sufficient statistics, leaving the precise event undefined, covering the models of Merton (1974), Longstaff-Schwartz (1995), and an application of the model by Madan, Carr and Chang (1998). We then survey the models by Duffie and Singleton (1999), Madan and Unal 1 (1998), Jarrow, Lando and Turnbull (1997), and Madan and Unal 2 (2000).

State contingent zero coupon bonds

For each name that is an individual or a legal entity empowered to write financial contracts in our economies with similar counterparties we are interested in the following events. The first is that name A defaults on obligations at some future time T, and the second is that there is partial recovery in default to the extent of y, i.e., $(1 - y)$ times the promised obligation is lost in default at T.

Events by themselves are not very interesting when they are possibilities, as they may happen or not, and we may describe the outcomes but there is little more to be said. We may live or die: so what is the issue? What concerns us now about these future events is their probability conditional on current information. We denote by $\pi(t, A, T)$ the probability at time t that name A defaults on a dollar obligation at time T. This function assesses for us the real timing risk of default.

Furthermore, as there may be partial recovery in default, we are also interested in $f(y; t, A, T)$, the conditional probability that the recovery level is y in this time T default. The default magnitude is assessed by this conditional probability distribution.

Two securities may be associated with these two events. These are zero coupon state contingent bonds, one of which pays out a dollar if the event of default occurs while the other pays out a dollar only if the default occurs and the recovery level is y. Just as the events have probabilities that we may determine today, the securities have prices that we may determine today. We denote by $p(t, A, T)$ the price at time t of the security paying a dollar if name A defaults at time T. We also have the prices of the securities paying a dollar if there is default at T and the recovery level is y that we denote by $h(y; t, A, T)$,. It is clear that

$$p(t, A, T) = \int_0^1 h(y; t, A, T)\, dy \tag{1}$$

and hence the counterpart in the world of prices to the conditional probability distribution $f(y; t.A.T)$ is

$$g(y; t, A, T) = \frac{h(y; t, A, T)}{p(t, A, T)} \tag{2}$$

which is the number of default timing bonds one must sell to finance the purchase of bonds at recovery level y. After all, one may finance all the recovery level bonds for all recovery levels by one timing bond. The timing bond is the appropriate numeraire asset for the recovery level bonds.

We have associated the conditional probabilities and current market prices with our events of default timing and magnitude. A natural question is the relation between these numbers. Should not the market price for a state contingent zero coupon bond just reflect its probability? More precisely, will the ratio of market prices equal the ratio of probabilities. It is one of the founding principles of modern finance to observe that the answer to this question is no. The difference is termed a risk premium. The rationale for this terminology may be explained briefly.

Consider holding the zero coupon state contingent bond, contingent on some event X for which the outcome will be known in a year. There are two payouts, one if the event happens and zero otherwise, and hence the expected cash flow is just the probability of the event or $P(X)$. Consider now the two claims that pay a dollar if X occurs, while the other pays a dollar if X does not occur. The sum of their prices must be the value of a bond or say $1/(1 + r)$ where r is the annual compounding spot interest rate for a one-year term. The prices are also non-negative and when multiplied by $(1 + r)$ they sum to unity and behave like probabilities. These are called risk-neutral probabilities and for the event X occurring are denoted by $Q(X)$. The price, say $V(X)$, of the claim paying a dollar if X occurs is then

$$V(X) = \frac{Q(X)}{1 + r} \qquad (3)$$

The gross rate of return on the claim, $1 + R(X)$, is the ratio of the expected cash flow to the price and is

$$1 + R(X) = \frac{P(X)}{Q(X)}(1 + r) \qquad (4)$$

whereby the excess return or risk premium is precisely the ratio of probability to risk-neutral probability $P(X)/Q(X)$.

Price and probability ratios are equal when events have no risk premia. Events for which probability exceeds risk-neutral probability have a positive risk premium and vice versa for events with the higher risk-neutral probability. If events have a positive risk premium, their complements have a negative risk premium. It is useful to consider some examples. Consider the term security that pays out in case of death, such as life insurance. The probability of death is low relative to its price and the security has a negative risk premium, which is why it makes sense to short this security and sell life insurance. The complementary security that pays out on living has a positive risk premium with a high probability of living and a low price for the claim that pays out in this event. Hence we wish to be long this security and this explains the absence of markets selling claims that pay out on living as opposed to death. In fact, insurance companies are long life as they collect monies during life and short death by paying out in this eventuality. Individuals go long on the death security and short the life security with a view to extending the consequences of life in death.

With the aim of appreciating these differences in the context of default, Table 1 contrasts probabilities, prices and implied risk premia in basis points on the event of no default for n years by firms in the rating categories AAA and B. The probabilities are obtained from a study of S&P default rates reported by Lucas (1995). The prices are inferred from rates of return earned on managing portfolios of bonds by rating category as reported in Altman (1989).

Table 1: Probability, prices and risk premia for no default on bonds by rating and maturity in basis points

Rating	Item	Maturity				
		1	3	5	8	10
AAA	Probability	1	1	1	0.9922	0.9861
AAA	Price	0.9955	0.9835	0.9656	0.9228	0.8755
AAA	Risk premia	45	168	356	752	1263
B	Probability	0.9430	0.8306	0.7680	0.7165	0.6802
B	Price	0.9618	0.8540	0.7840	0.5942	0.5533
B	Risk premia	−195	−274	−204	2058	2294

We observe that no default in n years by AAA is an event like life, one with a relatively high probability compared with its price. There is therefore a market in shorting the security that pays out on such defaults, as then we access a high-price and low-probability event. For the rating category B and a short maturity, say three years, the situation is reversed and we have a high price and low probability for the event of no default as opposed to default. Hence we might consider selling a security that pays out unit face if a B-rated firm does not default in a short time span. For the longer maturity the risk premium is positive on no default. In general, the risk premium rises with maturity and downgrading.

Understanding the rationale for the risk premia on various securities is an important exercise of modern finance theory. In many situations the cost of default is in excess of the dollars lost and hence the premium on price over probability. The welfare or replacement cost of a babysitter not showing up is often in excess of the dollars involved in the price of the service and sellers can charge a premium price for the service if it is coupled with reliability of delivery. Markets pay more than probability for events that are of particular concern to them. In the context of Table 1, we note that the market is not too concerned in the default of a B-rated firm in three years, but the failure of an AAA is a matter of concern.

The activity of managing portfolios of cash flow promises by a multitude of names requires us to understand the determinants of the probabilities $\pi(t, A, T)$, $f(y; t, A, T)$ and prices $p(t, A, T)$, $g(y; t, A, T)$ of events associated with default. For the purposes of trading it is the price that is the primary focus of attention, but if the portfolio is to be held to maturity, forecasting the cash flow experience requires an understanding of the probabilities. We anticipate that models for these prices and probabilities would include as explanatory variables the dynamic structure of the asset backing for the firm, the term structure of interest rates in the market, the priority structure of the debt, its rating, and other firm-specific and macroeconomic variables that impact on the fortunes of the names in question. Our focus here will be primarily on pricing models as they have developed in the finance literature.

An important consideration in this regard is the use to which the model is to be put. If one is marking to market the default risk exposure, a particular model and its set of explanatory variables may be adequate; however, if one wishes to hedge the exposure as well, it is important to include among the explanatory variables the prices of traded securities in which one may take risk management positions. Alternatively, one needs to relate the prices of other traded securities to the set of explanatory variables in the model.

Option theoretic models

This class of models defines default as a contingent claim by describing precisely when default occurs and then prices the default security using the methods of derivative security pricing. We will consider three models in this class: the model by Merton (1974), an application of the model of Madan, Carr and Chang (1998), and the Longstaff-Schwartz (1995) model. Models in this class are differentiated by the way in which the default event is defined and particular definitions may well be better suited to describing particular defaults. All these models relate default to the process for the firm's asset backing and define the default event in terms of boundary conditions on this process. A major deficiency of these models noted in Madan and Unal (1998) is that they treat the value of asset backing as a primary asset of the economy when in fact it may be a derivative asset in its own right with exposure to other more primitive state variables of the economy. Prices should be reduced to exogenous state variables of the economy and it is unclear that a firm's asset value is such a variable.

The Merton model

Default in this model occurs only at maturity if at all. Hence the timing of default is a particularly simple random variable that is either T or ∞, where T is the maturity of the debt. Default occurs at T if at this time the firm value is below the face value of the debt at issue and the default magnitude is the extent of the shortfall. It is supposed that the initial firm value V evolves under risk-neutral probabilities as a geometric Brownian motion with a drift equal to a constant interest rate of r per unit time and a constant volatility of σ per unit time. Firm value at time T, $V(T)$ then has a ln normal distribution with $ln\,(V(T))$ normally distributed with a mean of $(r - \sigma^2/2)\,T$ and a variance of $\sigma^2 T$. The payoff to the defaultable bond is that of a treasury risk-free bond less the value of a put option with a strike F equal to the face value of the debt. Defining leverage by $d = Fe^{-rT}/V$ one may write the credit spread, cs, for the price of the defaultable debt over the constant interest rate r as

$$cs(d, \sigma, T) \;=\; -\frac{1}{T}\,ln\left(N(h_2) + \frac{1}{d}\,N(h_1)\right)$$

$$h_1 \;=\; \frac{ln(d)}{\sigma\sqrt{T}} - \frac{\sigma\sqrt{T}}{2}$$

$$h_2 \;=\; -\frac{ln(d)}{\sigma\sqrt{T}} - \frac{\sigma\sqrt{T}}{2}$$

$$N(x) \;=\; \int_{-\infty}^{x} \frac{1}{\sqrt{2\pi}}\,\exp\,(-u^2/2)du$$

We may verify that credit spreads rise with leverage, and rise with maturity for low values of leverage. For values of leverage below unity, credit spreads are hump shaped with respect to maturity, rising at first and then falling. For leverage levels above unity, credit spreads fall with maturity. Increases in volatility raise the value of the short put option and thereby raise credit spreads.

A feature of the model that is countered in data is that short maturity credit spreads are near zero in the model. This is a consequence of the fact that a continuous process requires some passage of time before it may enter the defined region of default. Other deficiencies include inconsistencies in the treatment of debt with multiple maturities as in the model they default at different times, each at its own maturity, while in reality they default all together. Finally, the assumption of constant interest rates and a flat yield curve are contrary to realistic term structures of interest rates. Since defaultable bonds are bonds, they must have an embedded exposure to interest rates that is here modeled unrealistically in terms of movements in a flat yield curve.

Risk premia in the Merton model are also unrealistically large. For a two-year debt on a 20 percent volatility with leverage (F/V) at $\frac{2}{3}$ in a 5 percent interest rate market and an equity risk premium of 10 percent, the statistical probability of default is given by $N(h_2)$ on replacing the interest rate in the expression for h_2 by the mean rate of return. For the data cited this is .009, while the corresponding risk-neutral probability is .0476, or a risk premium on the no default security of $(1 - .009)/(1 - .0476) - 1 = 405$ basis points. Realistic values would be below 100 basis points.

The Madan, Carr and Chang model

The deficiencies of the Black-Scholes-Merton model as an option pricing model are well known to participants in equity derivative markets. The *ln* normal distribution at any maturity fails to calibrate to the market skew and kurtosis, where the former is significantly negative in fact and zero for the *ln* normal and the latter is significantly above the *ln* normal value of 3. An option pricing model that calibrates well to risk-neutral distributions at each maturity was proposed by Madan, Carr and Chang (1998). This model has two extra parameters over the asset volatility and calibrates to the market skew and kurtosis. The model is called the variance gamma model in which the logarithm of the stock price is a Brownian motion with drift θ and volatility σ evaluated at an independent random time given by an increasing process with independent increments that have a gamma distribution of mean 1 and variance υ for the increment over unit time. The parameter θ allows for control over skewness while υ calibrates the kurtosis. The resulting process is purely discontinuous and the jumps in value can take asset value into the default region immediately with positive probability. This solves the problem with short maturity credit spreads witnessed in the Merton model.

For leverage defined as in the Merton model, the variance gamma credit spread, $csvg$, may be written as

$$csvg\,(d,\,\sigma,\,\upsilon,\,\theta,\,T) \;=\; -\frac{1}{T}\,ln\left(1 - \frac{1}{d}\,vgp(1,\,d,\,0,\,0,\,\sigma,\,\upsilon,\,\theta,\,T,\,0)\right)$$

$$vgp\,(p,\,k,\,r,\,q,\,\sigma,\,\upsilon,\,\theta,\,t,\,u)\;=\;VG\text{ option pricing function}$$

The VG option pricing function has arguments of the spot price, p, the strike price, k, the interest rate, r, the dividend yield, q, the process parameters, σ, υ, θ, the maturity, T, and a flag u that is 1 for calls and 0 for puts. Matlab code for this function is available upon request.

We present a graph of VG credit spreads against maturity for leverage .75 and process parameters of $\sigma = .25$, $\upsilon = .15$, and $\theta = -.33$. The short maturity credit spread is seen to be substantial in contrast with what would be found in the Merton model. The humped shape for this leverage level is consistent with the Merton model.

The Longstaff and Schwartz model

This model attempts to address a number of shortcomings of the Merton model. By allowing for early default time, consistency is attained in pricing multiple maturities. Default is defined as occurring at the first time that asset values reach a threshold level K and at this time all maturities still outstanding default simultaneously. The possibility of early default may also induce higher credit spreads and eliminate the problem of no short maturity credit spreads. Furthermore, by allowing for stochastic interest rates one may better calibrate to existing term structures of interest rates. The model supposes that asset values, $V(t)$, follow a geometric Brownian motion while interest rates, $r(t)$, follow a Vasicek (1977) process with movements that are correlated with the stock. Specifically it is supposed that

$$dV = rVdt + \sigma V dW_V(t)$$

$$dr = \kappa(\theta - r)\,dt + \eta dW_r(t)$$

$$dW_V dW_r = \rho dt$$

At the first passage time of V to K, the default threshold, we have a default in which the recovery level is some constant write-down of the face and creditors receive $(1 - w)F$.

In pricing the defaultable claim one may account for correlation between interest rates and asset values by following Jamshidian (1989), and Geman, El Karoui and Rochet (1995), and expressing the dynamic evolution of asset values and interest rates using the price of the risk-free bond, $p(t, T)$, as the numeraire. Hence we let Q^T be the probability under which asset prices discounted by the price of the risk-free bond price, $p(t, T)$, are martingales. The price of the defaultable bond, $v(t, T)$, may then be written as

$$v(t, T) = p(t, T)\,[G(t, T) + (1 - w)\,F(1 - G(t, T)] \tag{5}$$

where $G(t, T)$ is the probability of no default in the interval (t, T) and in this case we receive the unit face, while under default, with probability $(1 - G(t, T))$, we receive $(1 - w)F$ at time T by definition. The claim is priced on determining the probability of no default $G(t, T)$ under the measure Q^T.

The explicit dynamics for asset values and interest rates under Q^T may be determined by an application of Girsanov's theorem as

$$d\ln V = (r - \sigma^2/2 - \rho\sigma\eta\,M(T - t))dt + \sigma\,d\tilde{W}_V,$$

$$dr = (\theta - \kappa r - \eta^2 M(T - t))dt + \eta d\tilde{W}_r,$$

$$M(t) = \frac{1 - \exp(-\kappa(T - t))}{\kappa}$$

where $\tilde{W}_V$, $\tilde{W}_r$ are Brownian motions under Q^T.

To determine G, Longstaff and Schwartz present and solve an integral equation that equates the Gaussian probability of $\ln(V/K)$ being negative at T to the integral over first passage times to zero of the first passage probability to zero times the Gaussian probability of then ending up below zero, starting now at zero at the first passage time. It is now recognized that this integral equation is incorrect as one must also integrate over the level of the random interest rate at the first passage time of $ln(V/K)$ to zero. It is simple to show using characteristic functions, for example, that with two independent Brownian motions the distribution of the first Brownian motion at the first passage time of the second Brownian motion to zero is a Cauchy random variable with an infinite mean. The Longstaff and Schwartz model is, at the time of writing, unsolved.

Hazard rate models of default

This class of models focusses directly on describing the evolution of the probability of default in the next instant without defining the exact default event. Hence, at all times there is a probability that default will occur and a positive probability that it will not. We do not have a specification of variables with the property that if these variables are in a particular constellation then default happens with certainty immediately. The instantaneous likelihood of default is referred to as the hazard rate of default.

The motivation for this shift in focus was that default is often a complicated event and it is easy to misspecify the precise conditions under which it must occur. The conditions one writes down may be too stringent so that default often occurs before these conditions are met, or the conditions are too weak and default fails to occur when all the requisite conditions have been met. A useful analogy can be made with the arrival of customers in a queue – one may hope to describe the evolution of the likelihood of the arrival rate of customers but may not be in a position to pinpoint exactly when the next arrival will take place. Similarly, one may describe variations in the likelihood of a patient suffering a heart attack without being able to write down precisely when it will occur. The exact event is by construction outside the span of observables.

In keeping with the previous notation, we denote by $p(t, T)$ the price at t of a risk-free zero coupon bond maturing at T, while we let $v(t, T)$ be the price of a defaultable zero coupon bond. We also suppose the existence of a money market account paying a continuously compounded interest rate of $r(t)$ at time t. The time t value of the money market account is given by

$$B(t) = \exp\left(\int_0^t r(u)du\right).$$ (6)

The basic valuation equation of this class of models is that obtained on invoking the martingale principle whereby asset prices discounted by the money market account are martingales under a risk-neutral measure denoted here by Q. We may then write that

$$v(t, T) = B(t)E^Q\left[\frac{X(T)}{B(T)}\right]$$ (7)

where $X(T)$ is the payout of the claim, in default or otherwise, as seen in T dollars.

The literature has formulated three distinct conventions for transferring early dollars in default to dollars at time T. Suppose in an early default creditors receive a dollars. Jarrow and Turnbull (1995) transfer this to payment in T dollars of

$$X(T) = \frac{a}{p(u, T)}$$ (8)

as the a dollars may be immediately invested in risk-free bonds in the amount $X(T)$ for a time T receipt of $X(T)$ dollars. Madan and Unal (1998) place the a dollars in the money market account to receive at T

$$X(T) = a \frac{B(T)}{B(u)}. \tag{9}$$

Duffie and Singleton (1999) place the money in equivalent risky bonds to receive at T

$$X(T) = \frac{a}{v(u,\, T)}. \tag{10}$$

Since full payment amounts to having $X(T) = 1$ we have full payment in Jarrow and Turnbull on the delivery of a zero coupon Treasury bond of maturity T and unit face value. Full payment in Madan and Unal takes account of the actual money market experience in the interim, while in Duffie and Singleton one only has to deliver a risky bond with the same face and maturity as the original bond pre-default. If we take the view that full payment is precisely the cost of replication of the original promise at time T, the definitions of Jarrow and Turnbull and Madan and Unal accomplish this objective in different ways, while this objective is not attained in Duffie and Singleton as there may be another default. We further comment that as by Jensen's inequality

$$p(u,T) = E^Q \left[\frac{B(u)}{B(T)} \right]$$

$$\geq \frac{1}{E^Q \left[\frac{B(u)}{B(T)} \right]}$$

the cost of full replication is lower on average using the Madan and Unal investment strategy than that of Jarrow and Turnbull.

If we now fix the recovery rate in T dollars at the level y, we may write the price of the defaultable bond as

$$v(t,\, T) = p(t,\, T)E^Q [F(t,\, T) + y(1 - F(t,\, T))]. \tag{11}$$

assuming independence of the interest rate process and the default event to factor out the bond price. Alternatively, one may change numeraire to the Treasury bond of maturity T and construct the forward adjusted probability measure Q^T and write

$$v(t,T) = p(t,\, T)E^{Q^T} [G(t,\, T) + y(1 - G(t,\, T))] \tag{12}$$

$F(t,\, T)$ is the probability of no default under Q, while G is the probability of the same event under Q^T. Most of the earlier papers assumed independence and worked with F, while for example Madan and Unal (2000) use a calculation under Q^T.

The problem is now reduced to determining the probability $F(t,\, T)$. We will continue to discuss the situation for $F(t,\, T)$, noting that similar calculations hold for $G(t,\, T)$ after one has altered the dynamics to reflect the measure change.

Modeling the probability of no default

Jarrow and Turnbull consider the case of a constant hazard rate of default λ for which it follows from classical arguments for Poisson processes that

$$F(t,T) = \exp\left(-\lambda\,(T-t)\right). \tag{13}$$

Madan and Unal generalize this result to the case when the hazard rate is adapted to a Brownian filtration and is given by a continuous process $\lambda(t)$ for the hazard rate at time t, showing that in this case

$$F(t,\,T) = E^Q\left[\exp\left(-\int_0^t \lambda(u)du\right)\right]. \tag{14}$$

Duffie and Singleton generalize this result and show that when recovery is defined as a proportion $\theta(u)$ of the pre-default value of the defaultable bond, then

$$v(t,T) = E^Q\left[\exp\left(-\int_0^t (r(u) + \lambda(u)(1 - \theta(u))\,du\right)\right]. \tag{15}$$

The importance of these results is that they teach us how to value defaultable bonds using the mathematics of risk-free bonds as similar calculations have been done for risk-free bonds with just the interest rate process constituting the instantaneous discount process. We now learn that once the discount rate has been adjusted to reflect the exposure to the hazard of default, one may essentially treat defaultable bonds as if they were risk-free and in particular value coupon bonds are portfolios of zeros. In the absence of such an adjustment in the discount rate, the coupons of coupon bonds had cumbersome linkages in default, as all coupons subsequent to the default time defaulted together while a portfolio of zeros approach would give them independent default times.

To appreciate these results we consider two increasing and complete information filtrations $\mathcal{G}_t \subseteq \Im_t$ such that the default time is outside the span of $\mathcal{G} = \mathcal{G}_T$ but is adapted to $\Im_t$ while the hazard rate process is adapted to $\mathcal{G}_t$. We next define the default process by $\Delta(t) = 1_{\tau \leq t}$ where τ is the random default time. The process $\Delta(t)$ jumps to unity at the default time and is zero prior to this time. Clearly $\Delta(t)$ is an increasing process and it is not a martingale. The hazard rate process $\lambda(t)$ is the precise compensating process such that

$$\Delta(t) - \int_0^t (1 - \Delta(u))\lambda(u)du \tag{16}$$

is a martingale under Q. Note that once Δ has reached unity and default has occurred, the compensation automatically stops on account of the term $(1 - \Delta(u))$.

An important result that plays a crucial role in eliminating the jump process $\Delta(t)$ from our calculations states that

$$E[1 - \Delta(t) \mid \mathcal{G}_t] = \exp\left(-\int_0^t \lambda(u)du\right) \tag{17}$$

In deriving this result we shall use the result of a simple calculation using iterated expectations and the natural information inclusions that shows that if $M(t)$ is an $\Im_t$ adapted martingale then $M(t) = E[M(t) \mid G_t]$ is a G_t adapted martingale. We call this the drop-down lemma as it lets us drop $\Im_t$ martingales down to G_t martingales.

We now note that by the definition of the hazard rate process

$$m(t) = -\Delta(t) + \int_0^t (1 - \Delta(u))\lambda(u)du \tag{18}$$

is a $\Im_t$ adapted Q martingale. It follows that its Doleans-Dade exponential, $M(t)$, is also an $\Im_t$ adapted Q martingale. But we explicity write this exponential as

$$M(t) = \exp\left(\int_0^t (1 - \Delta(u))\lambda(u)du \right)(1 - \Delta(t)) \tag{19}$$

We now observe that we may delete the jump process from the exponential as it is unity while $\Delta(u) = 0$ and once $\Delta(t)$ is 1 then $(1 - \Delta(t)) = 0$ and the exponential is no longer relevant. Hence we may write

$$M(t) = \exp\left(\int_0^t \lambda(u)du \quad (1 - \Delta(t))\right) \tag{20}$$

and applying the drop-down lemma we have that

$$\bar{M}(t) = \exp\left(\int_0^t \lambda(u)du\right) E[1 - \Delta(t) \mid G_t] \tag{21}$$

is a G_t adapted martingale. But $\bar{M}(t)$ is easily seen to be a predictable process of integrable variation and hence it must be constant and equal to its initial value of unity and the result follows.

We are now in a position to model the price of a defaultable claim paying a face value of F at T and a stochastic coupon $c(u)$, for $u \leq T$, through time till the default time when the payment is $y(u)$. Writing the price as expected discounted future claims under the measure Q we have

$$v(t,T) = E_t \left[\begin{array}{c} \int_t^T \exp\left(-\int_0^u r(s)ds\right)[1 - \Delta(u)u]\,c(u)du + \\[2mm] \exp\left(-\int_0^T r(s)ds\right)[1 - \Delta(T)_r]\,F + \\[2mm] \int_t^T \exp\left(-\int_0^u r(s)ds\right)[1 - \Delta(u)_u]\,y(u)\lambda(u)du \end{array} \right] \tag{22}$$

We note in this expression how the jump process $\Delta(t)$ accomplishes the accounting for coupon payments till the default time and the default payout precisely at the default time for it is then that $d\Delta(t) = 1$. Now using iterated expectations and conditioning on the filtration G_t we may write

$$v(t,T) = E_t \left[\begin{array}{c} \int_t^T exp - \int_0^u r(s)ds \; E \; [1 - \Delta(u) \mid \mathcal{G}u] \, c(u)du \; + \\[2mm] exp\left(-\int_0^T r(s)ds\right) E \; [1 - \Delta(T) \mid \mathcal{G}_r] \, F \; + \\[2mm] \int_t^T exp\left(-\int_0^u r(s)ds\right) E \; [1 - \Delta(u) \mid \mathcal{G}_u] \, y(u)\lambda(u)du \end{array} \right] \qquad (22)$$

now apply our main result replacing $E[1 - \Delta(u) \mid \mathcal{G}_u]$ by $exp\left(-\int_0^u \lambda(s)ds\right)$ to deduce a pricing equation that eliminates all reference to the jump process $\Delta(t)$ as

$$v(t,T) = E_t \left[\begin{array}{c} \int_t^T exp\left(-\int_t^u (r(s)+\lambda(s))ds\right) c(u)du \; + \\[2mm] exp\left(-\int_t^T (r(s)+\lambda(s))ds\right) F \; + \\[2mm] \int_t^T exp\left(-\int_t^u (r(s)+\lambda(s))ds\right) y(u)\lambda(u)du \end{array} \right] \qquad (24)$$

This expression allows us to price defaultable coupon bonds now using the mathematics of default free bonds as the default jump process has been eliminated from the calculations.

In the further special case defining

$$y(u) = \theta\,(u)v(u,T) \qquad (25)$$

the Duffie and Singleton recovery definition we have that

$$v(t,T) = E_t \left[\begin{array}{c} exp\left(-\int_t^T (r(s)+\lambda(s))ds\right) c(u)du \; + \\[2mm] exp\left(-\int_t^T (r(s)+\lambda(s))ds\right) F \; + \\[2mm] \int_t^T exp\left(-\int_t^u (r(s)+\lambda(s))ds\right) \theta(u)\lambda(u)v(u,T)du \end{array} \right] \qquad (26)$$

The associated discounted gains martingale is

$$N(t) = \int_0^t exp\left(-\int_0^u r(s)+\lambda(s))ds\right) c(u)du \; +$$

$$\int_0^t exp\left(-\int_0^u r(s)+\lambda(s))ds\right) \theta(u)\lambda(u)v(u,T)du \; +$$

$$exp\left(-\int_0^t (r(s)+\lambda(s))ds\right) v(t,T)$$

It follows from an application of Itô's lemma that

$$c(t) + \lambda(t)\theta(t)v(t,T) - (r(t) + \lambda(t))v(t,\ T) + E[dv] = 0 \qquad (27)$$

or equivalently that

$$c(t) - (r(t) + \lambda(t)(1 - \theta(t)))v(t,\ T) + E[dv] = 0 \qquad (28)$$

and hence by Itô's lemma that

$$L(t) = \int_0^t exp\left(-\int_0^u (r(s)+\lambda(s)(1-\theta)(t)))ds\right)c(u)du +$$

$$exp\left(-\int_0^t (r(s)+\lambda(s)(1-\theta(t)))ds\right)v(t,T)$$

is a discounted gains martingale and so

$$v(t,T) = E_t \left[\begin{array}{l} \int_t^T exp\left(-\int_t^u (r(s)+\lambda(s)(1-\theta(t)))ds\right)c(u)du + \\ exp\left(-\int_0^t (r(s)+\lambda(s)(1-\theta(t)))ds\right)F \end{array} \right] \qquad (29)$$

Having reduced default pricing in the hazard rate formulation to the mathematical calculations used for default free models, we now consider some specific models – Duffie and Singleton (1999), Madan and Unal models 1 and 2 (1998), (2000), and Jarrow, Lando and Turnbull (1997).

The Duffie and Singleton model

The literature on pricing default free bonds has witnessed the application of two successful classes of models: the exponential affine models and the Heath, Jarrow and Morton models. Duffie and Singleton consider the development of defaultable bond pricing models along these lines. We briefly present the results of this approach.

Exponential affine models

For this purpose we introduce a vector of state variables $y(t)$ that represent unobservables driving the term structure of defaultable bond prices. In practice these would be inferred from the existing level of credit spreads and the model seeks to explain the universe of credit spreads from a finite set of such spreads. The state variables are constructed to be a vector of positive random variables through time.

We suppose that these state variables follow a vector stochastic differential equation that generalizes the Cox, Ingersoll and Ross (1985) model for the instantaneous spot rate to the vector case. Let K denote a diagonal matrix of speeds of mean reversion while Θ is a vector of long term levels to which the state variables are reverting. The matrix Σ is a covariance matrix between the state variables, and $W(t)$ is standard vector Brownian motion of dimension equal to that of y. The stochastic differential equation governing the evolution is given by

$$dy(t) = K (\Theta - y(t)) \, dt + \Sigma \, diag(y(t))^{1/2} dW(t) \tag{30}$$

where $diag(y(t))$ is the diagonal matrix with diagonal given by the state variable vector $y(t)$.

Both the instantaneous spot rate and the exposure to default measured by the hazard rate times the loss rate are supposed linear in the state variables.

$$\begin{aligned}
r(t) &= \delta_0 + \delta' y(t) \\
\lambda(t)(1 - \theta(t)) &= \gamma_0 + \gamma' y(t).
\end{aligned}$$

For such a formulation one may derive in closed form an exponential affine expression for the joint characteristic function of the integral of the process $y(t)$. Specifically,

$$E \left[\exp \left(i\xi' \int_0^t y(u)du \right) \right] = \exp \left(a(t, \xi) + b(t, \xi)' \, y(0) \right) \tag{31}$$

where the coefficient functions $a(t, \xi)$ and $b(t, \xi)$ may be explicitly solved for. Since the price of a defaultable bond requires that we evaluate the expectation of an exponential of the integral of a linear function of the state variables, these prices may be obtained in closed form by evaluating the joint characteristic function at an appropriate point. The result is a closed form model for defaultable bonds that may be empirically evaluated.

Defaultable HJM models

The Heath, Jarrow and Morton (1992) models, for the purposes of pricing fixed income claims, require a specification of the dynamics of the forward rates under the risk-neutral measure associated with the money market discounting process. For defaultable bonds we specify directly the dynamics of defaultable forward rates. Let $g(t,T)$ be the forward rate prevailing at time t for a defaultable loan at time $T > t$. Let $W(t)$ be a standard vector Brownian motion of dimension appropriate for describing the stochastic evolution of forward rates. In practice this would be determined by a principal components analysis of the covariance matrix of defaultable forward rates. The function $g(0,T)$ is the initial forward rate curve. It is supposed that

$$g(t, T) = g(0, T) + \int_0^t \mu (u, T)du + \int_0^t \sigma(u, T)dW(u) \tag{32}$$

Given a model for the martingale component, that is a choice by the modeler for the functions $\sigma(u, T)$, one needs to determine the drift coefficients $\mu(u, T)$ that enforce the condition that discounted prices are martingales under the risk-neutral measure. Using the definition of prices in terms of forward rates, and applying Itô's lemma, one deduces that the martingale condition determines completely the forward rate drifts $\mu(u, T)$. When recovery in default is defined as a proportion of the pre-default price of the bond, this drift restriction is seen to be identical to its counterpart in default free bond pricing and is

$$\mu(t, T) = \sigma(t,T) \left(\int_0^T \sigma(u, T)du \right)'. \tag{33}$$

When recovery is a proportion of the price of a Treasury or default free bond, this restriction is slightly more involved. Letting $f(t,T)$ be the default free forward rates, one obtains that

$$\mu(t, T) = \sigma(t, T) \left(\int_0^T \sigma(u, T) du \right)' + \theta(t)\lambda(t) \frac{v(t, T)}{p(t, T)} (g(t, T) - f(t,T)). \qquad (34)$$

These drift restrictions may be imposed in simulations designed to determine claim valuations, or in the construction of risk-neutral trees for the same purpose.

Madan and Unal 1

Madan and Unal take as a sufficient statistic on the well-being of a firm its equity value measured in units of the money market account. The hazard rate of default is modeled as a decreasing function of this relative price. If $S(t)$ is the process for the stock price, $s(t) = S(t)/B(t)$ is the value of equity in units of the money market account. This discounted price is modeled as a martingale with

$$ds(t) = \sigma s(t) dW(t) \qquad (35)$$

where $W(t)$ is a standard one-dimensional Brownian motion. Madan and Unal further suppose that

$$\begin{aligned} \lambda(t) &= \phi(s(t)) \\ &= \frac{c}{\left(ln \left(\frac{s(t)}{\delta} \right) \right)^2} . \end{aligned}$$

If δ lies below the current value of $s(t)$, λ is a decreasing function of the equity value with the hazard rate tending to infinity as $s(t)$ approaches δ. On the other hand if δ is above current equity values, a positive relation is possible. This is appropriate if increases in equity value are seen as signals of greater risk increasing the value of equity viewed as an option. The exact location of δ is left to be empirically determined.

The price defaultable debt is easily determined in terms of the probability of no default as explained earlier. For this probability, we now have a Markov setting in which the probability of no default in the interim t,T is of the form

$$F(t,T) = \psi (s,t). \qquad (36)$$

It is easily observed that $\exp \left(-\int_0^t \lambda(u)du \right) \psi(s,t)$ is a risk-neutral martingale and hence by Ito's lemma one must have that ψ satisfies the partial differential equation

$$\frac{\sigma^2 s^2}{2} \psi_{ss} + \psi_t = \phi(s)\psi \qquad (37)$$

subject to the boundary condition

$$\psi(s,T) = 1. \qquad (38)$$

The solution is given by

$$\psi(s,T) \;=\; G_a \frac{2}{d^2(s,T)}$$

$$d \;=\; \frac{ln(s/\delta)}{\sigma\sqrt{T}} - \frac{\sigma\sqrt{T}}{2}$$

$$a \;=\; \frac{2c}{\sigma^2}$$

and $G_a(y)$ satisfies the ordinary differential equation

$$y^2 G'' + \left(\frac{3y}{2} - 1 \right) G' - aG = 0 \tag{39}$$

subject to $G(0) = 1$, $G'(0) = -a$.

The Jarrow, Lando and Turnbull model

Jarrow, Lando and Turnbull consider a finite state discrete time model with states represented by rating categories, modeling default as a transition to the default state. They incorporate information on statistical rating transition matrices into default pricing. Suppose there are m states, with state m being the default state, and let Q_{ij} be the observed statistical probability of a transition from state i to state j in a single period. From what we have noted, assuming a default payout of a proportion y of the value of a Treasury bond, we may write

$$\frac{v(t,\,T)}{p(t,\,T)} = 1 - (1 - F(t,T))(1 - y) \tag{40}$$

and hence the risk-neutral probability of no default may be inferred from market prices as

$$1 - F(t,T) = \frac{1}{1-y} \left(1 - \frac{v(t,\,T)}{p(t,\,T)} \right). \tag{41}$$

This information is employed to build the risk-neutral transition probability matrix that is central to risk-neutral calculations of default. Theoretically, the risk-neutral probability of default is given by the mth column of the product of the single- period risk-neutral transition matrices in the interim, or

$$\frac{1}{1-y} \left(1 - \frac{v_i(0,\,T)}{p(0,\,T)} \right) = \left(\prod_{n=1}^{T} \tilde{Q}(n) \right)_{im} \tag{42}$$

where the subscript i denotes the ith rating category. It remains to determine the risk-neutral transition matrices from market data.

For this identification it is supposed that the relative transition probability to different states is risk neutrally equal to their statistical counterparts and so we may write

$$\tilde{Q}(n)_{ij} = \pi_i(n) Q_{ij} \text{ for } i \neq j \tag{43}$$

while

$$\tilde{Q}(n)_{ii} = 1 - \sum_{j \neq i} \tilde{Q}_{ij}(n)$$

$$= 1 - \pi_i(n) \sum_{j \neq 1} Q_{ij}$$

$$= 1 + \pi_i(n)(Q_{ii} - 1)$$

and hence we have that

$$\tilde{Q}(n) - I = diag(\pi(n))(Q - I). \tag{44}$$

One may employ the prices of zero coupon bonds by rating category by maturity to recursively identify the vector $\pi(n)$. For this we solve the following equation, linear in $\pi(T)$,

$$\left(\prod_{n=1}^{T-1} \tilde{Q}(n) \right)^{-1} \frac{1}{1-y} \left(1 - \frac{v_i(0, T)}{p(0, T)} \right) = [I + diag(\pi(T))(Q - I)]e_m \tag{45}$$

where e_m is the mth column of the m dimensional identity matrix.

Madan and Unal 2

Madan and Unal in their later model take a structural approach to default in hazard rate models and define default as occurring when a cash flow event triggers a short-fall of equity. This approach avoids the necessity of building a complicated jump component to the firm's asset value process with the resultant complexities of the associated first passage times that are typical of structural default models allowing for early default. They also allow for stochastic interest rates correlated with the value process and obtain closed forms for the prices of defaultable bonds.

Default is here viewed as arising from the occurrence of a single unforeseen loss of magnitude L that triggers default if L dominates the existing continuously evolving equity. The loss arrival rate is a constant λ and the loss distribution, $F(L)$, is exponential with mean loss μ_L.

Equity on the other hand is composed of non-financial assets of value V and financial assets less liabilities in the amount $g(r)$ where r is the spot interest rate. This formulation importantly allows for duration considerations in assessing the impact of interest rate changes. In the classical models, an increase in interest rates is always good news for the firm as it lowers the value of liabilities, leaving assets untouched at V. Equity is then given by

$$E = V + g(r). \tag{46}$$

Taking a local linear approximation of equity in $ln\,(V)$ and r around an expansion point V_0, r_0, the hazard rate is derived as

$$\lambda(t) = a - b\,ln\,(V(t)) + cr(t)$$

$$a = \lambda(1 - F(E_0)) + b\,ln\,(V_0) - cr_0$$

$$b = \exp \frac{\lambda}{\mu_L} - \left(\frac{E_0}{\mu_L}\right) V_0$$

$$c = \frac{b}{V_0} D$$

where D is the firm's net asset duration.

Modeling the firm's non–financial asset value as

$$dV = rVdt + \sigma VdW_V(t) \tag{47}$$

and assuming a Vasicek interest rate model

$$dr = \kappa(\theta - r)dt + \eta \, dW_r(t) \tag{48}$$

that is correlated with the value process with correlation ρ, supposing a recovery of y as proportion of Treasury value, simple closed forms are derived for the prices of defaultable coupon bonds. Calibration is illustrated on data from Bloomberg on credit spreads by rating category.

Conclusion

A variety of models have been proposed in the literature, ranging from direct option theoretic approaches linked to the dynamics of the firm's asset backing to the class of hazard rate models that relate credit spreads and their evolution to existing credit spreads, credit ratings, and asset values. Much of the literature has concentrated on zero coupon bonds, while the majority of claims trading are coupon bonds. At this stage we clearly need a comprehensive empirical study evaluating the performance of this wide array of models in explaining the implied prices of traded coupon bonds. The results of such a study would point the way for research in developing model improvements.

The focus of attention has been almost exclusively on assessing the time of default, with little attention paid to recovery rates. Madan and Unal (1998) present an attempt to assess recovery rates from market data, but clearly more needs to be done in this direction.

Summary

Dilip B. Madan looks at the developments in the finance literature with respect to pricing default. A broad description of the issues is followed by a detailed summary of the main points and features of the models proposed. Both option theoretic and hazard rate models are presented and critically reviewed.

Suggested further reading

Altman, E. (1989) "Measuring corporate bond mortality and performance," *Journal of Finance*, 44, pp. 909–922.

Cox, J., Ingersoll, J. and Ross, S. (1985) "A theory of the term structure of interest rates," *Econometrica*, 53, pp. 385–408.

Duffie, D. and Singleton, K. (1999) "Modelling term structures of default risky bonds," *Review of Financial Studies*, 12, pp. 687–720.

Geman, H., El Karoui, N. and Rochet, J.C. (1995) "Change of numeraire, changes of probability measures and pricing of options," *Journal of Applied Probability*, 32, pp. 443–458.

Heath, D., Jarrow, R. and Morton, A. (1992) "Bond pricing and the term structure of interest rates: a new methodology for contingent claim valuation," *Econometrica*, 60, pp. 77–105.

Jamshidian, F. (1989) "An exact bond option formula," *Journal of Finance*, 44, pp. 205–209.

Jarrow, R. and Turnbull, S. (1995) "Pricing derivatives on financial securities subject to credit risk," *Journal of Finance*, pp. 53–85.

Jarrow, R., Lando, D. and Turnbull, S. (1997) "A Markov model for the term structure of credit risk spreads," *Review of Financial Studies*, 10, pp. 481–523.

Longstaff, F. and Schwartz, E. (1995) "A simple approach to valuing risky fixed and floating rate debt," *Journal of Finance*, 50, pp. 789–819.

Lucas, D. (1995) "Measuring credit risk and required capital" in *Derivative Credit Risk: Advances in Measurement and Management*, Risk Publications, London.

Madan, D., Carr, P. and Chang, E. (1998) "The variance gamma process and option pricing," *European Finance Review*, 2, pp. 79–105.

Madan, D. and Unal, H. (1998) "Pricing the risks of default," *Review of Derivatives Research*, 2, pp. 121–160.

Madan, D. and Unal, H. (2000) "A two-factor hazard rate model for pricing risky debt and the term structure of credit spreads," *Journal of Financial and Quantitative Analysis*, 35 (1), pp. 43–65.

Merton, R. (1974) "On the pricing of corporate debt: the risk structure of interest rates," *Journal of Finance*, 29, pp. 449–470.

Vasicek, O. (1977) "An equilibrium characterization of the term structure," *The Journal of Financial Economics*, 5, pp. 177–188.

The estimation of default probabilities: a review of alternative methodologies and why they give different results

by John Hull and Alan White

Estimating the probabilities that corporations and sovereign entities will default on their obligations has become a key part of credit risk management. When combined with estimates of future exposures and recovery rates, the probabilities enable a company to derive probability distributions for its credit losses over future time periods. This, in turn, allows credit Value-at-Risk measures to be calculated. As the methods used by regulators to calculate credit risk capital continue to evolve, those financial institutions that have developed sophisticated internal models for quantifying credit risk and calculating credit Value-at-Risk measures are likely to find themselves well positioned to keep their credit risk capital to a minimum.

Another important use for default probabilities is in the valuation of credit derivatives. Credit derivatives are relatively recent innovations in financial markets. Their aim is to allow credit risks to be traded and managed in much the same way as market risks. The most popular credit derivative is a credit default swap. In its simplest form, this is an instrument where one party (the buyer) makes periodic payments to another party (the seller) and in return receives a payoff if a third party (the reference entity) defaults on its obligations. In the event of a default, the payoff is effected by either a cash settlement or a physical settlement and is designed to mirror the loss incurred by creditors who are owed a particular dollar amount by the reference entity. Credit default swaps can be used by credit risk managers to reduce the exposure to a particular counterparty without closing out any transactions with the counterparty.

In this article, which is an extension of the material in Hull and White (1999), we explain alternative approaches for estimating default probabilities. We point out that estimates based on historical data are generally much lower than those based on bond prices and explain the reasons for this.

Using bond prices

The prices of bonds issued by a corporation provide one source of information on its probability of default.[1] If we assume that the only reason a corporate bond sells for less than a similar Treasury bond is the possibility of default, it follows that:

Value of Treasury bond − value of corporate bond = present value of cost of defaults

---

[1] For ease of exposition we will assume that we are estimating the probability of default for a corporation, but the approaches are equally appropriate for sovereign entities.

By using this relationship to calculate the present value of the cost of defaults on a range of different bonds issued by a corporation, and making some assumptions about recovery rates, we can estimate the probability of the corporation defaulting at different future times.[2]

We start with a simple example. Suppose that a five-year zero-coupon Treasury bond with a face value of $100 yields 5 percent and a similar five-year zero-coupon bond issued by a corporation yields 5.5 percent. (Both rates are expressed with continuous compounding.) The value of the Treasury bond is $100e^{-0.05 \times 5}$ or 77.8801 and the value of the corporate bond is $100e^{-0.055 \times 5} = 75.9572$. The present value of the cost of defaults is, therefore,

$$77.8801 - 75.9572 = 1.9229$$

Assume that the risk-neutral probability of default during the five-year life of the bond is p. If we make the simplifying assumption that there are no recoveries in the event of a default, the impact of a default is to create a loss of 100 at the end of the five years. The expected loss from defaults in a risk-neutral world is, therefore, $100p$ and the present value of the expected loss is

$$100pe^{-0.05 \times 5}$$

It follows that:

$$100pe^{-0.05 \times 5} = 1.9229$$

so that $p = 0.0247$ or 2.47 percent. (The fact that we get an answer close to 2.5 percent should be no surprise. The 0.5 percent spread earned on the corporate bond is worth about 2.5 percent of the bond's principal over the five-year life of the bond. This means that expected default losses must be about 2.5 percent of the bond's principal. Because there are no recoveries in the event of a default, the probability of default over the five-year period must also be about 2.5 percent.)

There are two reasons why the calculations for extracting default probabilities from bond prices are, in practice, usually more complicated than that just given. First, the recovery rate is usually non-zero. Second, most corporate bonds are not zero-coupon bonds.

When the recovery rate is non-zero, it is necessary to make an assumption about the claim made by bondholders in the event of default. Jarrow and Turnbull (1995) and Hull and White (1995) assume that the claim equals the no-default of the bond. (As we will see later, this is largely for analytic convenience.) As pointed out by J.P. Morgan (1999), this does not correspond to the way bankruptcy laws work in most countries. A better assumption is that the claim made in the event of a default equals the face value of the bond plus accrued interest.

A general analysis

We now present a general analysis that can be used for any assumptions about the claim amount. We assume that we have chosen a set of N bonds that are either issued by the corporation under consideration or issued by another corporation that

---

[2] We assume that Treasury rates are the benchmark zero-default-risk rates. Some analysts argue that because of the tax treatment of Treasury bonds in the United States and other issues, it is more appropriate to assume that LIBOR rates are the benchmark. Our analysis can easily be adjusted to do this.

is considered to have the same risk of default as the corporation under consideration. Suppose that the maturity of the ith bond is t_i with $t_1 < t_2 < t_3 \ldots < t_N$. We assume that defaults can happen only on bond maturity dates. When a default occurs on a particular date, bond payments due on that date and any subsequent dates are not made.

Define:

B_j: price of the jth bond today
G_j: price of the jth bond today if there were no probability of default
r_i: risk-free rate for maturity t_i
p_i: the risk-neutral probability of default at time t_i
F_{ij}: forward value of the jth bond for a contract maturing at time t_i assuming no probability of default ($j > i$)
C_{ij}: claim made by holders of the jth bond if there is a default at time t_i
R_{ij}: recovery rate for holders of the jth bond in the event of a default at time t_i.

For ease of exposition, we first assume that interest rates are deterministic, and that both recovery rates and claim amounts are known with certainty. Later, we explain how these assumptions can be relaxed. Because interest rates are deterministic, the price at time t_i of the no-default value of the jth bond is F_{ij}. If there is a default at time t_i, the bondholder makes a recovery at rate R_{ij} on a claim of C_{ij}. The present value of the loss on the jth bond arising from defaults at time t_i ($j \geq i$) is, therefore,

$$e^{-r_i t_i} p_i (F_{ij} - R_{ij} C_{ij})$$

The total present value of the losses on the jth bond is given by:

$$G_j - B_j = \sum_{i=1}^{j} e^{-r_i t_i} p_i (F_{ij} - R_{ij} C_{ij}) \tag{1}$$

This equation allows the ps to be determined inductively:

$$p_j = \frac{G_j - B_j - \sum_{i=1}^{j-1} e^{-r_i t_i} p_i (F_{ij} - R_{ij} C_{ij})}{e^{-r_j t_j} (F_{jj} - R_{jj} C_{jj})} \tag{2}$$

(Note that F_{jj} equals the face value of the jth bond plus its final coupon payment.)

These results have been produced on the assumption that interest rates are constant, recovery rates are known, and claim amounts are known. It can be shown that if a) the probabilities of default, b) Treasury interest rates, and c) recovery rates are mutually independent, equations (1) and (2) are still true with the recovery rate set equal to its expected value in a risk-neutral world.[3]

In practice, it is probably reasonable to assume that there is no systematic risk in recovery rates so that expected recovery rates observed in the real world are also expected recovery rates in the risk-neutral world. This allows the expected recovery rate to be estimated from historical data. Table 1 shows some estimates produced by Carty and Lieberman (1996). As might be expected, the mean recovery rate is heavily dependent on the seniority of the bond.

[3] This assumes that the claim amount for a particular bond at a particular time is at most dependent on interest rates.

173

Table 1: Recovery rates on corporate bonds estimated by Carty and Lieberman (1996)

Class	Mean (%)	Standard deviation (%)
Senior secured	53.80	26.86
Senior unsecured	51.13	25.45
Senior subordinated	38.52	23.81
Subordinated	32.74	20.18
Junior subordinated	17.09	10.90

As mentioned earlier, the N bonds used in the analysis are issued by either the company under consideration or by another company that is considered to have the same risk of default as the company under consideration. This means that the p_i should be the same for all bonds. In theory, the recovery rates can vary according to the bond and the default time. In practice, an analyst is likely to choose bonds that have the same seniority in the event of default and assume that the recovery rate on a bond is the same regardless of when the default occurs. The parameter R_{ij} is then the same for all i and j.

Claim amounts and value additivity

We now investigate the impact of different assumptions about the claim amount, C_{ij}. As mentioned earlier, Jarrow and Turnbull (1995) and Hull and White (1995) assume that in the event of a default the bondholder claims the no-default value of the bond. This is an attractive assumption. It implies that $C_{ij} = F_{ij}$. If the recovery rate is a constant, R, equation (2) can be used to estimate

$$p_i(1 - R)$$

directly from observable market variables. This is the percentage of the no-default value lost through defaults at time t_i. Furthermore, an analysis of equation (1) shows that, in this case, the value of the coupon-bearing bond B_j is the sum of the values of the underlying zero-coupon bonds. We will refer to this property as value additivity. It implies that it is theoretically correct to calculate zero curves for different rating categories (AAA, AA, A, BBB, etc.) from actively traded bonds and to use them for pricing less actively traded bonds.

The more realistic assumption suggested by J.P. Morgan (1999) is that C_{ij} equals the face value of bond j plus accrued interest at time t_i. It is interesting to note that value additivity does not apply when this assumption is made (except in the special case where the recovery rate is zero). There is no zero-coupon yield curve that can be used to price corporate bonds exactly for a given set of assumptions about default probabilities and recovery rates.

How much difference does the assumption about C_{ij} make to the probabilities that are estimated? In most cases, the difference is relatively small. Table 3 illustrates this, showing the default probabilities estimated from the six bonds in Table 2. The bonds have maturities ranging from one to ten years and yields ranging from 6.5 percent to 10 percent (continuously compounded). The coupon is assumed to be paid semi-annually, the Treasury zero curve is assumed to be flat at 5 percent (continuously compounded), and the recovery rate is assumed to be 30 percent.

Table 2: Bond data

Bond life (years)	Coupon (%)	Yield (%)
1	9.0	6.5
2	9.0	7.5
3	9.0	8.0
4	9.0	8.5
5	9.0	9.0
10	9.0	10.0

Table 3: Implied probabilities of default for data in Table 2 (recovery rate = 30 percent)

Time of default (years)	Default probability (%) Claim=no-default value	Default probability (%) Claim=face value + accr int
1	2.17	2.17
2	5.07	5.04
3	5.63	5.51
4	6.86	6.66
5	7.96	7.66
10	39.94	37.63

Since the coupon rates in our example are higher than the Treasury rate, the claim made in the event of default under the "C_{ij} equals no-default value assumption" is greater than that under the "C_{ij} equals face value plus accrued interest assumption." This leads to higher implied default probabilities if we assume C_{ij} equals the no-default value.

It is interesting to note in passing that the assumption of a particular recovery rate imposes a lower limit on the yield on a bond. In the example in Table 2, it can be shown that when the recovery rate is 30 percent, a 20-year bond with a coupon of 9 percent must have a yield greater than 9.53 percent when the claim amount equals the no-default value of the bond and a yield greater than 10.01 percent when the claim amount equals the face value plus accrued interest.

Historical data

Historical data provides another way of estimating default probabilities. Table 4 is typical of the information produced by rating agencies. It shows the default experience of bonds that started with a certain credit rating. For example, a bond with an initial credit rating of BBB has a 0.18 percent chance of defaulting by the end of the first year, a 0.44 percent chance of defaulting by the end of the second year, and so on. The probability of a bond defaulting during a particular year can be calculated from the table. For example, the probability of a BBB-rated bond defaulting during the second year is 0.44 − 0.18 = 0.26 percent.

It is interesting to note that for bonds with good credit ratings, the probability of default in a year tends to be an increasing function of time. For bonds with a poor credit rating, the reverse is often true. In Table 4, the unconditional probabilities, as seen at time zero, of an AA bond defaulting during years 1, 2, 3, 4, and 5 are 0 percent, 0.02 percent, 0.10 percent, 0.13 percent, and 0.18 percent, respectively. The corresponding probabilities for a CCC bond are 19.79 percent, 7.13 percent, 4.71 percent, 4.34 percent, and 4.18 percent. This phenomenon can be explained as

Table 4: Average cumulative default rates (%)

Term (yrs)	1	2	3	4	5	7	10	15
AAA	0.00	0.00	0.07	0.15	0.24	0.66	1.40	1.40
AA	0.00	0.02	0.12	0.25	0.43	0.89	1.29	1.48
A	0.06	0.16	0.27	0.44	0.67	1.12	2.17	3.00
BBB	0.18	0.44	0.72	1.27	1.78	2.99	4.34	4.70
BB	1.06	3.48	6.12	8.68	10.97	14.46	17.73	19.91
B	5.20	11.00	15.95	19.40	21.88	25.14	29.02	30.65
CCC	19.79	26.92	31.63	35.97	40.15	42.64	45.10	45.10

Source: S&P CreditWeek, 15 April 1996

follows. For a bond with a good credit rating, some time must usually elapse for the fortunes of the issuer to decline to such an extent that a default happens. This leads to default probabilities being an increasing function of time. For a bond with a poor credit rating, the next year or two may be critical. If the issuer survives this period, the probability of default per year can be expected to decline. This leads to default probabilities being a decreasing function of time.

There are some anomalies in the data in Table 2. For example, the cumulative probability of an AA-rated bond defaulting during a ten-year period is 1.29 percent – less than the 1.4 percent experience for a AAA-rated bond. Analysts often smooth the data to eliminate these types of anomalies before using it for forecasting.

Bond prices vs historical default experience

The default probabilities calculated from bond prices are invariably significantly greater than those estimated from historical data. Consider, for example, A-rated bonds. Table 4 shows that the probability of a default during a five-year period is 0.67 percent. If we assume that the spread over Treasuries for a zero-coupon five-year A-rated corporate bond is 50 basis points and there are no recoveries in the event of a default, the estimated probability of default during a five-year period is 2.47 percent.[4] This is almost four times as much.

The two key assumptions we have made in arriving at the 2.47 percent estimate are that (i) A-rated bonds yield 50 basis points above Treasuries, and (ii) the recovery rate is zero. Both assumptions are conservative. In practice, the yield on A-rated bonds is often more than 50 basis points above Treasuries and the recovery rate is non-zero. As we increase either the yield above Treasuries or the assumed recovery rate, the probability of default calculated from bond prices increases.[5]

Altman (1989) was one of the first researchers to comment on this apparent discrepancy between bond prices and historical default data. He showed that even after taking account of the impact of defaults, an investor could expect significantly higher returns from investing in corporate bonds than from investing in Treasury bonds. One interesting pattern in Altman's results is that as the credit rating of the corporate bonds declined, the extent of the higher returns increased.

Why do bond prices give much higher probabilities of defaults than historical data? One reason may be that investors require higher average returns on corporate

---

[4] The calculations leading to the 2.47 percent estimate are given early in the first section of this article.

[5] For example, if the recovery rate equals 30 percent and the spread of corporate bond over Treasuries is 70 basis points, the probability of default rises to 4.91 percent.

bonds to compensate for their lower liquidity than Treasury bonds. Another reason may be that bond traders are allowing in their pricing for the possibility of "depression scenarios" much worse than anything seen during the time period covered by the historical data. However, the key reason is that the probabilities backed out from bond prices are risk-neutral probabilities while those calculated from historical data are real-world probabilities.

To illustrate what is going on we return to the five-year A-rated zero-coupon bond example. The price of a five-year zero-coupon A-rated bond is 2.47 percent less than the corresponding Treasury bond, but the probability of an A-rated bond defaulting during the five-year period is 0.67 percent. One way of getting the pricing difference is by assuming:

1. The expected cash flow from the corporate bond at the end of five years is 2.47 percent less than the expected cash flow from the Treasury bond at the end of the five years; and
2. The discount rates appropriate for the two cash flows are the same.

The second of these two assumptions is correct in a risk-neutral world because the expected return required by all investors on all investments in this world is the risk-free rate. The first assumption corresponds to a probability of default of 2.47 percent. This characterization of the pricing difference confirms, therefore, that the prices of the Treasury and corporate bonds are consistent, with 2.47 percent being the probability of default in a risk-neutral world.

The 2.47 percent price difference between the corporate and Treasury bonds can also be obtained if we assume:

1. The expected cash flow from the corporate bond at the end of five years is 0.67 percent less than the expected cash flow from the Treasury bond at the end of the five years; and
2. The discount rate appropriate for the expected corporate bond cash flow is about 0.36 percent higher than the discount rate appropriate for the Treasury bond cash flow.

This is because a 0.36 percent increase in the discount rate leads to the corporate bond price being reduced by approximately $5 \times 0.36 = 1.8$ percent. When combined with the corporate bond's lower expected cash flow we get a total difference between the corporate bond price and the Treasury bond price of approximately $1.8 + 0.67 = 2.47$ percent.

The 0.67 percent estimate of the probability of default is therefore correct in the real world if the correct discount rate to use for the bond's cash flows in the real world is 0.36 percent higher than in the risk-neutral world. Arguably, a 0.36 percent increase in the discount rate when we move from the risk-neutral world to the real world is not unreasonable. A-rated bonds do have some systematic (that is, nondiversifiable) risk: when the market does badly they are more likely to default; when the market does well they are less likely to default.

The excess expected return of the market over the risk-free rate is about 5 percent. Using the capital asset pricing model, a 0.36 percent excess expected return for the corporate bond is consistent with the corporate bond having a beta of about $0.36/5 = 0.072$. It is interesting that what seems to be a large discrepancy between default probability estimates translates into a relatively small, and quite reasonable, adjustment to expected returns for systematic risk.

This explanation of the difference between estimates calculated from bond prices and those calculated from historical data is consistent with the pattern of Altman's results, mentioned earlier. As the credit rating of a bond declines, it becomes more similar to equity, and its beta increases. As a result, the excess of the expected return required by investors over the risk-free rate also increases.

At this stage it is natural to ask whether we should use real-world or risk-neutral default probabilities in the analysis of credit risk. The answer depends on the purpose of the analysis. When valuing credit derivatives, or estimating the impact of counterparty default risk on the pricing of other derivatives, we should use risk-neutral default probabilities. This is because we are likely to be implicitly or explicitly using risk-neutral valuation in our analysis. When calculating credit value at risk or carrying out scenario analyses to calculate potential losses from defaults, we should use real-world default probabilities.

Merton's model

The approaches we have examined so far for estimating a company's probability of default have relied on the company's credit rating. Unfortunately credit ratings are revised relatively infrequently, which has led some financial engineers to argue that equity prices can provide more up-to-date estimates of default probabilities.

Merton (1974) proposed a model where a company's equity is an option on the assets of the company. Suppose for simplicity that a firm has one zero-coupon bond outstanding and that the bond matures at time T. Define

V_0: value of company's assets today

V_T: value of company's assets at time T

E_0: value of company's equity today

E_T: value of company's equity at time T

D: amount of debt interest and principal due to be paid at time T

σ_V: volatility of assets

σ_E: volatility of equity.

If $V_T < D$, it is (at least in theory) rational for the company to default on the debt at time T. The value of the equity is then zero. If $V_T > D$, the company should make the debt repayment at time T and the value of the equity at this time is $V_T - D$. Merton's model therefore gives the value of the firm's equity at time T as

$$E_T = \text{Max}(V_T - D, 0).$$

This shows that the equity is a call option on the value of the assets with a strike price equal to the repayment required on the debt. The Black-Scholes formula gives the value of the equity today as

$$E_0 = V_0 N(d_1) - De^{-RT} N(d_2) \tag{3}$$

where

$$d_1 = \frac{ln\ (V_0/D) + (R + \sigma_V^2/2)T}{\sigma_V \sqrt{T}}$$

$$d_2 = d_1 - \sigma_V \sqrt{T}$$

and R is the risk-free interest rate for maturity T. The value of the debt today is $V_0 - E_0$.

The risk-neutral probability that the company will default on the debt is $N(-d_2)$. To calculate this we require V_0 and σ_V. Neither of these is directly observable. However, we can observe E_0. This means that equation (3) provides one condition that must be satisfied by V_0 and σ_V. We can also estimate σ_E. From Itô's lemma

$$\sigma_E E_0 = \quad \sigma_V V_0.$$

or

$$\sigma_E E_0 = N(d_1)\sigma_V V_0. \tag{4}$$

This provides another equation that must be satisfied by V_0 and σ_V. Equations (3) and (4) provide a pair of simultaneous equations that allow V_0 and σ_V to be estimated.

Up to now we have assumed that all of the company's debt is repayable at one time. In practice, debt repayments are likely to be required at a number of different times. This makes the model relating V_0 and E_0 more complicated than equation (3), but in principle it is still possible to use an option pricing approach to obtain estimates of V_0 and σ_V. The probability of the company defaulting at different times in the future can then be estimated.

How well do the default probabilities produced by Merton's model agree with historical default experience? The answer is that there is a significant difference between the two. However, Crosbie (1998) reports that there is a good empirical relationship between the probability of default calculated from Merton's model and either real-world or risk-neutral probabilities. This suggests that Merton's model can be used in an indirect way to estimate either of these two probabilities.[6]

Conclusion

This chapter has examined alternative approaches for estimating the probability of default. It points out that the probabilities estimated from bond prices are risk-neutral probabilities while the probabilities estimated from historical data are real-world probabilities. Risk-neutral default probabilities are higher than real-world default probabilities because investors require a higher return in the real world than in a risk-neutral world.

In practice, analysts are likely to be interested in both risk-neutral and real-world probabilities. Risk-neutral probabilities should be used to value credit derivatives and quantify the impact of default risk on the market prices of traded instruments. Real-world probabilities should be used when scenario analyses are carried out and credit Value-at-Risk measures are calculated.

Summary

John Hull and **Alan White** review three approaches for estimating the probability that a corporation or sovereign entity will default on its obligations during a specified time period. The first is based on bond

---

[6] KMV, a company in California, and has pioneered the use of Merton's model in this way..

prices; the second is based on historical data; the third is based on equity prices. The chapter explains the reasons for the large differences between the "risk-neutral" probability estimates calculated from bond prices and the "real-world" probability estimates obtained from historical data.

© John Hull and Alan White

Suggested further reading

Altman, E.I. (1989) "Measuring corporate bond mortality and performance," *Journal of Finance*, 44, pp. 902–22.

Carty, L.V. and Lieberman, D. (1996) "Corporate bond defaults and default rates, 1938–1995," *Moody's Investors Service, Global Credit Research*, January.

Crosbie, P. (1998) "Modeling default risk," Chapter 8 in *Credit Derivatives: Trading & Management of Credit & Default Risk*, edited by S. Das, pp. 299–315, Singapore, John Wiley and Sons.

Hull, J. and White, A. (1995) "The impact of default risk on the prices of options and other derivatives," *Journal of Banking and Finance*, 19, pp. 299–322.

Hull, J. and White, A. (1999) "Quantifying credit risk: why different approaches give different answers," *Canadian Journal of Administrative Studies*, September, Vol. 16, No. 3.

Jarrow, R. and Turnbull, S. (1995) "Pricing options on derivative securities subject to default risk," *Journal of Finance*, 50, pp. 53–85.

Merton, R. (1974) "On the pricing of corporate debt: the risk structure of interest rates," *Journal of Finance*, 29, pp. 449–470.

Morgan, J.P. (1999) *The J.P. Morgan Guide to Credit Derivatives,* London, RISK Publications.

OPERATIONAL RISKS

3

Contributors

Marcelo Cruz has over six years of experience in operational risk modeling and derivatives trading. His most recent position was in operational risk research at UBS-Warburg, New York. Currently, Dr Cruz works as a consultant to several large financial institutions. He has many publications in professional journals and academic texts on risk management.

Carol Alexander is Professor of Risk Management at the ISMA Centre at the University of Reading, UK. She was also formerly a Director and Head of Market Risk Modeling for Nikko Global Holdings and Academic Director of Algorithmics Inc. Her research interests include volatility and correlation analysis, high frequency price prediction, alternative investment strategies and quantification of operational risks. She is the author of *Market Models: a guide to financial data analysis* (Wiley, 2001).

Anthony Peccia is a Vice President at the Canadian Imperial Bank of Commerce (CIBC). He is responsible for developing best practice operational risk policies, methodologies and infrastructures. This includes developing operational risk metrics for quantifying operational risk, developing operational risk predictive factors, regularly reporting operational risk profiles with attention to recommended action plans for achieving the right reward for risk taken.

David Murphy is Director of product and business development at Merrill Lynch. He began his financial career at SFA, working in the risk assessment unit. From there, he was global risk manager at Paribas before joining Merrill Lynch as Global Head of Product Control, first for Equity Derivatives and latterly for Equity and Debt Markets. He takes a keen interest in risk management and regulatory policy matters, and sits on a number of bodies including the FSA consultative committee on the new Basel Accord.

Contents

Introduction

This last part of the book presents some of the recent advances in the very difficult area of measuring and managing operational risks. There are many different types of operational risks and they have quite diverse characteristics; consequently a variety of financial and mathematical models have been proposed. Some types of operational risks (e.g. human risks) are not well represented by operational loss distributions. Instead they may be better measured by performance indicators so standard actuarial based techniques that might carry over from market and credit risks will not apply. Consequently new methods are being developed that have their roots in disciplines such as management and the decision sciences.

The four chapters have been chosen in this part of the book to represent quite different aspects of operational risk. The first chapter in this section is by Marcelo Cruz on the pricing operational risk linked bonds using actuarial based techniques from extreme value theory. It also shows how discriminant analysis, traditionally used for credit risk scoring, can be applied to generate operational risk indicators (see pp. 187–199).

The chapter by Tony Peccia of CIBC, Toronto shows how to design a framework for measuring and managing operational risk in a large investment bank. Many banks already use qualitative risk indicators based on questionnaires and quantitative approaches to measuring operational risk that have their roots in actuarial methods are now becoming more common. Because of the scarcity of internal loss data on low frequency high impact operational risks, Monte Carlo simulation is often used to generate operational loss distributions. This chapter reviews the effectiveness of these and other statistical methods for quantifying operational risk. Finally it considers the managers perspective, from operational risk capital to pro-active portfolio management (see pp. 200–218).

Bayesian methods have an important role to play in the assessment of operational risks, where data are scarce and the values of model parameters may be very uncertain. The next chapter, by myself, introduces Bayesian statistics and reviews its applications to operational risk measurement and management. In particular, Bayesian belief networks and Bayesian decision networks are shown to have wide-ranging applications; from modeling loss distributions or multivariate densities for a loss event probability, to understanding and managing human risks using networks for key performance indicators. These models lend themselves to scenario analysis so that operational risk managers can assess maximum operational loss; and although there is no unique Bayesian network they are easily back tested so that optimal architectures and node probabilities can be validated (see pp. 219–238).

The final chapter by David Murphy assesses the regulatory developments for operational risk capital requirements in the forthcoming Basel 2 Accord. It provides a critical overview of the current proposals for the new regulations and their likely impact on the industry (see pp. 239–250).

Carol Alexander
Professor of Risk Management,
ISMA Centre, University of Reading, UK

Mathematical models for pricing and hedging operational risks

by Marcelo Cruz

Operational risk (OR) has earned considerable attention from the financial industry recently. A huge number of seminars, and discussions between the industry and regulators have culminated in the Basel Consultative Paper (Basel 2001), which openly supports OR measurement and states that operational risk will have a formal charge in 2004.

OR measurement will enable the allocation of risk capital to cover OR losses to be determined from loss data. It will highlight risky business activities, and assist management in reducing the risk. The development of models for measuring OR begins with a thorough database modeling. Events therein should carry their losses or potential losses, the business activity giving the losses and other risk indicators. The creation and management of a diverse operational losses and key risk indicators database is key to understanding the control environment in which financial institutions process their operations. In investment banking, most losses will be from processing a high volume of transactions, and will show up as interest payments to counterparts, fees and fines paid to exchanges, etc. Retail banks will be exposed to frauds, legal and liability problems, and small claims arising from processing errors. The database should allow separate analysis for each business unit and for each potential loss-making activity.

The aim of this article is to demonstrate briefly how robust mathematical and statistical techniques using these databases of operational losses can help in measuring, managing and even pricing OR. Given the multidimensionality of OR, many different methodologies may be envisaged. Here we present just two: first, a statistical model using extreme value theory to measure extreme events, with re-sampling techniques, and applied to the pricing of an operational risk derivative; second, econometric techniques to suggest an OR rating scheme, developed by the application of discriminant analysis.

Statistical modeling using extreme value theory

A mathematically robust way to approach the measurement of operational risk could involve the use of statistical/actuarial methods (by using an internally built operational loss database to estimate the joint and marginal distributions of severity and frequency loss) combined with econometric techniques (such as multiple regression and discriminant analysis). In addition we have borrowed quantitative methods developed for hydrology and engineering, where the rare events having major financial consequences are floods, storms, etc.

An OR database would typically show high-impact events at low frequency among events of high frequency but low impact. A financial institution might therefore sort its losses into "expected loss" to be absorbed by net profit, "unexpected loss" to be

This paper shows the personal research of the author and does not necessarily reflect the opinion of any institution to which the author may be affiliated.

covered by risk reserves (or even using captives), and "stress loss" requiring core capital or hedging for cover. A more formal statistical method to deal with those extreme and rare events uses extreme value theory.

In extreme value distributions, the normal distribution that forms the basis of much of statistical inference is replaced by a loss distribution showing a thicker upper tail. We might have chosen to work with any heavy-tailed model, but we have selected the Generalized Extreme Value distribution (GEV – see Embrechts et al., 1997), which encompasses the Weibull, Frechet and Gumbel distributions that arise as limit distributions for the largest observation in a sample.

We used a database from frauds in a large retail bank. The estimation procedure takes the largest loss observed in each of the preceding 12 months, and obtains the parameters of the GEV best fitted by these 12 values. Estimation procedures are described in Embrechts et al. (1997). The results can be updated daily, weekly, or monthly on a rolling 12-month basis. The estimated 100p percent quantile is called the value-at-risk at confidence level p (VaR$_p$). In view of the heavy-tail characteristics, a very high quantile such as 99 percent can give very high figures, suggesting an economic capital allocation beyond that which would be deemed appropriate, so the 95 percent quantile might prove more suitable.

Table 1: Maximum amount at risk (£ million) at year-end

Year	1992	1993	1994	1995	1996
Loss frequency	586	454	485	658	798
Stress loss frequency	21	17	17	19	21
VaR 95%	2.9	5.9	14.0	1.1	5.1
VaR 99%	12.9	29.2	122.9	3.3	28.1

Table 1 shows values similar to those that were obtained from a typical fraud database of a clearing bank handling millions of transactions per day, with about 20 frauds in excess of £100,000 attempted each year, and only one massive fraud (in 1994) over a period of five years. The single extreme case in 1994 is seen to distort the shape of the fitted distribution. However, formal tests of fit for any particular heavy-tailed distribution such as Kolmogorov-Smirnov would lack power to detect a lack of fit, and this was seen in our studies (see Cruz et al., 1998). We deepen the analysis in the next section.

Pricing an OR-linked bond using extreme value theory

The topic of hedging operational risk became especially interesting after the Basel Committee stated in its paper "The New Basel Capital Accord" (see Basel Committee, 2001) that a capital charge must be implemented for operational risk. This surcharge will demand more earmarked capital from the banks and will be especially challenging for banks with problems in their capital ratio.

Currently, the hedging alternatives are very limited. Broadly speaking, the operational risk manager has the following options:

1. Risk mitigation.
2. Insurance.
3. Capital allocation.

The first option is not a financial one. It is the most commonly used and the risk management decisions are constantly based on qualitative or even intuitive measures. Several banks have operational risk managers that work with the business lines to mitigate operational problems. The problem is that risk mitigation decisions by themselves will not necessarily protect a bank from an operational risk catastrophe. Such managerial risk mitigation decisions need to be complemented with some financial instrument.

The second option is already used by banks but hitherto has played an unsatisfactory role in risk mitigation/hedging. There are various reasons for this. One is that traditional policies offered by insurance companies address only very specific and limited areas of operational risk. The insurance market itself is fragmented and the policies and coverage are not uniform – the coverage is barely appropriate to cover the multidimensional risks that operational risk represents. Second, the risk pricing is not transparent, which is a sensitive question for financial institutions. Insurance requires a large premium to be paid each year in advance or after a covered event, and this has a negative effect in the cash flow. Third, in the event of an operational risk catastrophe, even if a bank were insured and the loss was clearly inside the policy, the insurer would take several days to pay the bank.

Insurers bear credit risk and it may be considered that eventually they may default on the payment of a large loss. Even if this does not happen, the payment can take much longer if there is litigation on the origin or cause of the loss. A central bank or a consortium of investors will not bail out a financially insoluble bank for very long. Given the time constraint, in the case of a catastrophic event insurance may not in fact save an institution, although it does reduce earnings volatility caused by operational losses.

The third option is to allocate capital against operational risk. This is probably the most expensive way of protecting the bank against earnings volatility, but can be very efficient if used in a context of performance measurement and adjusting returns inside the organization to the appropriate level of risk. Retaining risk internally can tie up corporate capital, and since the frequency and severity of loss events are stochastic, the capital allocated for the bearing of risk has to be invested in liquid assets and cannot be used operationally, which obviously reduces the return. Capital allocation means also having a reliable quantitative measurement model inside the organization: capital must be estimated based on a very objective basis using sound statistical/mathematical techniques.

In this section we suggest a fourth alternative: the securitization of operational risk by developing operational risk-linked (ORL) bonds. The objective here is to suggest the introduction of this instrument and prove the feasibility and robustness of the pricing of ORL bonds, but we will not detail legal aspects such as the creation of special purpose vehicles (SPVs). ORL bonds are inspired by the recent development of insurance and catastrophe-linked bonds. Nevertheless, the pricing is slightly different, in the sense that the simulations used in insurance and catastrophe-linked bonds consider variables such as extreme weather conditions.[1] The basic structure can be seen in Table 2.

The advantage of ORL bonds over the hedging alternative is that the insurance helps avoid swings in earnings volatility, and it may even save the institution in the

---

[1] Some of CatBonds' variables could be inflation in building costs, population growth, cost of lands, etc.

Table 2: The structure of an ORL bond

Agent	Financial institution	Risk transfer company or SPV	Capital market
Instrument	Insurance policy offered by RTC	Takes the Risk and issues *bond* linked to operational event at the financial institution	Buy the *bond*
Financial results	Paid a premium	Receives a commission	Receives high yield
Risks	None up to the limit insured	None	If the operational event described in the *bond* happens in the financial institution, loss of some or all the principal or interest

event of an operational risk catastrophe. Looking from the bond investor point of view, the ORL bonds offer the same benefits as CatBonds, as operational risk events are uncorrelated with market or credit occurrences. In other terms, this means that buying regular bonds or even shares of the issuer bank does not bring significant diversification benefits.[2] In this respect ORL bonds offer better diversification opportunities since their expected betas are near zero. A study on the correlation of PCS options, a type of reinsurance-linked security traded at CBOT, proved no correlation with the S&P 500 (see Canter et al., 1996). In this case the efficient frontier of the investment is raised with no substantial increase in the risk. Investment institutions are competing more fiercely to produce consistent, high returns on capital, so diversification is becoming one of the hot buzz-words among asset managers.

The intention here is to price the bond from the issuer point of view. There are basically two methods being considered to price CatBonds that can be adapted to ORL bonds: the actuarial and the financial. Embrechts and Meister (1997) provide a good summary of the discussion of these alternatives. The aim in derivative pricing is to protect against market conditions and price swings through dynamic hedging. The distribution under the real-world probability measure of some financial risk is not used for pricing this risk; instead prices are estimated using some artificial martingale measure whose existence is closely associated to the economic notion of no-arbitrage. These models are called *complete*. For models of the type we are studying here, in general no unique martingale price exists, and holding the derivative is a genuinely risky business. This condition is called *incomplete markets*. The pricing of uncertain cash-flow streams under these conditions is substantially weaker in the interpretation of the pricing results that can be obtained than is the case for pricing in complete securities markets. The price can no longer be justified by arbitrage considerations alone, i.e., the cost of a portfolio of existing assets that provides the appropriate payoffs, as there is no such portfolio. The uniqueness of the prices is lost. A more simple explanation can be that the payments of an ORL bond cannot be hedged by a portfolio of traditional bonds or shares due to the fact that they are uncorrelated with other economic variables. Therefore the original derivatives pricing scheme cannot be used in the present case.

---

[2] A recent study showed that if 5 percent CAT risk is added to a portfolio of 60 percent equities and 40 percent bonds, the return of the portfolio increases by 1.25 percent and the volatility (risk) decreases by 0.25 percent.

The methodology envisaged here will explore an actuarial parametric approach for pricing ORL bonds. As mentioned before, the pricing of ORL bonds can be very similar to the pricing of insurance CatBonds and the parametric approach has been chosen by some issuers of CatBonds (see Schmock, 1998). We are particularly interested in estimating the tails of loss severity and aggregate distributions. In this situation it is essential to find a reliable statistical model for the largest observed operational losses. A model chosen for its overall fit to whole distribution may not provide a particularly good fit to the large losses, and such a model would fail in pricing ORL bonds. Our modeling for catastrophic operational losses is based on extreme value theory. It is important in these models to understand the sensitivity of the price if distributions or parameters – particularly the shape – are changed: the shape parameter can make the loss and the aggregate distribution quite unstable, especially in high quantiles. We try to overcome this problem by testing the results against different distributions and using resampling techniques such as bootstrapping and jackknife to check the stability of the parameters. The pricing methodology follows four steps.

1. Estimate the parameters of the frequency and severity distributions

The most common frequency distribution is the Poisson, and its parameter can be estimated by maximum likelihood (ML). However, we opted to use the "probability weighted" or "L-Moments" method in estimating the parameters of the severity distributions. One advantage of L-Moments in relation to ML is its simplicity and straightforwardness. It also has a better applicability in small samples than ML (see Landwehr et al., 1979). Hoskings and Wallis (1997) have demonstrated asymptotic efficiency of the individual L-Moments estimators. It is important that the conclusion they reached was in terms of the small sample properties of L-Moments because our interest here is to study small samples of the largest operational losses. As Hoskings et al. (1985) noted, although probability-weighted estimators are asymptotically inefficient compared with ML estimators, no deficiency is detectable in samples of 100 or less. The biases of L-Moments estimators are small and they decrease rapidly as the sample size increases. The standard deviations of the L-Moments estimators are comparable with those of ML estimators for moderate sample sizes ($n = 50, 100$) and are often substantially less than those of the ML for small samples.

2. Analyze the sensitivity of the parameters by using resampling techniques

Limiting the analysis to tail events in general means working with small samples. Therefore, the inclusion or exclusion of a single operational loss event may influence the shape of the tail, which is quite crucial in the analysis. Hence, it is important to test the robustness of the parameters estimated.

Two techniques may help in this sense: bootstrapping and jackknife (see Efron and Tibshirani, 1993). Bootstrapping is used to obtain a description of the sampling properties of empirical estimators using the sample data themselves, rather than broad theoretical results, which are in general not yet developed for tails of the distribution. Let $\hat{\Theta}_n$ be the estimate of a parameter vector θ based on a sample of operational loss events $X = (x_1, ..., x_n)$. An approximation to the statistical properties of $\hat{\Theta}_n$ can be obtained by studying a sample of bootstrap estimators $\hat{\Theta}(b)_m$, $b = 1, ..., B$, obtained by sampling m observations, with replacement, from X and recomputing $\hat{\Theta}$ with each sample. The bootstrap sample size, m, may be larger or smaller than n.

This is done a total of B times, and the desired sampling characteristic is computed from $\hat{\Theta} = [\hat{\Theta}(1)_m , ..., \hat{\Theta}(B)_m]$. We might approximate the asymptotic covariance matrix of the estimator $\hat{\Theta}$ by using

$$\text{Estimated asymptotic variance } [\hat{\Theta}] = \frac{1}{B} \sum_{b=1}^{B} [\hat{\Theta}(b)_m - \hat{\Theta}_n][\hat{\Theta}(b)_m - \hat{\Theta}_n]'$$

Jackknife is a simulation technique similar to bootstrapping. In this technique we have to re-estimate the parameters by successively dropping a single observation from the operational loss events, getting n alternative parameters estimates $\{\hat{\Theta}_{-1}, ..., \hat{\Theta}_{-n}\}$. The pseudo-parameters originated by the jackknife can be useful to estimate the variance (or bias) of the parameters as well as standard errors.

3. Find the aggregate distribution through simulation

We are aiming to structure and price a bond that covers the aggregate losses during one year and therefore we estimate the aggregate loss distribution. For bonds covering just the largest loss above a certain threshold there is no need to estimate the aggregate distribution. Previously we estimated the severity and frequency of the operational losses. Now we need to aggregate them through simulation. The simulation results are then used to construct an artificial loss experience, which may substitute for an actual history of losses when necessary. In order to perform a risk and return analysis of the investment, the prospective investor may use a forward-looking scenario simulation if a historical database is not disclosed. For the bank issuing the bond or the pricing consultant, the internal historical database of losses should be used as much as possible. The objective with the simulation is to get the compound distribution of operational losses, considering the number and the size of losses. Traditionally S denotes aggregate sum of losses associated with a set of n observed claims $X_1, X_2, ..., X_n$

$$S = X_1 + X_2 + ... + X_n, \ (n = 0, 1, 2, ...) \ (S = 0 \text{ if } n=0)$$

where n has a counting distribution (such as the Poisson distribution). The random sum S has a distribution function:

$$\begin{aligned} F_S(x) \ &= \ Pr(S \leq x) \\ &= \sum_{n=0}^{\infty} p_n Pr(S \leq x \mid N = n) \\ &= \sum_{n=0}^{\infty} p_n F_x^{*n}(x) \end{aligned}$$

Here N is the random variable for the number of claims of the period of study, and $F_x^{*n}(x)$ is an n-fold convolution of $F_x(x)$, the distribution function for a typical loss X. In most cases there will be no analytical method to obtain separate expressions for $\{p_n\}$ and $F_x(x)$ from $F_s(x)$, where p_n is the probability of n losses given, for example, by the Poisson or the negative binomial counting distribution and $F_x^{*n}(x)$ is the aggregate claim size distribution function for a fixed number of n claims fitted by extreme value distributions.

4. Structure the ORL bond

There are several possibilities for structuring the ORL bond, depending on the level of risk and coverage desired. The principal can be totally or partially at risk and so can the interest (in the case of coupon bonds). For the purpose of simplicity, in this article it will be priced a zero-coupon ORL bond in which the principal is fully at risk and linked to the risk of yearly aggregated losses higher than a certain threshold. In this case the price of the bond will be defined by the following formula:

$$P = \frac{(1 - \alpha)\ par\ value}{(1 + r)^t}$$

where r is the risk free interest rate, t is the number of years and ψ is the probability of an operational loss event in excess of X happening during the holding period of the bond. By including α we include a risk premium to the security equivalent to the operational event risk. The following relation holds:

Prob[Bond Default] = Prob[Aggregated (Yearly) Interest Expenses > X]

If the bond is issued for terms longer than one year, the variable ψ needs to be modified because the probability of an event occurring obviously grows as the holding period of the bond is increased. The return period of the event $\{X >$ Aggregated Yearly Interest Expenses = $Y\}$ can be defined as Excess Loss $(Y) = p^{-1} = (F(Y))^{-1}$. The relevant questions concerning the return period can now be answered through the corresponding properties of the geometric distributions (for details, see Embrechts et al., 1997). Given that we can define:

$$\alpha = p_k = p \sum_{i=1}^{k} (1 - p)^{i-1} = 1 - (1 - p)^k, \quad k \in N$$

where α is the probability that there will be at least one exceedance of Y before time k. p is the probability of excess aggregated losses to a certain threshold.

With the intention of showing the pricing of a securitization of operational risk we used a database from a medium-sized investment bank[3] on interested claims expenses risk[4] in just one location. Those expenses happened from 1994 to 1998. Following the methodology above, the first activity was to choose a distribution[5] and the level of threshold at which we should work. After performing graphical test analysis (QQ and mean excess plots), it is apparent that the GEV fits the data slightly better. Figure 1 shows the QQ-plot for the GEV and GPD.

We then decided to pursue the analysis of the extreme losses using the GEV distribution. Extreme distributions can be very sensitive to the choice of the threshold. For this reason, we estimated the parameters of the distribution choosing different thresholds. The results are shown in Table 3.

---

[3] The data was simulated.
[4] Interest claims expenses are charges incurred due to problems in the processing, settlement or clearing of transactions. Banks are expected to compensate the counterparts for these errors.
[5] To test against model risk the analyst might want to test the pricing under other distributions.

Figure 1: QQ–plot for GEV and GPD

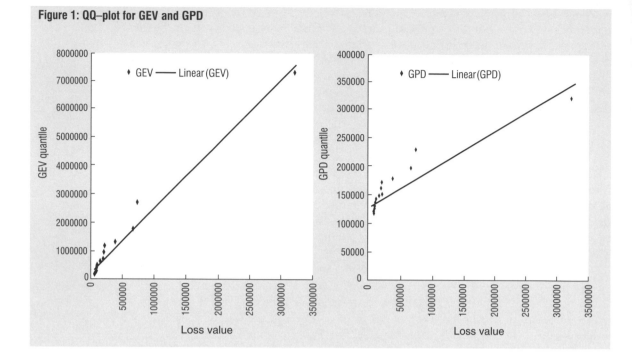

Table 3: Parameter estimation and excess loss quantiles

Threshold	Shape	Scale	Location	λ	1% Excess loss quantile (in US$m)
10	1.130	313,045.99	587,833.75	6.64	27.3
20	0.953	223,847.22	355,266.93	13.29	22.5
30	0.888	174,187.97	263,982.11	19.94	22.7
40	0.909	139,197.84	208,216.20	26.58	26.2
50	0.941	115,310.81	171,927.33	33.23	26.8
60	0.912	102,538.89	149,677.38	39.88	26.5

Four parameters were estimated for each of the six different levels of threshold: shape, scale and location for GEV, and λ for the Poisson distribution. We aggregated the distributions through Monte Carlo simulation. Each simulation was composed of 10,000 runs and then we ran it ten times for each threshold to see if there was any remarkable variance. The quantiles resulting from the runs seem very stable independently of the level of threshold chosen. Nevertheless, we performed a Hill plot to test the stability of the shape parameter, which is quite influential in estimating high quantiles of the severity distribution. The relative straight line at the 45–60 level indicates that this level of threshold would be a reasonable choice. We chose to use the 50 largest events. At this level of threshold the 1 percent aggregated excess loss probability is estimated at $26.8 million. As expected, it is a conservative figure as the worst year registered $3.8 million in accumulated interest expenses.

Following the methodology we proceeded with the jackknife and bootstrapping resampling techniques to analyze the sensitivity of the parameters of the severity distribution. The jackknife run shows that the parameters are quite stable but still influenced by the largest event. The bootstrap 95 percent confidence intervals were very close to those of the jackknife. Other simulations were run considering the top range of the confidence intervals and the results were just slightly above the initial ones. The 1 percent excess loss quantile was $28.2 million, just $1.4 million above the previous estimates.

We then used the level of 1 percent of probability of excess losses to price an ORL bond of $26.8 million. If the aggregate sum of interest expenses paid is higher than the value of the bond, the investors will not receive their principal back. Obviously if the bond is issued for periods greater than one year, the probability of losses will increase, as shown previously. The results of issuing the bond from one to five periods are shown in Table 4. We see that, given the current market conditions, for the issuer it is cheaper to reissue the bond every year than to issue a five-year one. The rate on line – a term used in the insurance industry meaning the premium divided by the underlying coverage – is also quite reasonable considering that we are buying insurance against a "catastrophic" bad year (approximately seven times worse than the worst recorded year so far) and the issuer must consider that in this case the money to cover this unexpected loss is already inside the institution. From the point of view of the investor it is a high-yield bond issued by a high-rated institution in which the risk embedded is not correlated to market or credit events.

Table 4: Pricing the ORL bond

Holding period (in years)	Excess of loss probability	ORL bond price (per 100 face value)	Risk premium (bps above risk free rate)	ROL equivalent
1	1.00%	94.286	104	1.04%
2	1.99%	88.898	124	2.47%
3	2.97%	83.818	143	4.29%
4	3.94%	79.028	163	6.52%
5	4.90%	74.513	183	9.17%

ROL stands for rate on line. Just the risk premium (above the regular borrowing cost) is considered as the price here

As a conclusion to this section, we believe that the financial institutions should optimize their operational risk hedging decisions by using the four options available. The alternative introduced in this article, the securitization of operational risk, can be interesting as it allows financial institutions to have cash available immediately after the operational loss event, thus limiting the earnings volatility. In the case of a catastrophic event this may be the only actual hedge.

Banks obviously tend to be secretive about their operational losses. As the disclosure of the internal losses database (if one were available) would not always be possible, the structuring and modeling process will need to be thoroughly checked by rating agencies and third parties such as audit companies. The choice of distribution and parameter estimation needs to be robust enough to avoid high variances in the definition of the risk premium and to reduce the model risk.

In the same way that banks have credit ratings and spreads, we believe that these instruments will allow the industry to distinguish the management of operational risk at financial institutions by accepting smaller premiums for institutions regarded as well-managed and overcharging those that are poorly perceived. Possibly this would provide incentives for the banking industry to improve the management of operational risk. These instruments also represent a good opportunity for investors, as they are uncorrelated to market or credit events.

Applying discriminant analysis to operational risk indicators

Transforming the qualitative analysis of operational risk into a more quantitative approach is one of the key problems facing operational risk managers. How can risk managers identify the relevant quantitative risk indicators? How can they weight risk factors to produce a more accurate risk rating for a business line or company? We try to show how to achieve this by means of a robust statistical technique known as discriminant analysis.

Solving the problem is important because qualitative risk scoring is being widely adopted by institutions as the most practical way of assessing operational environments across different business units. Several of the indicators used to score the risks of a unit – often known as key risk indicators – have been inherited or adapted from internal audit functions. These and other operational risk indicators differ from financial risk measures in that they are mostly based on subjective opinions. Often managers are simply asked to rank risks on a scale of, say, 1 to 5.

Even where quantitative risk indicators are employed, the usual methodology adopted acts to limit the risk analysis because it is univariate, i.e., the manager examines each risk indicator in isolation and then arrives at the – essentially qualitative – aggregate risk score or rating. It is thus not possible to determine the correlation between the indicators used by the manager to arrive at the score, or to examine how these indicators relate to the operational losses of a particular business unit over a period of time. This means that it is troublesome to adjust the relative value of each indicator as an input to the final score. It is also difficult to work backwards to find out why some business lines do so much better than others in preventing operational losses or risks.

Discriminant analysis is a statistical classification technique that has been used for some time in the world of credit risk management to solve similar problems. In particular, Altman (1968) employed the technique to develop one of the dominant models for predicting the likelihood of bankruptcy in firms. To build his model, Altman extracted 22 financial ratios from the financial statements of 66 companies (some of them bankrupt). Using discriminant analysis, he then identified the five ratios that contributed most to the accuracy of the model's predictions.

To apply the technique to operational risk, we must first devise a risk map that encompasses all types of operational risk (legal, compliance, operations, security, systems, etc.). This exercise is important because of the multi-dimensional nature of operational risk. For each dimension of risk, specify several quantitative risk indicators (for the sake of the discriminant model we might call them "factors" too). For example, two key factors in a system risk analysis might be "system downtime" (measured in minutes per day) and "system support" (the number of staff supporting a particular system). The same type of "conversion" from qualitative to quantitative should be done for each dimension of OR. It does not matter how many factors are developed, as the number can later be reduced using statistical techniques such as factor analysis or principal component analysis. (Alternatively, the multi-factor model itself will discard those factors that are not representative in explaining the variance of the model.)

For example, suppose that we wish to rank the business units of a financial institution in terms of the quality and risk level of the transaction processing in each business. As a first step, we might decide to make a daily record of the number of transactions that exhibited Nostro breaks[6] in each of the units. We could then create a simple rating for the business lines using the ratio of Nostro breaks to the total number of transactions. Business units that exhibited a 0 percent to 1.5 percent ratio might be deemed AAA, those which showed a 1.51 percent to 3 percent ratio might be considered AA, and so on. Table 5 shows how three simplified operational environments can be rated using three factors: systems, capacity, and people. The idea is to use the "real" measure – the level of Nostro breaks – to define the rating, and then to attempt to use various factors/indicators to explain this rating.

Table 5: Operations risk factors/indicators

| Breaks/ volume (%) | Rating | Systems | | Capacity | | People | |
		System downtime min/week	System factor	Volume/ employee	Capacity factor	% total employees present	People factor
0–1.5	AAA	$\vec{X}_{AAA}$	(...)	$\vec{Y}_{AAA}$	(...)	$\vec{Z}_{AAA}$	(...)
1.51–3	AA	$\vec{X}_{AA}$		$\vec{Y}_{AA}$		$\vec{Z}_{AA}$	
3.01–4.5	Rating n	$\vec{X}_n$		$\vec{Y}_n$		$\vec{Z}_n$	

Define ratings →   ← Predict ratings based on factors

Table 5 displays the factors characteristic of each rating in terms of the vectors of factors $\vec{X}_{AAA}$, $\vec{Y}_{AAA}$, $\vec{Z}_{AAA}$, and/or any other extra factor that represents any of the three environments. For example, if a financial institution has six business units, a possible description of system downtime might be $\vec{X}_{AAA}$ ={6,3,10,5,4,11}. The next step is to use discriminant analysis to identify the operational environment and indicators that are associated with good (or poor) operational risk ratings. We might expect an AAA-rated business unit to present lower system downtime, a higher ratio of employee presence, and so on – but without discriminant analysis we will not be able to weight or relate these factors to Nostro breaks (or loss) in any formal manner. Performing discriminant analysis, which is no more than a multiple factor econometric model having as dependent variable the ratings, leads to a discriminant function ($OR_{Rating\,n}$) equivalent to:

$$OR \text{ score} = \beta_1 x + \beta_2 y + \beta_3 z + \beta_n n$$

Here x is the system downtime factor, y is the volume/employee factor, z is the employees' presence ratio, and n can be any other factor. The next step is to define the scores associated with each rating by analyzing the scores across the full spectrum of business units. For example, we might look at the range of scores and decide that a business has to score higher than, say, 0.957 to achieve a rating of

[6] It would be better to use operational losses as our real measure, rather than the "loss proxy" of Nostro breaks, but most banks do not have sufficient data to attempt this.

AAA. Units with scores lower than this down to, say, 0.756 might then be ranked AA, and so on. This allows us to rate business lines for which the "real" measure is unavailable. Suppose, for example, that the analysis of the business units for which data is available suggests that the operational risk score of a business unit can be estimated by the relationship:

$$\text{OR score} = 0.12x + 0.0009y + 0.12z.$$

This suggests that a further business unit that exhibits risk indicator scores of, say, $x = 3$ (min/week), $y = 900$ (employees), and $z = 90$ (percent of the total), should be awarded a score of 1.278. It would be estimated as AAA even if we do not know the Nostro breaks/number of transactions figures.

The main benefits of such a model are that:

- the firm can begin to develop an understanding of the weight that should be attributed to the different risk factors/indicators and an understanding of the correlation between them (i.e., the method helps firms understand the statistical relationship between the indicators);
- if the institution is unable to produce loss data (or Nostro breaks information, in the context of our example), the risk indicators/factors derived previously from loss experiences within the organization can be used in the model to estimate the rating (and the level of losses);
- many firms already collect information on certain risk indicators. The approach outlined above allows a firm to use an incomplete loss record from certain business units to calibrate the model, and to estimate the likely size and frequency of losses.

The quantitative indicators that a firm needs to develop for this kind of analysis can also be used in other kinds of statistical models. For example, the frequency or severity of losses can be analyzed using multiple regression techniques. Cluster analysis could be employed to check which factors seem to determine when losses happen. Lastly, a methodology such as this has implications for the whole industry. It could be used to generate operational risk rankings for bank sectors. Rating agencies might use the methodology to rank financial institutions according to their operational environment. In turn, reliable ratings might improve the pricing of operational risk insurance or even support the pricing of operational risk derivatives (Cruz, 1999).

Conclusion

We have tried to show that a structured quantitative methodology can be developed to measure, manage, and price operational risk. Different mathematical methods can be used to quantify this emerging and important risk. Due to OR's multidimensional concept it is hard to envisage one mathematical method to capture all types of OR. A statistical/actuarial approach is viewed as the most appropriate one encompassing the measurement of the most important OR types. Nevertheless, given that large operational losses happen not very often and we may have not yet seen the "big one," we have shown that extreme value theory might be a useful extrapolation tool based on solid statistical techniques.

By describing a pricing scheme derived from extreme value theory, we have shown that OR can be hedged by transferring the risk to the capital markets, this eventually being the only safe haven from catastrophic events. The definition of the risk premium level may be helped if a rating methodology is devised for OR in the same fashion as for credit risk. The technique known as discriminant analysis helps to understand and forecast the factors which may determine this rating.

As a conclusion, we suggest that banks should concentrate their efforts on collating a loss event database that will allow them to apply these and other methods to understand the pattern of their operational losses and to try to predict them in the future.

Summary

A structured quantitative methodology can be developed to measure, manage and price operational risk. It is hard to envisage one mathematical method to capture all types of operational risks, but a pricing scheme derived from extreme value theory shows how operational risk can be hedged by transferring the risk to the capital markets. The measurement of the risk premium may be helped if a rating methodology is devised for operational risk in the same fashion as for credit risk, and **Marcelo Cruz** shows how discriminant analysis helps to understand and forecast the factors that determine this rating.

Suggested further reading

Altman, E. (1968) "Financial ratios, discriminant analysis and the prediction of corporate bankruptcy," *Journal of Finance*, pp. 589–609.

Basel Committee on Banking Supervision (2001) "The New Basel Capital Accord," Basel, Switzerland.

Canter, M., Cole, J. and Sandor, R. (1996) "Insurance derivatives: a new asset class for the capital markets and a new hedging tool for the insurance industry," *The Journal of Derivatives*, Winter, pp. 89–104.

Cox, S.H. and Pedersen, H.W. (1998) "Catastrophe risk bonds," Technical Paper, May.

Cruz, M. (1999) "Taking risk to market," *Risk*, Operational Risk Supplement, November, pp. 21–24.

Cruz, M., Coleman, R. and Salkin, G. (1998) "Modeling and measuring operational risk," *Journal of Risk*, Vol. 1, No. 1, pp. 63–72.

Efron, B. and Tibshirani, R. (1993) *An Introduction to Bootstrap,* New York, Chapman & Hall.

Embrechts, P., Kluppelberg, C. and Mikosch, T. (1997) *Modelling Extremal Events,* Springer-Verlag, Berlin Heidelberg.

Embrechts, P. and Meister, S. (1997) "Pricing insurance derivatives, the case of CAT-futures," Proceedings of the First Bowles Symposium, GSU Atlanta.

Hoskings, J.R.M. and Wallis, J. (1987) "Parameter and quantile estimation for the generalised Pareto distribution," *Technometrics*, 29, pp. 339–349.

Hoskings, J.R.M, Wallis, J. and Wood, E. (1985) "Estimation of the generalised extreme-value distribution by the method of probability-weighted moments," *Technometrics,* 27, pp. 251–261.

Landwehr, J., Matalas, N. and Wallis, J.R. (1979) "Probability weighted moments compared to some traditional techniques in estimating Gumbel parameters and quantiles," *Water Resources Research,* 15, pp. 1055–1064.

Schmock, U. (1998) "Estimating the value of the WinCat coupons of the Winterthur insurance convertible bond: a study of the model risk," Working Paper, ETH Zürich.

Designing an operational risk framework from a bottom-up perspective

by Tony Peccia

Most firms have been managing operational risk since their founding, otherwise they would not be around today. Those firms that were particularly bad at managing operational risk would have gone into bankruptcy or would have been acquired. The survivors are naturally good at managing operational risk. So why is there now such a heightened interest in managing operational risk, especially among financial institutions?

First, there are the widely reported attention-grabbing headlines about major operational risk loss, culminating with the destruction of Barings Bank. These headlines have been seen and discussed by senior management, boards of directors, and regulators, and they have naturally asked whether the same destructive events could happen to their institutions, and what can be done to prevent the disaster.

Second, most firms, either explicitly or implicitly, operate according to the rule that what gets measured gets managed. This is especially true if the firm is managed on a RAROC basis. Under the RAROC framework, a business has to either earn a return on all the risks taken or the risk has to be reduced or transferred. Most financial institutions have measured their market and credit risk, and therefore operational risk was the next risk area to be fitted into the RAROC framework. It is important to note that the RAROC framework engenders a dramatic paradigm shift in managing operational risk. This may not have been intended, but it is nevertheless a direct consequence of applying RAROC to operational risk. The traditional approach to operational risk has been to control it, which has meant to minimize it. Through the RAROC framework, attention can be shifted from control to management. Management of operational risk involves not only minimizing the risk but also looking at the associated cost of minimization. For example, good measures of operational risk should allow the firm to determine whether too much is being spent on controlling the risk, and may perhaps lead to a relaxation of the controls. Without an operational RAROC framework, such an action would have been unthinkable.

The third important reason for the increased attention to operational risk is the growing awareness that operational risk is already a substantial part of the current risks being assumed by the firm and will increase significantly in the future. As noted in Figure 1, most banks have 20 percent to 30 percent of their capital supporting operational risk, and it is growing closer to 30 percent at the bottom end of the scale; depending on the business mix, it can be as high as 100 percent of the total capital. For example, a financial institution that concentrates on asset management will have little market or credit risk but substantial operational risk.

Here are some of the reasons for this increase. As the margins from traditional lending are being eroded, banks are increasingly securitizing their loan portfolios, or

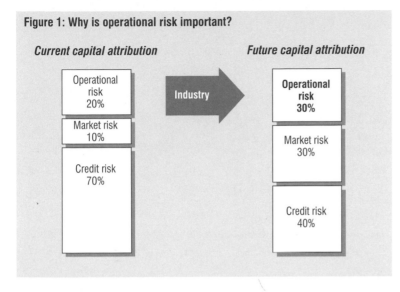

Figure 1: Why is operational risk important?

Current capital attribution → Industry → *Future capital attribution*

Current capital attribution:
- Operational risk 20%
- Market risk 10%
- Credit risk 70%

Future capital attribution:
- Operational risk 30%
- Market risk 30%
- Credit risk 40%

searching for new markets. Through securitization banks are transferring their credit and market risk associated with the loans and retaining the operational risk, and in many instances increasing that risk, if they become the servicing agent. Banks are entering new businesses such as e-commerce and advisory roles where most of the risk is operational, not credit or market. Also, they are facing intense competition for clients, coupled with rapidly evolving client needs, a situation which has led banks to create more tailored and complex products as well as more intricate matrix organizational structures and delivery channels. Again these developments improve the ability of the bank to meet the client need efficiently, but also either raise the level of existing operational risk or introduce new ones.

The fourth and perhaps most important reason for the increased attention to operational risk has to do with the realization by financial institutions that risk management (credit, market and operational) is not an add-on activity but rather a core competency, which can be used to create competitive advantage.

Because of the well-publicized losses, because of the desire to match reward with risk, and because operational risk is increasing, management, boards of directors and regulators have come to the conclusion that a new sophisticated approach to the management of operational risk is required.

What is operational risk?

Before a new sophisticated approach can be developed, it is important to be clear about what operational risk is. Most newcomers to operational risk are confronted by a wide variety of opinions about what is and what isn't operational risk. For example, is it the risk within the back office? Does it include strategic risk, i.e., the risk that business stategies will not achieve their objects? Are reputational and legal risk included? And so on.

Most banks understand credit and market risk. Therefore they begin by defining operational risk as what is left over after accounting for credit and market risk. This is a good starting point, but it is clearly not the desired end state. As Figure 2 illustrates, operational risk cannot be understood in isolation – there are significant

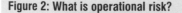

Figure 2: What is operational risk?

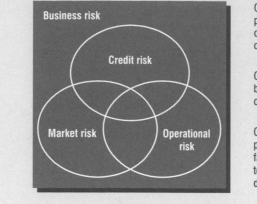

Operational risks are all potential losses that are not directly attributable to credit or market risk.

Operational risk comprises both strategic risk and operational failure risk.

Operational failure risk is the potential for loss due to the failure in people, process technology, and external dependencies.

interdependencies among the three risks. For example, the purchase of an option has credit risk associated with the potential default of the counterparty, market risk associated with changes in volatility, and operational risk (model risk) associated with the valuation model used to mark the position to market. Furthermore, a large market move may lead to the counterparty defaulting, which may lead to a discovery that the wrong model or wrong inputs were used. This inter-nesting of the three risks has some very important implications for how operational risk should be managed, which we will explore later. For now it is important to realize that there is a core of risks that are definitely operational risk, i.e., fraud and system failures, and around the core the risk has components of operational and market or credit, or both. For example, settlement risk has components of operational and credit risk. For these overlapping risks, it is important that they are identified and not double counted; it is less important that they be unambiguously labeled.

As a starting point it is useful to define operational risk as the residual risk, i.e., all that is not market or credit. However, this is too broad a category to make much progress, so it is also useful to divide it into two smaller yet still broad categories of risk: strategic risk and failure risk. Some institutions prefer to create a fourth category to capture strategic risk. This fourth category is sometimes confusingly referred to as business risk. Business risk is the universe of risks a business faces and therefore by definition includes market and credit and all aspects of operational risk. Whether strategic risk is a fourth category or part of operational risk is a matter of preference. The point is that it must be measured and managed. However, as we will see later, the methodologies and management and capitalization of this risk are different from operational failure risk.

Strategic risk refers to the potential for loss arising from a failure in the firm's strategies. These include strategies designed to address or anticipate changes in the competitive, client, political, or regulatory environments. This risk is meant to capture the potential loss from not doing the right things rather than from a failure while doing the right things. This latter risk is called operational failure risk and will form the bulk of the subject matter discussed here. Henceforth, operational risk will refer primarily to operational failure risk.

At a base level, running a business involves employing people carrying out